Perspectives in Professional Child and Youth Care

THE CHILD & YOUTH SERVICES SERIES:

EDITOR-IN-CHIEF

JEROME BEKER, *Director and Professor, Center for Youth Development and Research, University of Minnesota*

Perspectives
in Professional
Child and Youth Care

James P. Anglin
Carey J. Denholm
Roy V. Ferguson
Alan R. Pence
Editors

The Haworth Press
New York • London

Perspectives in Professional Child and Youth Care has also been published as *Child & Youth Services*, Volume 13, Numbers 1 and 2 1990.

The Haworth Press, Inc., 10 Alice Street, Binghamton, NY 13904-1580
EUROSPAN/Haworth, 3 Henrietta Street, London WC2E 8LU England

Library of Congress Cataloging-in-Publication Data

Perspectives in professional child and youth care / James P. Anglin, Carey Denholm, Roy Ferguson, Alan Pence, guest editors.
    p. cm.
    Published as Child & Youth services, volume 13, numbers 1/2, 1990'' — Verso t.p.
    ISBN 0-86656-891-3. ISBN 1-56024-055-5 (pbk.)
    1. Child care — United States. 2. Child care — Canada. 3. Child care services — United States. 4. Child care services — Canada. 5. Children — Institutional care — United States. 6. Children — Institutional care — Canada. I. Anglin, James P. II. Denholm, Carey J., 1951- . III. Ferguson, Roy. IV. Pence, Alan R., 1948- .
HQ778.7.U6P47   1990
362.7'0971 — dc20
                                              90-4051
                                            CIP

DEDICATION

To all students
of Child and Youth Care.
You are the future of the profession.

Perspectives in Professional Child and Youth Care

CONTENTS

SECTION 3:
KEY SUPPORT FUNCTIONS IN CHILD AND YOUTH
CARE PROGRAMS

SECTION 4:
DEVELOPING PROFESSIONALISM

SECTION 5:
CURRENT ISSUES IN EDUCATION AND TRAINING

SECTION 6:
THE CHANGING WORK ENVIRONMENT AND NEW
ROLES FOR CHILD AND YOUTH WORKERS

ABOUT THE EDITORS

James P. Anglin, MSW, is Associate Professor and Director of the School of Child and Youth Care at the University of Victoria, British Columbia, Canada. He has worked in a variety of areas of child care ranging from residential treatment and program evaluation to formulating family policy and developing curriculum. His current research interests include parent education and support, family development, and training needs. He remains active in the field by serving as the Canadian representative to the International Federation of Educative Communities (UNESCO). Mr. Anglin has published articles in several child and youth care journals.

Carey J. Denholm, PhD, MEd, is Associate Professor in the School of Child and Youth Care at the University of Victoria in British Columbia. Dr. Denholm has vast teaching experience with students in different developmental stages, educational settings, and with different degrees of handicaps. He has worked in primary education, counselling, and educational psychology. In his years at the University, he has been involved in writing course manuals and materials, as well as curriculum design and supervision/evaluation of undergraduate students in child care, social work, psychology, and education. Dr. Denholm has published recent research in child and youth care and related journals.

Roy V. Ferguson, PhD, is Associate Professor in the School of Child and Youth Care at the University of Victoria. He is also the founding director of the Department of Psychology at the Alberta Children's Hospital in Calgary, Alberta, Canada. Dr. Ferguson's research interests include hospitalized children, environmental design for children, pediatric psychology, children with developmental disabilities, and distance education delivery mechanisms and their application to the human service field.

Alan R. Pence, PhD, is Associate Professor in the School of Child and Youth Care at the University of Victoria. Dr. Pence is also the co-director of a major Canadian study on labor force participation, family life, and child day care. He has been involved with children's programs for preschool-age, school-age, and adolescents in both school and residential facilities. His current activities include developing curricula for First Nations Child and Youth Care Education and researching working families and their day-care needs.

Foreword

I have been told that at the height of the battle for the North Atlantic during World War II a "think tank" was asked to provide a plan for reducing the effectiveness of enemy submarine attacks on merchant shipping. After some deliberation, the group sent back its recommendation: "drain the ocean." When the report was received, an angry and perplexed senior officer asked, "how the Hell are we going to do that?!" The leader of the think tank replied, "that's a practical matter of implementation; we only deal with conceptual problems."

The story may be apocryphal, but its relevance to this book is clear. This is *not* a book that is alive only in theory, at the conceptual level and divorced from the nitty gritty issues of child care. It is an honest effort to come to terms with what it really means to think about caring for children. It insists upon child care as a serious topic of intellectual inquiry. In this, the book bears the fruits of several generations of practitioners, now increasingly reinforced by good conceptual thinking and empirical research.

Like the authors, I am very much encouraged that such a book as this *could* be written at all and not degenerate into *either* a montage of anecdotal accounts or glorified theoretical speculation. Being head of an institute dedicated to training professionals for work with children, I recognize the challenge confronted by this volume. To keep both feet firmly, responsibly, and respectably planted in the world of practice and theory/research is a triumph of will, as much as, if not more than, anything else.

I appreciate also that the book's authors do not flinch from recognizing the relevance of personal and social transformation in understanding quality care. Learning to care for children and youth changes you (or at least it should if your training succeeds). You become a different person through good instruction and properly supervised experiences "in the field." Training means confronting

xiii

yourself—as you were and as you might be. It should also lead to a confrontation with the dominant social realities of your community, the conditions of life that offer or deny opportunities, that nurture or erode basic human competence, that create justice or foster oppression. So it is that good child care training leads to advocacy and social action as much as it does personal transformation. This book comes to that position, and I hope each reader/user will as well. It's a place we need to be to live an ethic of caring as a profession and a policy.

James Garbarino, PhD
President
Erikson Institute for Advanced Study
in Child Development
Chicago, Illinois

Acknowledgements

The editors wish to thank all of the contributors who wrote, re-vised, and often re-revised their chapters in order to achieve some degree of commonality in the use of terminology and format. At the same time, the editors attempted to interfere as little as possible in order to allow each contributor to speak with her, or his, own voice. We trust that they will be as pleased with this volume as we are.

To Jerry Beker, wc owe a debt of gratitude for his continuing and inspiring leadership in the field of child and youth care. In particular, we are indebted to him in his capacity as an editor of the *Child & Youth Services* series for his immediate positive response to this book as a whole which has ensured that it will be readily and widely available to its intended North American audience. Warm thanks also goes to Mary Burnison for her helpful editing comments and suggestions.

Finally, we want to acknowledge you, the reader. Whether you have come across this book on a shelf somewhere, or have had faith enough to purchase it yourself, we sincerely hope you will find information, ideas, and inspiration which will help you in your daily struggle to provide better care for children, youth and families. In the end, it is this commitment to serve others which unites us all.

Introduction

BACKGROUND

This volume has been compiled to serve as a much needed sourcebook of readings on the current state-of-the-art of professional child and youth care in North America. The manner in which this collection was developed is worth noting. After some discussion of how best to compile such a collection, the editors decided to write to 40 of the leading practitioners, academics, researchers, and administrators in the field asking each of them to propose, in a one page outline, a topic of current importance on which she or he would be prepared to write a chapter. Based upon the proposals which came back, the editors made various comments and observations, and gave the go-ahead for the various chapters to be written. As a result of this process, the content of this book represents the cutting edge of the field of child and youth care as perceived by leaders in the field themselves.

To borrow a useful phrase from Karen VanderVen's chapter, what is represented in this volume is "the child care perspective"; a way of seeing and understanding the world that seems to evolve uniquely out of the day-to-day care of children and youth as a full-time occupation. Wherever the authors represented in this book are to be found at this moment, you can be sure that the experience and insights shared have been forged and moulded in the "blood, sweat and tears" as well as the incomparable joys of living and working with children, youth and families.

HOW TO USE THIS BOOK

It is anticipated that this text will be used in academic courses and training workshops, as well as read by individual child and youth care professionals and practitioners from related disciplines. In order to assist students and other readers in making the best use of the material in the various chapters, a chart has been prepared outlining a wide range of major themes covered, in varying degrees, by the chapters in the book (see Figure 1). Where a particular chapter deals explicitly with a theme, the degree of focus, or emphasis, given to the theme in the chapter is indicated as "high" (i.e., it is a major theme), "medium" (i.e., it is a significant theme, though not a predominant one), or "low" (i.e., it is considered to some degree).

This chart can assist the reader who is interested in pursuing a specific theme in selecting for review those articles which will be most pertinent. So, for example, the reader interested in considering the theme of "politics and the field of child and youth care" will note that the chapters by Peter Gabor, and Mary Lyon and Patricia Canning, treat this topic as a major focus (i.e., is rated as "High"), while the chapters by Douglas Powell, Carol Kelly, Roderick Durkin, Carey Denholm, and Carol Stuart and Mary Lynne Gokiert treat this as a significant issue (i.e., are rated as "Medium"), and the chapter by Sharon Moscrip and Adrien Brown discusses the theme to some degree (i.e., is rated as "Low"). Thus, by reading these eight chapters, the reader will be able to gain a variety of perspectives on the important theme of "politics." It should perhaps be mentioned at this point that this analysis deals only with the *explicit* consideration of each of the listed themes. Other chapters will inevitably deal with particular themes in an indirect, or implicit manner. As well, *other* themes not identified on the chart can also be found, and may be of considerable interest to the reader. In other words, the chart is offered as a *guide*; adventurous readers will (and should) explore and analyze the entire contents for themselves.

In addition to the theme analysis chart (Figure 1), each section of the volume is preceded by a brief introduction placing the chapters in the context of contemporary child and youth care practice. This collection of perspectives, although unique in its format and breadth of focus, is but one more addition to the swelling stream of books now being published by, and for, the child and youth care profession (however we may choose to define it). Indeed, the entire *Child & Youth Services* series, outlined at the front of this volume, repre-

Chapters   Themes

Degree of Focus:

★ = High
● = Medium
○ = Low

Chapters	Teamwork	Research / Knowledge Base	Professionalization	Future Directions	Politics	Media / Public Awareness	Context / Ecology of Child Care	Child / Youth Development	Ethical & Moral Dimension	Relationship	Structure of Work	Child & Youth Care Roles	Administration & Organizations	Education & Training	Historical Developments	Practice Skills & Issues	Worker Growth & Development	Supervision & Staff Relations	Relating to Parents & Families
Section 1: The Nature of Child and Youth Care																			
Chapter 1 - Maier		●					★	★	●	★			●	○		★	○		○
Chapter 2 - Fewster	○		●	○			●		●	★	○	★	●						○
Section 2: Therapeutic Program Issues																			
Chapter 3 - Arieli, Beker & Kashti		●		●			★				★	●	●				○		
Chapter 4 - Pratt							●			●		●				●	★		
Chapter 5 - Gauthier	●	●					○	○			★	●							
Chapter 6 - McMain & Webster			○				●		●	○	●	★	●						
Chapter 7 - Gershowitz & MacFarlane											★	★	●						★
Chapter 8 - Durkin	●		●	●	●		★	★	●	●	★	●	★	●	○				○
Section 3: Key Support Functions in Child and Youth Care Programs																			
Chapter 9 - Krueger	★						●			●	★	●	●	★		★	●	★	
Chapter 10 - Phelan										●	●	●	★			★	★	★	
Chapter 11 - Ing	●						○			●	★	○				★	★	★	
Chapter 12 - Manburg & Goldman	○	○	●	●			○			○			★	★	○		○	●	
Section 4: Developing Professionalism																			
Chapter 13 - Kelly		●	★	★	●	●	●		●		●	●	●	●	★		●		●
Chapter 14 - D. Powell		★	★	★	●	●	★		●		●	●	●	●					★
Chapter 15 - Lyon & Canning		★	★	★	★	★	★		○		●	★	●	●					●
Chapter 16 - Gabor	○	★	★	★	●		●				○	○	○	●					
Section 5: Current Issues in Education and Training																			
Chapter 17 - R. Peterson, S. Young & J. Tillman			●			○		★	●		●		★		★	★	○		
Chapter 18 - Pence	★					○					●		★		★	★	●		
Chapter 19 - Demers		○				○							★	●	★	★			
Chapter 20 - Stuart & Gokiert		○	○	●		★		●	○				●	★	●		○		
Chapter 21 - Ferguson		○	★							○			●	★	●				
Chapter 22 - Moscrip & Brown		●		○	○	●					★	●	●	★		●	★	○	
Section 6: The Changing Work Environment and New Roles for Child and Youth Workers																			
Chapter 23 - Savicki	●		●	★		★					★	★	★	○		●	○		●
Chapter 24 - Barnes & Bourdon	★		★	★		●					★	★	★	★	●	★	★		
Chapter 25 - Bagley & Young		★	★									★		○	○	★			
Chapter 26 - VanderVen			●	★							★	★	●	○		★	★		
Chapter 27 - Denholm	●	●	●	●	★	●	●	○		○	★	★	●	★	○	★	★		

FIGURE 1. Theme Analysis Chart

sents a wealth of recent material which is waiting to be mined and
refined by those who wish to pursue further the themes raised herein.

James P. Anglin
Carey J. Denholm
Roy V. Ferguson
Alan R. Pence

SECTION 1:
THE NATURE OF CHILD
AND YOUTH CARE

Introduction

It is fitting that Henry Maier leads off this collection of perspectives by introducing what he identifies as "the developmental perspective." Maier has been a recognized leader in the field of child and youth care for many years, and this chapter represents his most recent thinking on an essential core of knowledge for child and youth workers. As he himself observes, "this chapter introduces a developmental perspective decisively different from the child and youth field's previous alignments with psychodynamic, behavioral, or cognitive psychological stances."

In this foundational contribution, Maier interweaves several of the strands of lifespan developmental knowledge and ecological understanding with the experiential threads of daily child and youth care. It is characteristic of Maier's writing (and teaching) that he is able to knit together so deftly the grand universals of human growth and development with the "minutiae," the critically meaningful yet apparently insignificant moments, of human interaction. We encounter here the real world of messes and mistakes, of "heated disputes" and "temper tantrums," so familiar to child and youth workers. At the same time, we are inspired to develop our creativity, our sensitivity, and to renew our commitment to "that which is valuable in human existence."

In a companion piece on the nature of child and youth care, Gerry Fewster brings his extensive experience to bear in an intensely personal (in his words, "idiosyncratic"), yet broadly applicable, exploration of the worker-child relationship. As he vividly illustrates, this particular relationship becomes a unique crucible of growth and development for *both* parties. Fewster suggests that "the personalized relationship continues to be the greatest challenge in professional child and youth care" and, in so doing, reveals the reason why so many of us become hooked on child care, even if we only stumbled in to it "by accident," or began by thinking "it's just a job."

Only through relationships can we really come to know who we are and what we are to do with our lives, and for us, as child and youth workers, we oftentimes discover the most important parts of ourselves in what Fewster refers to as the "mystery" of our interactions with children. He reminds us that to be truly professional, at least in our profession, is also to be intensely personal. Perhaps more importantly, he offers us practical ways, through introducing us to "presence," "making judgements," "role-taking," "keeping things clear," and "establishing boundaries," to make this ideal into a reality.

These two pieces, by Maier and Fewster, set the tone for all those that follow. To quote Fewster himself:

> The words that express these thoughts come easily.
> The actions that the thoughts imply demand courage,
> commitment, creativity, and, most of all, discipline.

1

A Developmental Perspective for Child and Youth Care Work

Henry W. Maier

ABSTRACT. Child and youth care work is presented within a developmental perspective. Spelled out are a wide range of care activities, reflecting grounded (empirical) research and conceptualized by an ecological lifespan orientation. Such an approach is acknowledged as decisively different from the care fields' previous alignments and is seen as the most appropriate scientific source for child and youth care work.

Care work is very much akin to the subject matter in the discipline of child development, more correctly designated as *human development*. Human developmental knowledge emerges out of studies of the interpersonal and ecological life experience of children and adolescents, especially growth and development within family and communal matrices. Care work with children or youth requires an intense interpersonal involvement at whatever level of development a child or youth is operating. Consequently, human development knowledge can provide a solid backdrop for care workers engaged in revitalizing children's and adolescents' development (Beker & Maier, 1980; Bronfenbrenner, 1979; Gilligan, 1987; Maier, 1987; VanderVen, 1986; VanderVen, Mattingly, & Morris, 1982). Simultaneously care workers respond to ongoing contextual conditions in order to assure salutary life experience.

Henry W. Maier, Professor Emeritus, School of Social Work, University of Washington, Seattle, WA 98195.

7

This chapter introduces a developmental perspective decisively different from the child and youth care fields' previous alignments with psychodynamic, behavioral, or cognitive psychological stances. Carol Gilligan cogently pointed out this factor more recently:

> Two approaches currently characterize the response of professionals to . . . [young people's difficulties]. One relies on the imposition of control, the effort to override a tortuous reason with behavior modification and biofeedback, to focus attention simply on physical survival by teaching skills for managing stress and regulating . . . [behaviors]. The other approach reaches into reason and joins the humanistic faith in the power of education with the insight of modern psychology. Positing human development as the aim of education, it turns attention to the question: What constitutes and fosters development? (Gilligan, 1987, pp. 17-18)

The perspective advocated here relies upon lifespan developmental knowledge, grounded in empirical research and buttressed by an ecological orientation as the most appropriate scientific source for child and youth care work (Bronfenbrenner, 1979; Lerner & Busch-Rossnagel, 1981; Maier, 1979).

WHAT IS A DEVELOPMENTAL PERSPECTIVE?

Human development, especially child and adolescent development, is a universal process and at the same time, highly individualized. Studies of human development zero in on basic human functioning: the way a person grows and develops and what people do under various circumstances within their relevant environments. Development is viewed for a person's physical, behavioral, emotional, and cognitive functioning (Ivey, 1986; Maier, 1978). Developmental change is studied and understood for the reciprocal interactions between an individual and his or her active context. Just as the context changes the individual, so the reverse is true. Human life experiences are bi-directional (Lerner & Busch-Rossnagel, 1981, p. 9). In essence, by being both a product and a producer of their contexts, individuals effect their own development (Lerner & Busch-Rossnagel, 1981, p. 3). Human development is known as orderly and empirically predictable. Although they occur over time, few changes emerge simply as the result of the passage of time; instead, changes emerge out of relevant *experiences*.

Studies of human development are constantly expanded by new research data enlarging or replacing previous findings (Skolnick, 1986, p. 7). Various details of knowledge about human behavior and development may, for the present, be in a state of flux. Nevertheless, what is currently known provides ample backdrop for on-the-spot certainty and actions. In fact, in the behavioral sciences, lifespan developmental psychology is presently assuming the foreground (Balter, Reese, & Lipsitt, 1980; Gilligan, 1987; Kegan, 1982, p. 298; Lerner & Busch-Rossnagel, 1981; Maier, 1986; Schuster & Ashburn, 1986), superceding previous commitments to other earlier "schools" of psychology. Many of the research findings and concepts of these earlier formulations are now conceived as complementary rather than contradictory (Ivey, 1986; Izard, Kagan, & Zajonic, 1984; Maier, 1978, p. 7-10; Skolnick, 1986, p. 107). Contemporary helping orientation seems to foster a holistic approach where each person is recognized as a unique being functioning as a total entity (Maas, 1984).

It is reasonable to postulate then that no other spectrum of knowledge incorporates so closely and completely the very essence of professional child and youth care work. That is to say, a perspective which appraises *what* is happening in an individual's life and *how* interpersonal interactions and environmental alterations can change what is happening in order that children and youth can *experience* integrative growth in their development toward adulthood.

ILLUSTRATIVE SELECTIONS OF DEVELOPMENTAL FINDINGS APPLIED TO CHILD AND YOUTH CARE

Several areas of developmental knowledge out of a vast "bin" of useful possibilities are presented to illustrate how such material can directly be applied to child and youth care work. They are: (1) attachment formation and "beginnings" early or later in life; (2)

rhythmicity as the underpinning for the mutuality of personal inter-actions; (3) transitional objects and how they are utilized in facing of new life situations; (4) trial-and-error learning as a fundamental learning mode; and (5) personal value acquisition.

Attachment Formation — and "Beginnings" Early and Later in Life

Basic to all child care is the formation of a solid interpersonal relationship between care giver and care receiver. Studies on attach-ment formation are useful here as an extension of that effort (Ains-worth, M.D., 1972; Sroufe, 1978). They also amplify processes of beginnings in human interactions. Attachment has to be nurtured through direct and predictable care giving. In the process of attach-ment formation in the beginning of a relationship, and at moments of crises, the support of attachment striving is particularly crucial. Interestingly, the more an individual feels certain of support (at-tachment), the less demand there will be for reinforcement of such support (Maier, 1987, p. 121-128).

It is useful to distinguish between attachment and attachment be-haviors. Attachment behavior occurs whenever a child, or in fact a person at any age, wishes to strengthen an attachment or feels the ongoing attachment in jeopardy. At that point, the individual will manifest attachment behaviors (e.g., physical or verbal contacts such as holding on, embracing, or clinging). Attachment behaviors are really efforts to maintain or increase attachment, they have to be seen and responded to as such.

Need and demand for attachment succorance is more apt to arise at points of personal stress, especially in periods of life transitions such as moves by the family. The need is particularly accentuated by a move from one environmental experience to another (e.g., change of school, homes, friendship groups, or other personal life reorienta-tions) (Ainsworth, M.D., 1982; Bronfenbrenner, 1979; Maier, 1987, pp. 22-23). In turn, attachment behaviors lessen as an indi-vidual feels more assured of the wanted attachment (Ainsworth, M.D., 1982; Sroufe, 1978).

These accounts of ordinary attachment formation speak to profes-sional child and youth care work where nurturing care enhances the possibility for attachment to the care worker. This is a fundamental for effective work and is a stepping stone in "permanency planning." Workers will need to welcome and actively support attachment strivings, hoping to normalize attachment behavior (Ainsworth, M.D., 1982; Maier, 1987, Ch. 5).

Rhythmicity as the Underpinning for the Mutuality of Personal Interactions

Recently, novel and prominent research at a large number of developmental study projects have concluded that both care givers and care receivers experience challenging *mutual* interactions of giving and taking, of coping together and apart, in an interweaving of rhythms (Lerner & Busch-Rossnagel, 1981). This potent force found in joint rhythmicity seems to enhance the very energy which links people together. It can bring about a symphony of human actions with a joint rhythm and fine tuning one to another (Maier, 1987, pp. 46-48).

With this concept in mind, the worker may attempt in the daily care tasks to energize a joint rhythm with each child and the group-as-a-whole in order to assure full engagement as a symphonic totality. Recognizing the developmental components of rhythmicity may encourage workers to search out activities and play with built-in rhythmic interactions. Rhythms in music, song and dance, push-and-pull playful activities, the rhythmic exchange in throwing a frisbee, ball or pillow, waving goodbye or exchanging solid handshakes have a strong potential for bringing about sensations of spontaneous togetherness (Maier, 1987, Ch. 1).

The Use of Transitional Objects for Facing New Life Situations

Studies describing the use of transitional objects (Maier, 1987, pp. 57-58) in crucial experiences requiring change in the childhood period, can cast light on the essence of making transitions later in life when a change to a new situation seems overwhelming for an individual (e.g., being with an unaccustomed care giver, having a room change, or whatever) (Maier, 1987, pp. 57-58). A "transitional object," as the blanket for Linus in the *Peanuts* cartoon, can give a person the extra symbolic assurance needed to ease the adaptation.

Workers can utilize such understanding and assist youngsters to manage severely uncertain conditions, whether momentary or long-term transitions. By supporting and incorporating the individuals' very special objects, the worker recognizes that these items serve as linkage to previous places, people, and memories of good as well as tough times. These items, possibly a scrap of paper, a piece of clothing, a picture, or remnant of a once stuffed animal might be clutched closely, slept with, etc. The transition objects may be worn out, possibly smelly or sometimes bizarre; but they are essential to the owners and are a source of strength. In addition, care workers themselves must plan to be on hand and available as vital and tangible links in transition.

Trial-and-Error Learning as a Fundamental Learning Mode

Developmental knowledge offers rich possibilities for understanding mastery of incremental and novel experiences. Progressive trial-and-error learning is the basic cognitive mode in infancy and childhood, and on occasions of substantial new learning later on in life. This developmental fact establishes that new learning has to be first concrete, visual, and open for experiment. Initial learning must follow the cognitive process of trying out where individuals see for themselves how something works or what it means. Above all, the person needs latitude to err without that being regarded as a devastating mark of failure but as a consequential step toward learning (Maier, 1978, pp. 36, 156 & 244).

With such understanding, care workers are challenged to foster and to invent situations so that what must be learned can be tried out, experimented with, to provide those opportunities where new behaviors or understanding can be attempted, failed, and tried again. Eventually the young people themselves may experience these tasks as manageable and safe. At this point, learning takes place and is eventually integrated. Actual learning rather than temporary compliance has the potential to occur with this model (Maier, 1987, Ch. 3). For instance, to learn "to wait for one's turn" can be acquired in specially created situations where young-sters can play out their capacity to wait. Later such playful give-and-take can be built-in into more and more daily life situations of waiting. Children can be playfully engaged in getting their "proper" turns in receiving their treats while being assured that no one is to be left out (Maier, 1987, Ch. 6).

Parenthetically, familiarity with the progression of cognitive processes serves not only as an eye-opener and practice guide for the care workers; it also introduces an advantageous "thinking screen" for masterminding the very training of these workers.

Personal Value Acquisition

In early childhood and later on in subsequent value acquisitions, individuals assume personal values, utilizing a progression of imitation and later identifying with highly visible, esteemed, powerful persons and culminating in an eventual alignment with the reference groups of these "heroes" (Jones, Garrison, & Morgan, 1985, Ch. 9). Values are adopted through personally satisfying experiences with selected key persons. The values a care giver holds are potentially transferrable, if such a person has been experienced as a dependable esteemed person by the care receiver. This awareness suggests for child and youth practice that it is the workers as *persons* who stand as the ultimate transmitters of values, not their moral edicts, admonishments, or rewards. In short, care workers must have personal satisfying meaning for the ones they serve, if they wish to effectively impact the youngsters' values.

Moreover, the importance of peers in value clarification, especially for those in their pre-adolescent and adolescent years cannot be overlooked in group care work. Research from developmental psychology establishes that in their adolescent years, youngsters devote much energy sorting out and integrating their basic personal values (Schuster & Ashburn, 1986). Also, in the teens, alignment with peers is nearly at par with ongoing identification with key elders (Washington, 1982). Consequently, frequent informal but full group deliberations, including heated disputes with the young people are in order. Such discussions serve the youngsters as opportunities for verbally trying out a range of notions for their "fit" as they do so easily with their wardrobe fantasies on a Saturday morning shopping spree: "nothing bought, just looking!"

WHAT ABOUT SO-CALLED "DEVIANT" OR "PATHOLOGICAL" DEVELOPMENT?

What were formerly viewed as pathological or deviant behaviors can, under this model, be conceived and approached as ordinary but inopportune and untimely developmental occurrences (Kegan, 1982, p. 298). Former preoccupation with children's "deviant" or "pathological" aspects of their lives easily resulted in seeing them as special classifications of persons; their thoughts, actions and affect were conceived as "defective" or "disturbed," because their thinking or actions seemed to be incomprehensible. The youngsters were "disturbing" because they could not fit into existing behavioral, cognitive, or affective continua of human development. This dilemma seemed to stem from the fact that major attention revolved around their incapabilities and adult's failures in connecting effectively with them. Little attention was given to these youngsters' capabilities. The individual as a *total* person got lost among efforts to combat the "deviations" (Schuster & Ashburn, 1986, pp. 23-24).

In a developmental approach, in contrast, children are appraised and understood for their response to their daily life situations, their patterns of coping, and their way of encountering supposedly unmanageable situations. The child's affective, behavioral, cognitive, and physio-motor interactive responses are then scanned to locate corresponding levels on the continua of development. They then can be spotted for their specific point of developmental status and transitions. They can consequently be "fitted-in" and a decision can be made with some predictive clarity about what needs to happen to reinforce development (Ivey, 1986; Maier, 1978, Ch. 6). For example, a big, boisterous Paul, 13, demands continuous adult approval as if he were a four-year-old. He goes to pieces with temper tantrum explosions when he feels slighted, and in particular when he thinks that he cannot predict what is going to happen at a particular moment of his life. In other words, he "lets go" emotionally, of rational perception and even bodily inhibitions when he feels *out of control*. His demands for adult approval and his temper outbursts are not necessarily "deviant" behaviors; they also can be conceived as a desperate outreach for adult care when he feels at a complete loss. His intensity directed toward getting clarity about what is going to happen, is also a valiant self-maintenance effort. None of these are apropos for expectations of a 13-year-old fellow. Yet, these youngsters strike out for adult nurturance and a search for subsequent certainty within their lives. These life experiences would be akin to very young children whose behaviors are conceived as acceptable while full reassuring support is rendered to them.

Armed with such understanding, workers can find directions for their work with such situations. For instance, Paul, in the illustration above, could find *and experience* his connectedness to others who cared and sense a predictable outcome. This strategy is developmentally sound and more useful than pushing him off and isolating him for his untimely, and consequently unwanted, behavior.

In many ways the sputtering of an automobile motor due to the coldness of its engine or the strain of a steep incline can be drawn as analagous to the difficulties people experience while encountering stressful situations. In the case of the automobile motor, nobody questions the "properness" of a shift to a lower gear to allow the car to apply its energy in a more fundamental way. Before shifting to a higher gear, the driver wants to be sure that the engine is operating at a higher pace than needed for the lower gear still in place. The same is relevant in the expenditure of human energy. A recourse to earlier forms of functioning is appropriate when this more fundamental level is at the moment the more facilitating one. Such a recourse needs not then to be defined as "regression." It is most natural to kick a tire when the car "lets one down," or rely on finger count when one is unsure of one's ability to keep track of something, and so on.

This important notion has implications in other ways as well. In a good number of group care situations, care work involves as much an effort to *maintain* an individuals' ongoing functioning as it does to enhance developmental progress. Moreover, placements into a group setting, part or fulltime, transitions to a new community and a new group life culture, etc., all represent experiences which cause a person to function most naturally on a less adequate level than before (Maier, 1987, Ch. 1). A case could be made here for youngsters with severe disabling physiologic or somatic complications. For some of these, developmental knowledge can be applied toward helping to maintain their ongoing level of functioning in order that these children can survive *at all*.

TUNE-UP RATHER THAN SPEED-UP

In a quite different aspect, over the past 30 years there has been an eagerness to accelerate children's learning processes as if children had to compensate for their society's shortcoming. In the field of group care, recent concerns with proving behavioral changes as outcome and effectiveness of child tending, has as a by-product unleashed what Frank Ainsworth (1987) calls "the rush to independence—a new tyranny."[1] David Elkind (1981) also warns that pushing persons to independence can have serious consequences, or is at least unkind. Although pushing may bring about adequately functioning persons, they do not necessarily become people with satisfying life experience. A developmental lifespan orientation would lead workers to more keenly gauge their care receivers' readiness for relevant learning progressions.

CHANGE AND INTEGRATED CHANGE

A developmental approach to child and youth care is further enlivened by two recent but very separate findings. First, Bandura's (1977) studies on "self-efficacy achievement" bring forth clearly that actual integrative learning does not take place until the learners themselves have become aware of their changes in behavior, thinking, or affect. This suggests that it is not the observations of the workers or other fellow professionals alone, nor the attainment of sufficient points or tokens which ultimately count; instead, much depends upon the person's own level of recognition and acceptance of his or her newly acquired efficacy.

Second, Carol Gilligan calls attention to the fact that males and females respectively emphasize and value different aspects of growth in others. Men tend to stress change and quantitative growth while women lay greater value upon connectedness and integration, that is, qualitative growth (Gilligan, 1987; Kegan, 1982, p. 5). These differences in value expectations may suggest that, in general, male and female workers hold potentially somewhat different care objectives. Such differences can be viewed as welcome variations or as potential sources of tension. At times, behavioral improvements, that is, "quantitative" change, is desired. At other times, it is desirable to promote integrated growth, "qualitative" change, with an advance in developmental overall capabilities. The latter then demands a greater reliance upon dependency nurturance by child and youth care; whether a worker happens to be male or female. The above tendencies can be recognized and utilized in group care and beyond.

A DEVELOPMENTAL PERSPECTIVE AS A CHILD AND YOUTH CARE PRACTICE STANCE

Care Work Involves Proactive Intervention

Developmental knowledge not only provides an empirically-grounded practice framework for child and youth care work, it also entails the practice stance most in tune with actual tasks performed by these care givers. Workers are challenged to deal with the ordinary care demands and social surveillance basic for children and adolescents in general, at each particular period in their lives. They are also responsible for specific care needs of each individual on the basis of the child's special personal requirements and existing circumstances. The basic care demands are rooted in *general* human development knowledge and overall practice experience with children and youth; *individual* requirements are based upon specific assessment of each child's particular unique situation. These efforts on the part of care workers entail a combination of informed practice wisdom and clinical[2] thinking.

Developmental orientation, by its solid person-in-the-situation orientation, helps to lessen the ever-existing strain between personal requirements of the care receivers and care givers and those of the institutional (organizational) setting (Maier, 1987, Ch. 9). Integral to the workers' task performances is for them to observe, to assess, and to respond to each individual as well as to the way the particular living group is functioning. Importantly, care workers not only respond, but they themselves continuously initiate interactions and design programs which enhance the children's or youth's ongoing development. This may involve support or redirection of ongoing activities. At other times, they initiate expectations which reach beyond the children's immediate ongoing functioning *as if* they could also manage a slight shift to a more advanced level (Maier, 1987, p. 18). In all of these and other care activities, the worker proceeds on the basis of her or his assessment (diagnosis) of an individual's functioning (coping) and an understanding of what is needed for a step onwards in development, personal competency, and situational effective living.

Focus Upon What a Person Is Doing Rather Than What Is "Deficient"

A developmental perspective enhances a worker's interest to discern what is each individual's current performance. A worker's focus then naturally looks at what a person *is doing*, rather than not doing. To put it another way: full attention is directed to *what* is the observable activity and *how* he or she is "making a go." This requirement might sound rather self-evident. Yet, in much of everyday accounting of children's or adolescents' behavior, thinking or feelings, a common tendency is to report either what the youngsters are *not* doing or what they *ought* to be doing, feeling, or thinking. Such accounts are apt to define the adults' expectations; they yield little awareness into what the youngsters are all about. A worker may report, for example, that Carolyn does nothing;[3] "she absolutely paid no attention to whatever I told her." Such a statement reveals that the worker believes a girl like Carolyn should listen and obey. But it leaves one helpless in this situation, because one does not learn anything about Carolyn. In inquiring further into what actually happened *between* the two, it is revealed that Carolyn, 14, was apparently intently listening to her records, swaying with the music, as the worker approached her. When the worker started to speak to her from the door entry, the girl turned her back halfway to the worker. Carolyn did a lot! And with these observations, a worker may be prepared to find a number of possible points of entry: (1) joining in space and rhythm momentarily with Carolyn after acknowledging her entry into Carolyn's sphere; (2) waiting for a brief period before asking for her attention, (3) then gauging her readiness to receive, or (4) after momentary appraisal, deciding the message does or does not warrant the intrusion. This approach, observing and sharing in what the youngster *is* doing, while simultaneously staking out the necessary steps in the long process toward achievement brings about increased potency to the workers' efforts.

The Minutiae of Child Care Are the "Biggies"

While working with children or youth with a focus upon their feelings and ways of interactions, attention needs to be paid to the minutiae of interactions. It is these small details of interplay which tell by the actual variation in behavioral, thought, or affective processes, what is going on. In the preceding paragraph Carolyn was listening intently to music when the worker approached her. "She turned her back halfway to the worker." Thus, it is known that she did respond to the worker's intrusion. She acknowledged the worker while communicating her lack of readiness to be engaged with her, by turning halfway, leaving a partial frontal contact with the worker. Possibly the worker's announcing herself, momentary sharing in the rhythmic experience of Carolyn's recorded music, or seriously responding to her half acknowledgment, might result in a different outcome with some potential for movement.

Cognizant of these minutiae, concrete directions for the next interaction can be readily established and carried out. These small active interventive engagements, built upon minutiae of interactions by the care workers, as Albert Bandura (1977) points out, rather than any set of masterful techniques, clever verbal input, or major breakthrough tactics, make for effective change.

Development occurs then, by small steps through the minutiae of ordinary human experience, and within the context of daily events. In care work, apparently inconsequential activities might be some of the more potent ones such as the wink of an eye, a casual hand on a youngster's shoulder, a clear and honest expression of disagreement, or stopping at the bedside after lights are out for an extra squeeze after an earlier tough conflictual time. These minute acts can indeed be very significant in child or youth care work.

A Situational/Contextual Emphasis

A developmental perspective goes hand-in-hand with concrete effective care work—work which is flexible, adaptive, and hopefully deals with each care event in the *context* of the overall situation. Care work needs to be appropriate developmentally *and* situationally targeted rather than merely behaviorally or theoretically programmed. An honest word of praise (or a reprimand) may be effective if the individual and care worker are figuratively together in the same place. By contrast, if the same youth is amidst his or her peers, the worker's well-intended comments may achieve just the opposite effect. A reprimand may then be envisaged by the youngster and peers as a badge of achievement. Context, as ecological thinking demands, spells out the relevant meaning to all personal interactions. A situational definition makes or breaks the impact of a person's activities however valid or logically sounding the intent might have been (Bronfenbrenner, 1979).

Equally important is the workers' recognition of environmental factors and the *bi*-directional flow of human interactions. The individual's impact upon his or her environment and the powerful influence of the same environment upon these inherent interactions require of the care workers that their intervention includes efforts which "make the environment safer, more developmentally sound, and more nurturant" (Whittaker, 1986, p.78).

A DEVELOPMENTAL STANCE FALLS WITHIN AN OPEN SYSTEM APPROACH

A developmental approach leaves the way open for linkages with other systems of knowledge. If children and adolescents are observed, studied, understood, and dealt with as multi-functional but solitary beings within a social matrix and covered by powerful environmental forces (Maas, 1984), then it follows that other frameworks of psychological knowledge and their respective interventive techniques could be applied. Behavioral shaping may be appropriate when specific forms of *behaviors* are to be impacted; this could be accomplished without necessarily adopting a concentrated behavior modification or token economy program. Relaxation techniques can be very fruitful while dealing with facets of somatic tensions. Similarly, cognitive structuring or imagery work may be applicable when efforts are directed toward altering selected thought processes. In these illustrations, and in the potential utilization of the vast array of other psychological modalities and interventive procedures, the target is a specific human *process* which addresses the person-as-a-whole. Such interventive activities are supplementary to continued care activities which need to proceed simultaneously because children and adolescents require the *consistent* nurturing and enhancing care, protection, and challenges of instrumental adults *who are fully available* for them.

IMPLICATIONS FOR TRAINING
AND CHILD AND YOUTH CARE EDUCATION

It is almost redundant to point out that child and youth care workers have to be versed in human developmental knowledge, while observing and assessing and actually being engaged in work with the youngsters, ready to amass a vast repertoire of techniques, applied as these situations demand on the basis of on-the-spot assessment. Such competencies, for the most part, have to be acquired in prior training where knowledge and application of knowledge is fused. Practice skills have to be initially learned within the context of simulated skill-building practice experiences and afterwards in step-by-step, well-selected and supervised actual practice experience in order to avoid that children or youth become the "guinea pigs" of the workers-in-training.

Training has to focus upon the minutiae of practice: what is actually involved in the specific care activities instead of merely acquainting trainees with the tasks at hand. So simple a task as "calling youngsters in from the playground," represents a complexity of possible interactions. The same is true for physically separating oneself from a child while conveying in action to the child: "I am still with you!"

Training before and on the job is essential to mastery of at least beginning competence. Continuous learning and refinement of know-how should be further demanded in order to keep somewhat abreast with the exciting new findings from developmental studies (conceptual and empirical research). Hopefully before too long, research findings will be accumulated from care workers' own repertoire.

CLOSING COMMENTS

A *developmental* perspective is appropriately advocated because the subject matter and research undertaking of contemporary lifespan developmental psychology deals with the very questions that engage child and youth care workers in their daily work. They come up against the lives of children and youth in their immediate contextual situations. They confront the ways care givers and care receivers impact each other and their joint environment. These encounters intrinsically are reflective of the child's or youth's developmental course and current status.

However, a developmental perspective is not merely preferred for this commonality; it is particularly suitable because of its rich resources of immediately applicable knowledge, based upon empirically verifiable research. This is the kind of knowledge foundation which is directly necessary for the work with children and youth and their immediate care givers.

Also, a developmental perspective is at this point not only advocated as a specialty for direct care work, it is currently emerging as the orientation of choice in the wider human relations fields. Child and youth care workers can be challenged to be group care practitioners who are at the forefront rather than late in utilizing such an orientation. They have the potential to emerge as creators of practice experience, hopefully yielding research data for their own fellow professionals.

Finally, a developmental perspective is confidently introduced for its essential humanistic and ecological approaches, its scientific (research) explorations, and its consistency with that which is valuable in human existence. Children, youth or adults, researchers, teachers, or *child and youth care workers* who can join their creative efforts in advancing developmental knowledge and its application will also advance their own future.

NOTES

1. "Some of the short-term residential programs which specialize in teaching independent living skills are insufficiently clear about developmental issues, especially the place of nurturing experience in that process. They try to force growth. Growth cannot be forced through some kind of hothouse process and to attempt it, may do harm" (Ainsworth, F., 1987).

2. "Clinical thinking" has nothing to do per se with a white coat, medical model, or use of any one brand of psychological or psychiatric nomenclature. Instead, *clinical* thinking pertains to a judgment made on the basis of actual observation and painstaking study of the particular circumstances in order to obtain for each case a distinct assessment (diagnosis) of the case-specific conditions. "Clinical" stands for data obtained by other than class or categorical ordering, theory, or by a belief system.

3. Please note the contradiction: nobody can *do* nothing!

REFERENCES

Ainsworth, F. (1987). The rush to independence—a new tyranny. *Australian Social Work*.

Ainsworth, F., & Fulcher, L. C. (Eds.) (1981). *Group care for children: Concept and issues*. London: Tavistock Publications.

Ainsworth, M. D. (1982). Attachment: Retrospect and prospect. In C. M. Parkes & J. Stevenson, *The place of attachment in human behavior* (pp. 3-30). New York: Basic Books.

Baltes, P. B., Reese, H. W., & Lipsitt, L. P. (1980). Lifespan and developmental psychology. In M. R. Rosenzweig & L. W. Porter (Eds.), *Annual review of psychology: Volume 31* (pp. 65-110). Palo Alto, CA: Annual Review.

Bandura, A. (1977). Self-efficacy: Toward a unifying theory of behavioral change. *Psychological Review, 84*(2), 191-215.

Beker, J. & Maier, H. W. (1980). Emerging issues in child and youth care education: A platform for planning. *Child Care Quarterly, 10*(3), 200-209.

Bronfenbrenner, U. (1979). *The ecology of human development*. Cambridge, MA: Harvard University Press.

Elkind, D. (1981). *The hurried child: Growing up too fast too soon*. Reading, MA: Addison Wesley.

Gilligan, C. (1987). *Adolescent development reconsidered* (The Tenth Annual Gisela Konopka Lecture Monograph). St. Paul: Center for Youth Development and Research, University of Minnesota.

Ivey, A. (1986). *Developmental theory: Theory into practice.* North Amherst, MA: Microtraining Associates.

Izard, C. E., Kagan, J., & Zajone (1984). *Emotions, cognition, and behavior.* London: Cambridge University Press.

Jones, F. R., Garrison, K. C., & Morgan, R. F. (1985). *The psychology of human development.* New York: Harper & Row.

Kegan, R. (1982). *The evolving self.* Cambridge, MA: Harvard University Press.

Lerner, R. M., & Busch-Rossnagel, N. A. (1981). *Individuals as producers of their development: A lifespan perspective.* New York: Academic Press.

Maas, H. S. (1984). *People in context.* Englewood Cliffs, NJ: Prentice-Hall.

Maier, H. W. (1987). *Developmental group care of children and youth: Concepts and practice.* New York: Haworth Press. (Paperback, 1988).

Maier, H. W. (1986). Human development: Psychological basis. In A. Minehan (Ed.), *Encyclopedia of social work* (18th ed.) (pp. 850-856). New York: National Association of Social Workers.

Maier, H. W. (1981). Rhythms of care. In F. Ainsworth & L. C. Fulcher (Eds.), *Group care for children: Concept and issues* (pp. 28-30). London: Tavistock.

Maier, H. W. (1979). Child care workers' development from an interactional perspective. *Child Care Quarterly, 8*(2), 94-99.

Maier, H. W. (1978). *Three theories of child development* (3rd ed.) New York: Harper & Row; (1988 - A paperback by Lanham, MD, University Press of America.)

Schuster, C. S., & Ashburn, S. S. (1986). The holistic approach. In C. S. Schuster & S. S. Asburn, *The process of human development: A holistic lifespan approach* (2nd ed.) (pp. 23-41). Boston: Little, Brown, & Company.

Skolnick, A. S. (1986). *The psychology of human development.* New York: Harcourt Brace Jovanovich.

Sroufe, A. (1978). Attachment and the roots of competence. *Human Nature, 1*(10), 50-57.

VanderVen, K. (1986). From child care to developmental life cycle caregiving: A proposal for future growth. *Journal of Child and Youth Care Work, 2*(2), (Spring), 53-63.

VanderVen, K., Mattingly, M. A., & Morris, M. G. (1982). Principles and guidelines for child care personnel preparation programs. *Child Care Quarterly, 11*(3), 221-244.

Washington, R. O. (1982). Social developments: A frame for practice and education. *Social Work, 27*(1), 104-109.

Whittaker, J. K. (1986). The ecology of child and family helping and expanded practice roles for child and youth care workers. *Child Care Quarterly, 15*(2), 77-79.

2

Growing Together:
The Personal Relationship
in Child and Youth Care

Gerry Fewster

ABSTRACT. The term "relationship" is used to describe many forms of interaction between youngsters and adults. In this chapter it is suggested that the "personal" relationship provides the critical learning context in the field of child and youth care. The nature of this relationship is analyzed and discussed.

This chapter is about relationships. In the broadest sense, it is concerned with the most critical of all learning contexts: that complex inter-personal arena in which we struggle to know who we are and where we stand in relation to the world around us. Here is the universal crucible that inevitably consumes all of our personal experiences and blends them into complex and wondrous configurations of understanding and meaning. Only through relationships, real or imagned, past or present, near or far, do we come to know our qualities, potentials, vulnerabilities and, ultimately, our humanness and our mortality. Only through relationships can we come to understand the existence of others and the paradox of how, through our very individuation, we begin to discover the network of connections that forever draw us toward each other.

More specifically, this chapter is about a very special kind of

---

Gerry Fewster, Executive Director, Hull Foundation, 117 Woodpark Blvd. SW, Calgary T2W 2Z8.

relationship. In all societies, the continuity of the culture is founded upon the ability of the children to learn the ways of their elders and understand the meanings that emerge from individual and collective experience. Children who are fortunate enough to learn and understand through personal encounters with adults are able to acquire the competence, confidence and knowledge to establish their own unique pathways toward self-discovery, esteem, autonomy and responsibility. Children exposed to inadequate or coercive teachers and those who are denied access to the personal meanings and experiences of their elders become prisoners of their own incompetence, self-depreciation and confusion. Unable to come to terms with themselves and the worlds in which they live, they may choose pathways of dependence, resentment, hostility or despair. For the most part, these are the young people who find themselves in encounters with professional child and youth care workers. Potentially, these very critical and challenging relationships always contain the hope that the adult-child connection can be successfully established to the personal benefit of *both* participants.

Having suggested that the inter-personal encounter embodies the essence of all that we come to know and understand about ourselves and our worlds, it would be impossible to present an adequate analysis of the worker-child relationship within the scope of this chapter. The thoughts expressed here offer no more than a very brief and very idiosyncratic introduction to the topic. Bound up in the personal and professional experience of the author, they are not presented as "truths" or universal realities. The suggested approaches are not infallible, although they do have time-tested validity within a relatively limited sphere of experience. Behind all that is said here, however, is a fundamental belief that the personalized relationship continues to be the greatest challenge in professional child and youth care. From this perspective, it is suggested that child and youth care workers are in a unique position to explore new ways of connecting children with themselves and the adults that assume responsibility for caring and nurturing. To achieve this through relationships means that such practitioners must first become open to their own experiences and be prepared to examine their own meanings that emerge through their encounters with young people. The words that express these thoughts come easily. The actions that the thoughts imply demand courage, commitment, creativity and, most of all, discipline.

WHAT IS A RELATIONSHIP?

The term "relationship" can be applied to almost any type of human encounter. In the field of humanistic psychology, it has always been assumed that personal growth and development is inextricably linked to a person's awareness and understanding of others (e.g., Rogers, 1951; Perls, 1951; Derlega, 1984). By the same token, social psychologists have long been fascinated by the relationships between social interaction and personality development (e.g., Smelser & Smelser, 1963). In child psychology particularly the influence of primary relationships on child development and socialization has been a major emphasis (e.g., Hoppe, Milton & Simmel, 1970) and such influences have been well established in the areas of social cognition (e.g., Leahy, 1985), self-concept (e.g., Coopersmith, 1967) and social behaviors (e.g., Bond & Joffe, 1982).

The serious reader or committed practitioner should certainly examine the relationship literature carefully and consider the findings and conclusions in terms of her or his own experience. In the present context, however, we are concerned with one particular perspective (i.e., that of the author), on one particular type of relationship (i.e., where interaction is both personal and enduring), within a narrowly prescribed context (i.e., the world of the child and youth worker).

The Personal Relationship

A personal encounter is one in which participants relate directly to their own experience as it occurs at that immediate moment in time. Any disclosure then becomes an expression of the self rather than of some covert agenda designed to create a particular impression or evoke a particular response. Where such intentions exist they are disclosed as elements within the immediate experience. Since child and youth workers are generally burdened with a multiplicity of intentions associated with issues of control, treatment and immediate task completion, this is not an easy stance to take.

Caught up in the activity of the moment, even the act of being in touch with personal experience may demand a supreme effort. If this is not achieved, however, there is no way that such experience can be made available to a young person and the learning potential of the personal encounter is lost. In many relationships between adults and children, particularly in "therapeutic" environments, both parties are more concerned with "impression measurement" than self-disclosure (see Goffman, 1963; Schlenker, 1980).

This is not to suggest that a personal encounter calls for a total and absolute act of self-disclosure. If we are to maintain any sense of self-integrity it is essential that, in each encounter, we determine how much we are prepared to share at any particular time with any particular person. A failure to establish such personal "boundaries" can have devastating personal and inter-personal consequences. It should be emphasized that a commitment to pursue a pathway of complete self-disclosure is a very serious decision to be made and agreed upon by two people who intend to experience a state of "intimacy." Within the context of the practitioner-child relationship this goal is considered to be both impossible and undesirable. On the other hand, relating from the personal is possible across a wide range of encounters and contexts, and inevitably contributes to the ongoing process of learning and discovery. Where it occurs, the person creates an opportunity for both participants to address the most critical existential questions of "Who am I?" and "How do I fit into the world?" It is essentially an interactional process to the extent that it brings together two unique sets of experiences within the same arena of analysis. Hence, the benefits accrue as much to the practitioner as to the child.

Through being personal an adult extends an invitation to the child to respond from her or his own place of immediate experience. Of course, the young person may not choose to do so and that decision must always be respected. To invade the boundaries of another person by assaulting her or his private world of personal experience is an act of disrespect that can only serve to depersonalize the encounter. On the other hand, the need to examine personal experience through the personal experiences of others is one of the most crucial developmental tasks and child care practitioners can do much to ensure that such opportunities are constantly available. A willingness to make use of these opportunities is clearly bound up in such issues as trust, self-worth and risk-taking but, even when strangers meet in suspicion, the potential for a personal encounter is built into the equation. Similarly, it is always possible for a child care worker to establish a personal way of relating to a child regardless of the conditions, deficits or developmental histories involved.

Existentially speaking, it is being suggested that in understanding ourselves and the worlds in which we live we have only our own experience to guide us. Personal relationships then become the most critical of learning contexts through which we all come to "understand." From this perspective they provide the foundation for self-awareness and development. In psychological terms, they are the very essence of self-esteem, personal autonomy and individual responsibility; notions that have become the cornerstones of contemporary child care practice. To fully appreciate the value of such concepts, however, it becomes necessary to abandon, or at least suspend, the traditional image of a practitioner "doing something to" a child. We must step away, at least temporarily, from the magic of "intervention" in order to fully experience the mystery of two lives, caught up within their own unique struggles, learning together by taking the risk to be personal.

This does not mean that roles and responsibilities should be cast upon the wind in a gesture of cathartic abandonment. On the contrary, it is a disciplined process of examination and analysis that brings together thought, feeling and action. In its most energetic form it involves an active and precise interchange where even the words employed are examined for their fidelity to experience and shared understanding. Roles and responsibilities become essential parts of the analysis to the extent that they enter into immediate experience. In its most evolved or developed form, the personal encounter actually requires very few words since immediate experience is quickly understood, communicated and acknowledged between people who know themselves and each other. Usually this is the experience of people who have spent many years sharing the journey of self-discovery and it should not be an expectation of child care practice. For the most part, we must be satisfied with the Airline's exhortation that "getting there is half the fun."

Why Do We Choose to Be Impersonal?

Despite our best intentions and the obvious benefits of developing personalized practices, it seems that we are often reluctant to take the risk. In this regard, we are no different from the children we serve. We also have our own self-doubts and confusions built into our personal struggle. At the professional level, however, child and youth care can also provide us with an effective impersonal cloak, if we choose to be seduced by its glamorous pretense. Grasping at its promise of invisibility, it is possible to enter a world where knowledge and understanding become matters of theory and concept rather than processes of discovery. Hiding behind the role that it offers, we can choose to accept a safe identity that is shared with others and evaluated according to prescribed performance criteria. In this way it is possible to avoid the more threatening prospects of self-evaluation. Then, when the action gets underway, we can happily fall back upon all of those skill-based intervention strategies that have become part of the trade. In this way, we always have the choice of attributing success to ourselves and failure to the tools. The real danger here is the sacrifice of the self in favour of the professional identity. As we objectify ourselves, so we turn children into objects to be treated, changed or otherwise controlled. At best, we create a sterile learning context and, at worst, we establish a climate for depersonalization and abuse.

For the practitioner who accepts the mantle of professionalism with humility and self-commitment, there are still many aspects of the world of practice that offer temptation toward depersonalization. From the outset, most practitioners must come to terms with the control functions of the agencies that employ them. Expectations are set and embodied in policies, regulations and procedures that promote accountability and standards, on the one hand, while encouraging routinization and control on the other. Where these influences cannot be recognized by the practitioner, it is easy to slip into the role of assuming responsibility for all that the individual child does while engaged within a particular program. Caught up in this expectation the practitioner has effectively taken away the autonomy of the young person and may well feel obliged to resort to strategies of coercion and manipulation in order to make sure that she or he complies with a set of agency standards or treatment outcomes. Here the youngster may be perceived as a threatening object who needs to be controlled from a distance. Many of the forces that have the potential to create these conditions are, in fact, legitimate aspects of service delivery and do not have to adversely affect practitioner-child relationships. Understanding how they operate, however, surely assists the person who wishes to place the personal relationship at the centre of child and youth care.

BECOMING MORE PERSONAL

In order to embrace the personal relationship within the core of child and youth care practice, it is necessary for practitioners to fully acknowledge that the primary commitment is to their own personal growth and development. If personalization is approached simply as an orientation for intervention strategies or treatment techniques, integrity is immediately lost and the scene is set for manipulation and control. Only when the self is fully invested in the process will the full potential of the relationship as a learning context be realized. Then it becomes possible to generate hypotheses, construct concepts and develop skill-based practices. As I have suggested elsewhere, "The practitioner who seeks to truly understand the nature of the relationship enters a world of intimidating complexity" (1982, p. 73).

For the person who is intent upon carving out a pathway through the forest of personal experience, there are many interactional theories and models that others have offered for consideration. Some have attained impressive empirical support while others seem to rely extensively upon intuitive appeal. They should all be examined from the perspective of personal experience at some point in any analysis. Then there are forestry guidebooks that point direction and teach basic survival skills without telling very much about the history or ecology of the environment. In child and youth care, the popularity of skill-based training approaches suggests that we will always have great needs for efficacy and survival in a context that we will never fully understand. Unfortunately, many of the solutions and prescriptions offered do not encourage self-involvement, personalization and relational practices. As such, they are generally low risk and control focused. The following suggestions are prescriptive to the degree that they move the person toward personalization. From that point, however, specific outcomes are unpredictable and risks are high. These are the costs of personal and professional growth.

Becoming Present

To be fully attuned to any immediate experience, the self must be totally invested in the process. This involves being exclusively attentive to the situation and in touch with all of the sensations and feelings experienced at that moment in time. In a personal encounter, this state of "presence" represents a condition of self-awareness from which the individual reaches out in an attempt to grasp and understand the experience of the other. It is not essential for all of the thoughts and feelings to be shared, merely that they be identified. In this context, a state of presence is a necessary precondition for any personal encounter.

For child and youth care workers caught up in their routines and responsibilities, becoming present generally requires both discipline and commitment. Previous activities, future aspirations and obligations, role-based ideals, long-term agendas, and the like, must all be suspended. Taking a moment before each "session" with a child to get in touch with the thinking and feeling self, should assist in making the transition from the pragmatic to the personal. Essentially, this involves a process of allowing thoughts and feelings to be acknowledged, and then letting them go with the security of knowing that they can be retrieved for future reference. In this way, the self becomes sensitized and "vulnerable" to the experience of the other person and aware of its own place in the moment. This is well exemplified by the Zen Master, Paul Reps, who when asked, "What are you doing this morning?" replied "Listening to you ask a question." For all who experience it, being present is an energizing rather than a draining experience. This is good news for all who work in the helping professions and fear the spectre of "burn-out."

Making Judgements

Given the perspective presented here, it is impossible for any one person to "know" another; all that is available is the personal experience of the encounter. Hence each person is the "owner" of her or his judgements and opinions. Such interpretations are a direct function of the self and not of the other . . . from an analytic perspective, they are self revelations. In this way, for example, the positive and negative qualities that we attributed to others turn out to be the likes and dislikes that we hold about ourselves.

For professionals trained to believe in clinical judgements, the above statement may seem offensive, bizarre and nonsensical. On the other hand, a person who accepts full ownership for personal judgements assumes a position of personal responsibility for all actions based upon such interpretations. As statements of self-disclosure, rather than fact, they are simply information for the other to consider without prejudice. In this way, both participants in an encounter are free to express judgements and interpretations without manipulation, coercion or condemnation.

While this seems like something of a lofty idea, experience suggests that children and young people can very quickly grasp the self-related function of judgements and learn by taking this perspective. Children with needs to protect their self-view learn to understand that they cannot be hurt directly by the judgement of others; they must take the dagger in order to stab themselves. By the same token, children with needs for acceptability can avoid losing autonomy to the imposter of flattery or "social reinforcement." Conversely, children can learn that their own attempts to manipulate through insults and flattery are more self-revealing than controlling. On the other side of the coin, once the ownership of judgements is understood, the adult or worker is free to be open without having to be "right," or responsible for the choices and interpretations made by the child. In an important way, this orientation gives people permission to be human.

Role-Taking Ability

"Role-taking ability" is a concept that emerges from the Symbolic Interactionist tradition in social psychology, particularly the work of George Herbert Mead. Briefly stated, it refers to the process through which we are able to look back at ourselves as if through the eyes of others. This ability represents a critical developmental task in the genesis of the self, but it continues to be fundamental in most forms of social interaction. One way or another, we are all interested in the images that others have of us, particularly those people whom we consider to be significant in our lives. This is an important aspect of self-awareness and discovery as long as we are clear about those images and understand them for what they are . . . the experiences of others.

Seen this way, information from role-taking becomes highly relevant in the process of understanding and deciding among the courses of action open to us. In child and youth care, for example, the young person who understands how she is perceived by the workers is aware of how they might respond to the choices she makes. In this way she is able to assess the possible consequences of her actions and is in a position to take control of her own destiny, rather than take pot luck. In the same way, this young person is also in charge of meeting her own self-esteem needs since she is able to choose how, and from whom, she would like to be accepted, recognized and cared for. Conversely, workers who understand how they are perceived by children are able to operate in a sensitive manner and continue to act in the best interests of the child. In its most effective form, role-taking is inter-personal understanding and is best exemplified by those individuals who, somehow, manage to move together in unison without verbal instructions or predetermined scripts.

Effective role-taking can undoubtedly enrich the personal aspects of the worker-child relationship. To some extent, it is a skill that can be enhanced through experiential training and practice. In its most basic form the role-taking person attempts to predict the responses of others by observing their behavior and assessing (1) that person's intentions; (2) that person's feelings about themselves and (3) that person's feelings about the role-taker. The training procedure involves an open disclosure of these assessments and interpretations within an interactional sequence. In this way, each person has an 'opportunity to check out such interpretations by inviting the other to attest to their "accuracy" and to provide further elaboration. Each participant can keep an accuracy score and may be encouraged to monitor progress over time through an accuracy chart. In the author's experience, where this procedure has been employed, role-taking has invariably improved and participants almost always report that their relationship has become more personal.

The benefits of role-taking training can often be quite dramatic, as participants move toward greater depths of personal disclosure and understanding. As more and more information is made available, people generally experience increased control over personal destiny, enhanced feelings of competence and esteem and expanded awareness of the needs of others. There seems to be little doubt that effective and accurate role-taking is an essential ingredient of any close relationship and a skill possessed by all people considered to be socially "successful."

Keeping Things Clear

In all relational networks, people carry around thoughts, beliefs, opinions and feelings about others that profoundly affect individual encounters. In many cases, this hidden "baggage" inhibits open and personal communication to the extent that it influences intentions and responses. In child care settings, many of the assumptions and interpretations made about children come to the surface in public bars or staff rooms, and may even become formalized in carefully guarded reports or closed case conferences. Similarly, people carry feelings and thoughts drawn from other experiences into relational encounters that have no legitimate place in that experience. We are all familiar, for example, with the husband who returns home from a frustrating day at work to "take it out" on his wife.

In child and youth care, it is easy for experiences with one child to be carried over into interaction with another or, even with the same child, it is possible to harbor resentments from one session to the next. The dangers of hanging on to such assumptions and beliefs, along with their associated feelings, are self-evident. Even so, for workers bound up in the pursuit of pragmatic goals and expectations, it takes considerable discipline and "presence" to take the time and the risk to confront this unfinished business. When external pressures prevail, such matters may be conveniently tucked away and dismissed as insignificant. A commitment to relationships would render this reaction intolerable.

To confront this issue directly, it is possible for child and youth care practitioners to incorporate a process of "clearing" into their daily practices and routines. This begins by specifically setting time aside to be with the young person for "personal" time. At the beginning of each session, both participants should have the opportunity to identify, acknowledge and express any carry-over assumptions, interpretations, thoughts, and feelings. Similarly, at the end of the session, each person should take the time to reflect upon the immediate encounter and clear anything that could potentially be carried over and, thereby, influence the course of subsequent interaction. Where judgements, interpretations, resentments or appreciations are offered, there should be no expectation that the listener must respond. This is not the purpose of the exercise and, in any case, over time it should be clear that such expressions and experiences belong entirely to the speaker and their acknowledgement is for her or his benefit. Once such procedures are incorporated as part of the normative interactional expectations, they readily become accepted and, just like dental flossing, their absence becomes immediately apparent.

Establishing Boundaries

Whenever people step beyond immediate tasks and roles in interaction with each other, the prospect of a personal encounter is presented and the rules become less clear. This can be anxiety producing and many opportunities for personal growth are lost or rejected in favour of a safe passage with a "goal and role" approach to life. On the other hand, the individual self and its private world of experience makes us who and what we are. Ultimately, it's all we have and there can be no sense of integrity or cohesion if it can be bombarded at any time by the forces of the external world. At the extreme, individuals who have no boundaries, who are unable to separate themselves from the world, are considered to be in a state of psychosis.

Within the helping professions, the inability of practitioners to establish clear boundaries for themselves is one of the most common areas of difficulty. In the terms of this chapter, it means that the worker has not decided how personally she or he wishes to be involved with children. In some cases, the practitioner becomes literally swamped with personal pressures and conflicts resulting in resentment, avoidance, fatigue and burn out. On the other side of the coin, the person may simply reject any temptation to become personally involved, preferring to reside in the impersonal world of "objectivity." Perhaps the most tragic of all is the person who constantly shifts personal boundaries in accordance with the perceived needs or demands of others. Relating to such a person is an exercise in acceptance and rejection, care and resentment or love and hostility. Where such a relationship cannot be avoided, as is often the case with children, the result may be one of learned anger or learned helplessness.

Being personal in relationships is more an issue of style than of content. In other words, it is possible to be personal without being particularly self-disclosing. The latter issue is a choice that we must all make for ourselves with particular people, in particular situations, at particular times. In no arena is this more important than in the field of child and youth care. This means that each practitioner must decide for herself or himself where the boundary lines are going to be drawn. In any situation where status roles and prescribed responsibilities exist, any move toward, or away from, the personal can readily upset the balance of the social equation. In a structured learning environment for children such a disruption may have consequences that should be considered.

From an individual perspective, there is no simple formula for establishing boundaries although it is crucial for all concerned that they be identified and communicated. As a simple rule of thumb, experience clearly attests to the conclusion that it is easier to work in the direction of "opening up" than "closing down." Although they will vary across individuals and situations, once established, they should be clearly communicated and maintained. If they change over the course of time, this must also be communicated through a process of renegotiation. Above all, it should be kept in mind that the learning, for both child and practitioner, is contained within the *process* and not in the location of the boundaries themselves. With this in mind, practitioners should be able to give themselves permission to establish boundaries according to their own particular needs and not according to some predetermined expectation of "openness." By the same token, the requirements and expectations of role responsibilities can, and should be, incorporated into decision making although this is usually more an issue of disclosure than personalization.

Maintaining a Personalized Workplace

The practitioner who is intent upon working through personal relationships with children must somehow manage to retain a fundamental commitment to her or his own sense of self-discovery and personhood. Unless this type of commitment is constantly addressed, the chances are that the pragmatic demands of the work environment will take over and create a climate of purposeful activity that is essentially impersonal. With this in mind, the person must be prepared to bring the real self into the role identity that is prescribed by the system and expected by colleagues. Once this position has been negotiated, the practitioner must then insist that the work environment becomes responsive to personal needs. To simply sit back and expect this of others would be an act of self-abandonment and diminished responsibility. This means that personal needs should first be identified and acknowledged. This will not occur unless time is made available for this purpose.

A child caring environment is not a factory of tasks and skills; it is an interactional milieu in which all of the primary benefits emerge from a sharing of individual knowledge, beliefs and experience. It is not a place where personal issues should be pushed aside since each one of these issues is a potential learning vehicle for all participants . . . adults and children. The environment should be responsive to the personal needs for competence, esteem and autonomy by providing ongoing feedback within all relational structures and configurations, while involving people directly in those decisions that impinge upon their daily lives. This is a dynamic, personalized environment that will only reach its full potential when all participants share a commonality of commitment to become fully human in recognizing their potential, individuality, and, above all, their relatedness.

SUMMARY

This chapter has attempted to present one idiosyncratic approach to the role of the relationship in child and youth care practice. From this perspective it is proposed that the personal relationship represents the primary vehicle through which we come to "know" ourselves and the worlds in which we live. In the field of child care, this proposition applies as much to the practitioner as it does to the child. The relationship is not, then, another tool or vehicle to be used by one person in relationship to another for the purposes of intervention, treatment or therapy.

At one level, the position taken here may be regarded as being "motherhood" and naive. On the other hand, the implications are both profound and sophisticated, since they penetrate the very nature of being and suggest explanations of monumental complexity. All of this makes for interesting speculation but, in working with children, the point of departure is the recognition that, in a personal relationship, practitioner and child are equal partners in a process of growth and development where the experience of one provides a learning context for the other. From this simple perspective, the objective has been attained when, after each encounter, each can say "thank you" to the other . . . and mean it.

REFERENCES

Bond, L.A., and Joffe, J.M. (1982). *Facilitating infant and early childhood development*. Hanover: University Press of New England.

Coopersmith, S. (1967). *The antecedents of self esteem*. San Francisco: W.H. Freeman.

Derlega, V.J. (1984). *Communication, intimacy and close relationships*. Orlando: Academic Press, Inc.

Fewster, G.D. (1982). You, me and us. *Journal of Child Care. 1* (1), 71-73.

Goffman, E. (1963). *Stigma: Notes on the management of spoiled identity*. Englewood Cliffs, NJ: Prentice-Hall.

Hoppe, R.A., Milton, G.A., and Simmel, E.C. (1970). *Early experiences and the processes of socialization*. New York: Academic Press, Inc.

Leahy, R.L. (1985). *The development of the self*. New York: Academic Press, Inc.

Mead, G.H. (1934). *Mind, self and society*. University of Chicago Press.

Perls, F., Hefferline, R.F., and Goodman, P. (1951). *Gestalt therapy*. Julian Press.

Rogers, C. (1951). *Client centered therapy*. Cambridge, MA: Riverside Press.

Schlenker, B.R. (1980). *Impression management*. Monterey: Brooks/Cole Publishing Co.

Smelser, N.J., and Smelser, W.T. (1963). *Personality and social systems*. New York: John Wiley and Sons, Inc.

SECTION 2:
THERAPEUTIC PROGRAM ISSUES

Introduction

In recent years, much reflection and critical reassessment has been taking place regarding all aspects of therapy and treatment across all the helping professions. Opinions in the formal literature and the public media vary all the way from "nothing works" to "we need more of the same." All but one of the chapters in this section either examines the child and youth worker's role in a specialized environment (i.e., court and emergency shelter) or reexamines the nature of therapy within a traditional mode (i.e., residential care, activity programming, and working with emotionally deprived children). The remaining chapter, which ends the section, takes a broad-brush approach in advocating a major restructuring of child and youth programs as a whole.

Leading off the section with a fresh look at the nature of residential care, Mordecai Arieli, Jerome Beker and Yitzhak Kashti confront the paradox that elite groups in many societies continue to favor residential group care settings, such as "prep" schools, for the care and socialization of their children, while the validity of such settings for children and youth at risk has come under serious questioning. The authors echo Maier's (see Section 1) contention that a developmental, or socializing, perspective is necessary for effective residential care, whatever the needs or problems of the youth. The characteristics of such a setting are examined, and a number of myths concerning residential care are dismissed.

Susan Pratt turns her attention to an integral dimension of all child and youth care work, therapeutic programming, and stresses that our focus in programming can sometimes be misplaced. Rather than becoming overly preoccupied with attempting to complete a planned activity successfully, Pratt reminds us that it is the process of interaction and learning occurring "on the road" to the completion of the activity that is of prime importance, not the activity itself. Therefore, we must be prepared to abandon or modify an activity at any point in the process for, as an advertisement for child and youth care might put it, "process is our most important product."

A collaborative study involving child care workers in France and Quebec focusing on emotional deprivation is described in the chapter by Pierre Gauthier. Using a variety of therapeutic techniques, including concentration exercises, non-verbal communication, relaxation, massage, spontaneous play, and verbal exchanges, the psycho-éducateurs (the term for professional child care workers in Quebec) implemented an integrated approach to working with emotionally deprived children. A major discovery of the project was the distant "professional" attitude of the Canadian éducateurs as compared with their counterparts from France. This stance, Gauthier records, quickly disappeared in favor of a warmer, more demonstrative approach. As well, the project's emphasis on the growth and development of the workers along with the research-and-development orientation allowed for the therapeutic process to evolve, respecting the primacy of the workers' personal creativity in their relationships with the children.

Shelley McMain and Christopher Webster, in their examination of the role of youth workers in the courts, address the tension between treatment and sanctions that exists in the judicial system for children and youth. Based upon their analysis, sound guidelines are offered for youth workers to ensure their therapeutic recommendations are accurate and relevant for the purposes of the court. Careless or biased reports can jeopardize the most efficacious disposition of the case and, contrary to the worker's therapeutic intent, result in unnecessary damage to the offender.

Michael Gershowitz and Alan MacFarlane demonstrate in their discussion of emergency shelters for youth that even short-term crisis-oriented residential care can be used as a therapeutic intervention. As a shelter program, by its very nature, has virtually no control over referrals, it must depend on the quality of its staff and the creation of its living environment for its success. The authors place particular emphasis on the role of the parents and family and the need for the shelter program to respond constructively to the opportunities for the family presented by the crisis. The demanding and volatile shelter environment offers to the student or beginning worker an intense introduction to many of the skills necessary in child and youth care.

Roderick Durkin completes the section by rethinking the *structure* of our children's programs. Assuming a developmental orientation and the central role of the worker-child relationship, Durkin argues forcefully that "restructuring programs as a strategy for change appears to be the quickest and most efficient way to change and improve programs"; his intention being to empower both the children *and* the workers. He also suggests that a number of changes to the profession and to education and training programs are necessary in order to bring about such widespread reorganization.

3

Residential Group Care as a Socializing Environment: Toward a Broader Perspective

Mordecai Arieli
Jerome Beker
Yitzhak Kashti

ABSTRACT. Residential group care has often been viewed as antithetical to healthy normalizing development processes for troubled or "at-risk" children and youth, yet it appears in other settings to be the method of choice for leadership preparation for the elite. This chapter examines group care generically and attempts to bring implications from programs in the latter category to bear on those in the former.

Much attention and energy have been devoted in recent years to questions concerning the validity of residential group care as an intervention modality with children and youth at risk, and the idea of "normalization" to dilute the supposedly negative consequences of institutional living. Yet residential group care in other settings — such as residential "prep" schools — continues to be the method of choice for developing the children of the elite for societal leadership roles. What implications might this paradox have for residential child and youth care work services?

Mordecai Arieli and Yitzhak Kashti, Professors, Tel Aviv University, School of Education, and Jerome Beker, Professor and Director, Center for Youth Development and Research, University of Minnesota, 386 McNeal Hall, 1985 Ruford Avenue, St. Paul, MN 55108.

In approaching this question, the analysis that follows proposes a new typology of residential settings, suggesting that currently ascendant models in child and youth care are closely associated with and have much to learn from the apparently successful approaches of group care programs that continue to serve more privileged elements of the population. It then suggests how this knowledge might be tapped for application in the child and youth care work domain.[1]

Organizational theorists as well as policy makers and practitioners in group care often suggest, explicitly or implicitly, that the central characteristic of residential settings for youth is their relative separation from the outside world. It is claimed, for example, that the greater the separation, the more capable the setting is of reducing the influence of potential conflicts (Wheeler, 1966), and the more effectively it operates. This notion seems to have guided the formulation of two key concepts in this field: "total institutions" (Goffman, 1961) and "powerful environments" (Bloom, 1964). The idea of normalization (Wolfensberger, 1972), on the other hand, suggests that isolation may promote efficiency but not effectiveness. In this connection, the objectives of the program in question are crucial. This is the focus of the typology to be proposed.[2]

CATEGORIES OF RESIDENTIAL GROUP CARE SETTINGS

From this perspective, there appear to be three broad categories of residential group care settings: those that seek simply to provide custodial "support" services to enable other, essentially unrelated processes to take place ("Incidental" group care settings); those that seek to use the group care setting to help to eliminate residential "traits" that are perceived as undesirable ("Remedial" settings); and those that seek to use the setting more broadly to promote some sort of socialization ("Socializing" settings). Most settings in the latter two categories share the assumption that prolonged and continuous stay in a residential setting can be used by those who maintain the setting to help them to achieve specific objectives. The assumption is that the group care setting itself can exert pressure on residents to internalize pre-selected modes of behavior and sets of norms through constant exposure to these influences, if the setting is "programmed" properly.

1. "Incidental" Group Care Settings

Although it can be argued that residential settings are people-changing organizations irrespective of the founder's and the staff's intentions, there are residential settings in which no *deliberate* use is made of the "power" of the residential situation. Those who run them are less interested in "changing" the inmates than in providing for physical needs, such as food, lodging, and protection, while other processes take place. These might simply be normal developmental processes, as in many traditional, custodial orphanages and correctional settings, or they might be curative ones, as in long-term hospitals for such ailments as tuberculosis. Some such institutions have, historically, provided shelter to residents suffering from chronic illnesses or severe physical handicaps assumed to be incurable; others (e.g., prisons) have been designed for punishment. Likewise, college dormitories provide residence away from home without, in most cases, the expectation that the group living situation will be used consciously (except perhaps by the resident himself or herself) to produce personal change.

2. Remedial Settings

Remedial settings function on the assumption that their residents suffer from a specific weakness, deficiency, or deviance. These characteristics define and constrain the resident's existential situation and must be eliminated if the inmates are to be "cured," or made "adaptive" to the environment, or made "normal." In this respect, remedial settings follow a medical or hospital model (Carlebach, 1970). Thus, the problem or deficit is perceived as stemming largely from within the resident rather than from social situations, although the latter may be viewed as an essential element in the "cure." Separation from the outside environment is viewed as beneficial because it allows the care givers to treat, rehabilitate, and cure the problem away from the potentially "re-infecting" influence of other social agents, such as peers, and because it reduces the likelihood of "infecting" others with the same condition ("isolation"). In general, this is the ideology that underlies much of the development of the residential treatment center model in the United States (Barnes & Kelman, 1974; Taylor, 1973; Weber & Haberlein, 1972), although less "clinically"-oriented residential "treatment" models have emerged over the last two or three decades (e.g., the Teaching-Family Model: Wolf, Phillips, Fixsen, Braukmann, Kirigin, Willner, & Schumaker, 1976, and the more socially contextual approaches described below). With few exceptions, similar personal deficit perspectives have governed not only custodial approaches in juvenile corrections, but also rehabilitation-oriented efforts in this domain until recent years (Ohlin, 1973).

3. Socializing Settings

Socializing settings have also been referred to as "mediatory settings" (Lubeck & Empey, 1968) and are frequently viewed as educationally or developmentally oriented and holistic in approach. Their modes of intervention focus on residents' social interactions among themselves and with others, rather than on remedying specific traits, presumed to be deficient, within the individual's personality. Although remedial and socializing settings sometimes cater to the same kinds of residents, the latter relate to the resident's problems as occurring as a result and in the context of social forces rather than as outcomes of particular personal traits or behaviors (e.g., Project Re-Ed: Hobbs, 1966).

Socializing institutions can be classified into three major groups: mainstreaming, autonomizing, and designating settings.

A. Mainstreaming settings are those intended to introduce children from weaker social and economic strata to the social and cultural mainstream of a given society. The idea is usually that rehabilitation will be achieved once residents have gained access to social resources, primarily involving education and training, characteristic of their mainstream peers. The assumption underlying such programs is that once residents gain adequate educational opportunity and achievement, their future position on the mobility ladder, in comparison to that of their parents, will improve: educational enhancement will lead to socioeconomic mainstreaming. Since they view education as central in residents' social habilitation, these settings often view themselves as residential schools. Most institutions for at risk and troubled youth that operate in the socializing rather than the remedial mode are in this category.

Israel's youth villages provide an example of mainstreaming residential settings. These institutions now primarily admit youths whose backgrounds are characterized by Oriental ethnicity, low parental level of education and income, and recent immigration to the country (first or second generation). The school within the youth village resembles an ordinary secondary school in the Israeli society. In addition, the daily schedule includes intensive social activities that allow for a great deal of peer interaction and modelling, and often several hours of work on the youth village farm. In spite of ideologies which attribute equal importance to schooling, work, and social interaction, however, it seems that the two latter fields of activity are frequently considered as means for assisting the students in the acquisition of schooling, which is perceived by staff, parents, and often by the students themselves as the key mainstreaming activity (Kashti, 1974). In the United States, the Job Corps program was developed to meet a similar need in the context of a high rate of youth unemployment (Smilansky, Kashti, & Arieli, 1982).

B. *Autonomizing settings* have emerged as a challenge to those who perceive education primarily as a means of preserving the culture and passing on the heritage to the younger generation. These settings, which seem to cater mainly to middle-class youth, maintain norms and values that emphasize the individual and his or her expressed needs. The resident's continuous exposure to expressive, non-competitive values is designed to help the setting achieve its aim. A radical example of a setting of this type is Summerhill (Neill, 1960), which was founded in Great Britain.

C. *Designating settings* are elitist residential settings that are designed and designated to prepare their students to assume positions of power and prestige in their respective societies, and they generally recruit from the higher strata in the society. They prepare their residents to assume the statuses, roles, and power characteristic of their families' social group, such as through political and economic leadership. American Prep Schools (Cookson & Persell, 1985), English Public Schools (Walford, 1986), and Israeli high school yeshivas (Smilansky, Kashti, & Arieli, 1982), are examples. Military or naval designating residential schools (e.g., West Point) also designate their students for specific roles, but they usually recruit them more on the basis of ability than on such ascriptive criteria as family background. Their curricula are designed to ensure the internalization of norms regarded as suitable for an army or naval officer.

"Avant-garde" designating residential settings are those that seek
to prepare their residents not for specific roles in a given class system, but for the presumed society of the future. Students are selected on the basis of distinctive personal characteristics or ideological affinities. An example is the Israeli Kibbutz, which has
functioned as an *avant-garde* setting for disadvantaged youth from
urban centers, who were admitted to the "Youth Society" affiliated
with the kibbutz to educate them in the light of its "pioneering"
and Zionist ideology.

OPPORTUNITIES AND RISKS
OF THE SOCIALIZING RESIDENTIAL SETTING

Early child and youth care settings were largely what has been
referred to above as "incidental," in which the specifics of group
life were viewed as important only in that they provided a setting in
which other, more crucial processes could occur. This orientation
survives today mostly in highly specialized programs dealing with
physical maladies and in maximum security, custodial residential
facilities. "Medical model" or what have been cited here as "remedial" programs have, in many cases, given way to broader, socializing or developmental orientations, the characteristics of which
frequently parallel those of organizations working with normal and
elite populations. Some of these characteristics are illuminated in
the following discussion of the opportunities and risks they share.

Opportunities

Alternative opportunities for achievement. Socializing residential
settings usually offer residents a multi-dimensional program (Kahane, 1981): residents are engaged together in several kinds of intrinsically satisfying and socially prestigious activities, the most
common of which, in addition to schooling, are social life and
work. As in a family, this range of activities opens a variety of
opportunities for experiencing achievement and success. Students
at a regular day school, on the other hand, are often evaluated in
that setting almost solely on the basis of their academic achievements in the context of an instrumental curriculum. In many academic day schools (as in most residential programs not in the

"socializing" category), they would be less able to experience achievement and to exhibit success in alternative domains, such as contribution to the community, group leadership, or excellence at work. These have been characterized as comprising the "expressive curriculum" of a socializing program — "expressive" in that they are viewed as satisfying in themselves (Lambert, Millham, & Bullock, 1970).

Thus, the expressive curriculum may be particularly important to educationally disadvantaged students in socializing residential settings. Since the level of self-esteem in one domain often influences its level in others, and since the level of self-esteem in a given domain often influences the level of the actual behavior in that domain — it seems reasonable to assume that high self-esteem in an expressive domain, such as leadership, will eventually lead to the development of high self-esteem in the scholastic field and, in turn, will be reflected in students' actual academic achievements.

The expressive curriculum can be criticized, however, on the grounds that it may serve as a control mechanism for residents who do not do well academically. Rather than continuing to strive to help students with a history of school failure to make academic progress, staff in the socializing residential setting may use the expressive curriculum (social activities, work, arts, etc.) as a means for keeping the "losers" somehow occupied and content. In spite of its "progressive" pedagogical connotations, critics may suggest, the expressive curriculum has very little to contribute toward the ultimate instrumental objective of education for much of the residential child and youth care work clientele, which is largely upward social mobility (Sharp & Green, 1975; Woods, 1979).

Self-governance. The continuous, collective life situation within the socializing residential setting provides ample opportunities for youth to experience leadership, responsibility, and sharing, both informally and through instruments of self-government (Grupper & Eisikovits, 1986). In discussions one of the authors held with both direct care workers and residents, however, several interviewees cynically or angrily pointed out that seemingly autonomous self-governance institutions are sometimes highly controlled by the staff (Arieli, 1988). Those residents who participate actively tend to be those who opt to support the powerful staff members who are ideologically interested in such "democratic presentations of the institutional self." This supportive attitude characterizes youths who have an interest in rewarding the formal order of the residential school for the prestigious position of "successful student" it allots them. Disadvantaged youths, on the other hand, tend not to enjoy such recognition and are less inclined to join the "democratic game" and to support a system which does not allot prestigious positions to them. Similar processes have been observed by Lacey (1970) in a day school and, one is tempted to add, by all of us in the world at large. They are often closely related to the referral that led to the placement in the first place, whether for manipulative youth who "play the game" too well or for resistive ones who reject it.

Belongingness. Group care practitioners often suggest that the continuous and intensive peer interaction within socializing residential settings tends to provide residents with experiences of reciprocity, collective commitment, identity, and sharing that transcend similar experiences in such other out-of-home programs as foster care (see, for example, Arieli & Feuerstein, 1987; Feuerstein, 1987). It is further suggested that this feeling is particularly enhanced in settings with ideologically unifying objectives (Wolins, 1980). Thus, in many countries, residential settings are sometimes called "homes" to denote the function they are expected to fill in their residents' emotional lives—but research on the roles of students in residential schools tends to refute this wide belief. In an Israeli study, for example, ten samples of residential school youth all demurred from the suggestion that their residential setting could be regarded as a home (Arieli, Kashti, & Shlasky, 1983).

Risks

Cultural and Family Severance. Goffman (1961) pointed out the tendency of total institutions to blur inmates' individual identities. More recent observers of residential care often claim that the intensive exposure of residents to the culture and value-system of the staff tends to result in the severance of children from their original collective identities and ethnic culture, although many residential agencies do try to recruit staff members who are culturally similar to the residents. Resocialization and reacculturation—processes enhanced by the total life situation—are considered by some to be psychologically hazardous and morally unjust, although from another perspective they are often viewed as the very purpose of the institution.

However, a symmetrically opposite process of cultural identity reinforcement, rather than dilution, may be operative. Most residential settings are populated largely by youth from relatively homogeneous socioeconomic and cultural backgrounds. Since residents are exposed to their peers more than to the staff, their shared cultural heritage may often be reinforced by their continuous and intensive interaction with one another. Polsky (1962) has also pointed out that, under certain circumstances, institutional residents can co-opt staff members into their "deviant" culture rather than being "co-opted" by what they view as the staff's "straight" cultural orientation.

Professionals in the behavioral sciences sometimes warn residential care agencies that not only young children, but also adolescents should not be involuntarily separated from home and parents and referred to residential programs. It is as if they might suffer from some kind of adolescent "parent deprivation," although this does not seem to be viewed as so significant an issue when the youth involved has chosen to go away, such as to school or to camp. The suggestion that the worst home is better than the best institution still seems to be widely accepted, although this may be viewed differently in the case of the elite socializing institutions, another source of suggestive insights for the child and youth care field. Further, as Dor (1973) and others have pointed out, parents from various backgrounds find it increasingly difficult to understand, empathize with, and guide their adolescent children. Perhaps parents will increasingly turn to professionals to perform traditional parental roles, outside the home if necessary. The sources and implications of such a development are beyond the scope of the present paper, although it should be noted that it is just this tendency among upper class families that was instrumental in the establishment of the elite socializing institution.

Cultural Homogenization. In counterpoint to the issue just discussed, critics of socializing residential settings often view the cultural and socio-economic homogeneity of the resident population, as well as the similarities in educational attainment, as a major problem, especially in settings which cater to the weaker social strata. Learning, particularly social learning, occurs largely through the process of modeling as young people select models for imitation and identification. For such models to be effective, they must be recruited by residents from among peers who have attained those features that are considered worth learning. In a homogeneous setting, critics claim, the availability of such models is too limited, although it seems that socializing residential settings are almost never closed to the extent that residents are entirely deprived of more advanced models.

In addition to other residents and the staff, residents usually interact with members of the encompassing social world. In residential settings that do not include school facilities, they attend neighboring day schools; in those with schools of their own, the school is very often open to day students from nearby communities. There seem to be relatively few socializing settings that do not initiate some kind of regular encounters between their residents and peers from the outside world (Shlasky, 1987), and this tendency appears to be increasing (Beker, 1981).

CONCLUSIONS AND IMPLICATIONS

If, as the authors perceive, the "socializing orientation" in residential group care is what such influences as normalization and deinstitutionalization are all about, then we will increasingly be concerned with socializing or youth development perspectives in residential settings for troubled young people and young people at risk. We view this as a positive development for the field of child and youth care work, partly because this orientation is shared by a variety of kinds of residential group care programs that deal with "normal" youth, including the elite, and are widely perceived as successful. On the basis of this common orientation, we can begin to examine their work systematically as a contribution to the knowledge base in the field, as well as to share ours, as appropriate, with this new set of colleagues.

For example, Cookson and Persell (1985), illuminate the dynamics of elite prep schools in the United States. National service and related programs around the world, many of which are residential in nature, are described by Danzig and Szanton (1986), Dickson (1976), Hebert (1979) [Katimavik, the Canadian Youth Corps], McMullan and Snyder (1986) [Katimavik], Rice (1985) [U.S. Peace Corps], Sherraden and Eberly (1982), and United Nations (1975). Organized resident camping, with a historical literature that addresses many of the concerns of the socializing institution rather directly (e.g., Blumenthal, 1937; Dimock & Hendry, 1929; Lieberman, 1931; Osborne 1937) has, significantly, been applied to populations of troubled and at risk youth as well (Loughmiller, 1965; McNeil, 1957), and has again begun to receive prominence as a resource from a residential socializing perspective (e.g., Robb, 1984, Teschner and Wolter, 1984). In the United Kingdom, Walford (1986) has described the elite British "Public" Schools, and Israeli residential group care settings are examined from this perspective by Arieli, Kashti, and Shlasky (1983), Kashti (1979), Smilansky, Kashti, and Arieli (1982), and Wolins and Gottesman (1971). Descriptions of other relevant group care programs are provided by Wolins (1974).

The future of residential group care has been viewed by many in the child and youth care work field as bleak, given the combination of ideological and fiscal restraints that have emerged in recent years, together with its spotty (we are generous!) record of effectiveness. The needs are not, however, being met elsewhere, and the socializing perspective can open our eyes and minds to a broader knowledge base that can be applied in our work as we seek to enhance the level of service we can provide to children and youth who are troubled or at risk.

NOTES

1. In this article, "child and youth care" is used to denote services — treatment, corrections, custody — for young people "in trouble" or viewed as "at risk"; "residential group care" refers to the full range of young people in residential settings, including the "elite."

2. The typology is partly based on a previous attempt by two of the authors of this chapter (Kashti & Arieli, 1976).

REFERENCES

Arieli, M. (1988). Cultural transition through total education: Actors' perspectives. In: Gottesman, M. (Ed.). *Cultural transition: The case of immigrant youth* (pp. 103-120). Jerusalem: The Magnes Press.

Arieli, M., & Feuerstein, R. (1987). The twofold care organization: On the combining of group and foster care. *Child Care Quarterly, 16*, 168-175.

Arieli, M., Kashti, Y., & Shlasky, S. (1983). *Living at school: Israeli residential schools as people processing organizations.* Tel Aviv: Ramot.

Barnes, F. H., & Kelman, S. M. (1974). From slogans to concepts: A basis for change in child care work (and accompanying comments). *Child Care Quarterly, 3*, 7-30.

Beker, J. (1981). New roles for group care centers. In Ainsworth, F., & Fulcher, L. C. (Eds.). *Group care for children: Concept and issues.* London: Tavistock. Pp. 128-147.

Bloom, B. (1964). *Stability and change in human characteristics.* New York: Wiley.

Blumenthal, L. H. (1937). *Group work in camping.* New York: Association Press.

Carlebach, J. (1970). *Caring for children in trouble.* London: Routledge and Kegan Paul.

Cookson, P., & Persell, C. (1985). *Preparing for power: America's elite boarding schools.* New York: Basic Books.

Danzig, R., & Szanton, P. (1986). *National service: What would it mean?* Lexington, Mass.: Lexington Books.

Dickson, M. (Ed.). (1976). *A chance to serve: Alec Dickson.* London: Dobsen Books, Ltd.

Dimock, H. S., & Hendry, C. E. (1929). *Camping and character: A camp experiment in character education.* New York: Association Press. (2nd Ed., 1939).

Dor, S. (1973). The residential school. In Urmean, Ch., (Ed.), *Education in Israel.* Jerusalem: Ministry of Education and Culture (in Hebrew).

Feuerstein, R. (1987). The foster home group care project (pp. 176-187). In Kashti, Y., & Arieli, M. (Eds.). *Residential settings and the community: Congruence and conflict.* London: Freund.

Goffman, E. (1961). *Asylums.* New York: Anchor Books.

Grupper, E., & Eisikovits, R. A. (1986). Student self-government in three Israeli youth villages: An ethnographic evaluation. In Kashti, Y., & Arieli, M. (Eds.). *People in institutions: The Israeli scene.* London: Freund.

Hebert, J. (1979). *Have them build a tower together: About Katimavik, a meeting place, about youth, about hope.* Toronto: McClelland and Stewart.

Hobbs, N. (1966). Helping disturbed children: Psychological and ecological strategies. *American Psychologist, 21*, 1105-1115. (Also in Wolins, 1974).

Kahane, R. (1981). Multi-modal institutions: A conceptual framework for the analysis of residential education centers. *Alim*, 3-15 (in Hebrew).

Kashti, Y. (1974). *Socially disadvantaged youth in residential education in Israel.* Unpublished doctoral dissertation, University of Sussex, U.K.

Kashti, Y. (1979). *The socializing community: Disadvantaged adolescents in Israeli youth villages.* Studies in Educational Evaluation, Monograph No. 1. Tel Aviv: School of Education, Tel Aviv University.

Kashti, Y., & Arieli, M. (1976). Residential schools as powerful environments. *Mental Health and Society, 3*(3/4), 223-232.

Lacey, C. (1970). *Hightown Grammar.* Manchester: Manchester University Press.

Lambert, R., Millham, S., & Bullock, R. (1970). *Manual to the sociology of the school.* London: Weidenfeld & Nicolson.

Leiberman, J. (1931). *Creative camping: A coeducational experiment in personality development and social living . . .* New York: Associated Press.

Loughmiller, C. (1965). *Wilderness road.* Austin: Hogg Foundation for Mental Health, University of Texas.

Lubeck, S. G., & Empcy, L. T. (1968). Mediatory versus total institutions. *Social Problems, 16,* 242-260.

McMullan, B. J., & Snyder, P. (1986). *Youth corps case studies: Katimavik, the Canadian youth corps.* Philadelphia: Public/Private Ventures.

McNeil, E. B. (Ed.). (1957). Therapeutic camping for disturbed youth. A special issue of *The Journal of Social Issues, 13*(1).

Neill, A. S. (1960). *Summerhill: A radical approach to child rearing.* New York: Hart Publishing Co.

Ohlin, L. E. (1973). Institutions for predelinquent or delinquent children. In Pappenfort, D. M., Kilpatrick, D. M., & Roberts, R. W. (Eds.). *Child caring: Social policy and the institution.* Chicago: Aldine. Pp. 177-199.

Osborne, E. G. (1937). *Camping and guidance.* New York: Association Press.

Polsky, H. W. (1962). *Cottage Six.* New York: Wiley.

Rice, G. T. *The bold experiment: JFK's Peace Corps.* Notre Dame, Indiana: University of Notre Dame Press.

Robb, G. (1984). *The Bradford Papers.* Martinsville, Indiana: Bradford Woods.

Sharp, R., & Green, A. (1975). *Education and social control.* London: Routledge & Kegan Paul.

Sherraden, M. W., & Eberly, D. J. (1982). *National service: Social, economic, and military impacts.* New York: Pergamon.

Shlasky, S. (1987). The Israeli youth village and its neighboring community (pp. 109-121). In Kashti, Y., & Arieli, M. (Eds.). *Residential settings and the community: Congruence and conflict.* London: Freund.

Smilansky, M., Kashti, Y., & Arieli, M. (1982). *The residential education alternative.* East Orange, New Jersey: The Institute for Humanist Studies.

Taylor, S. H. (1973). Institutions with therapeutic residential programs for children. In Pappenfort, D. M., Kilpatrick, D. M., & Roberts, R. W. (Eds.). *Child caring: Social policy and the institution.* Chicago: Aldine. Pp. 200-225.

Teschner, D. P., & Wolter, J. J. (Eds.). (1984). *Wilderness challenge: Outdoor education alternatives for youth in need*. Hadlyme, Connecticut: The Institute of Experiential Studies.

United Nations, Department of Economic and Social Affairs. (1975). *Service by youth: A survey of eight country experiences*. New York: United Nations.

Walford, G. (1986). *Life in Public Schools*. London: Methuen.

Weber, G. H., & Haberlein, B. J. (1972). Residential programs: Their components and organizing theories. In Weber, G. H., & Haberlein, B. J. (Eds.). *Residential treatment of emotionally disturbed children*. New York: Behavioral Publications. Pp. 54-63.

Wheeler, S. (1966). The structure of formally organized socialization settings. In Brim, O. G., & Wheeler, S. *Socialization after Childhood*. New York: Wiley.

Wolf, M. W., Phillips, E. L., Fixsen, D. L., Braukmann, C. J., Kirigin, K. A., Willner, A. G., & Schumaker, J. (1976). Achievement Place: The Teaching-Family Model. *Child Care Quarterly*, 5, 92-103.

Wolfensberger, W. (1972). *Normalization*. Toronto: National Institute on Mental Retardation.

Wolins, M. (Ed.). (1974). *Successful group care: Explorations in the powerful environment*. Chicago: Aldine.

Wolins, M. (1980). The successful institution: Some theoretical considerations. In Adiel, S., Shalom, H., & Arieli, M. (Eds.). *Fostering deprived youths and residential education*. Tel Aviv: Cherikover (in Hebrew).

Wolins, M., & Gottesman, M. (Eds.). (1971). *Group care: An Israeli approach*. New York: Gordon and Breach.

Woods, P. (1979). *The divided school*. London: Routledge & Kegan Paul.

4

Therapeutic Programming and Activities: Transitional Tools in the Treatment Process

Susan Pratt

ABSTRACT. Many child and youth care workers have found that a well-chosen and planned activity does not always ensure success. What this chapter will demonstrate is that the therapeutic benefits of any program occur within the interactions and processes that take place throughout the activity. Furthermore, refocusing on the dynamics of interactions actually enlightens the treatment process, as treatment goals take precedence over programming goals.

A therapeutic program was once considered successful as long as it achieved its goal without doing damage to the individual or the group (Redl & Wineman, 1957, p. 327). Many child and youth care workers, however, have found that a well-chosen and planned activity, matching both the client's level of functioning and the treatment goals, does not always ensure success. Just as a doctor can perform a surgically successful operation only to have the patient die, a child and youth care worker can implement a successful program only to have the client run away. In other words, the tendency has been to focus on the activity and its product or outcome rather than the process that occurs throughout the activity. What this chapter will demonstrate is that the therapeutic benefits of any program

Susan Pratt, Coordinator, Child and Youth Care Worker Program, Mohawk College of Applied Arts and Technology, Ferrell Ave. and West 5th, P.O. Box 2034, Hamilton, Ontario L8N 3T2.

occur within the interactions and processes that take place throughout the activity. Furthermore, refocusing on the dynamics of interactions actually enlightens the treatment process, as treatment goals
take precedence over programming goals.

AN OVERVIEW OF THERAPEUTIC PROGRAMMING

Therapeutic, or activity, programming has always been an integral part of child and youth care practice, contributing to the development of relationships, ego-building, psychomotor skills, sublimation, expression of feelings, social skills, education and fun
(Ouderkirk, 1980). The steps in therapeutic programming typically
include the following:

1. Collect information about the client – stage of development
   (normal vs. actual); clinical assessment and problem identification; life skills inventory; client interests. Ascertain
   whether the client's level of functioning is due to (a) lack of
   skills – doesn't know how, (b) lack of resources or environmental constraint – wants to do it but can't due to environmental circumstances (i.e., no time to be with friends after
   school due to family commitments), (c) lack of capacity,
   physically handicapped or delayed, (d) lack of motivation –
   knows how to do it and has the resources and capacity to do
   it, but doesn't want to. All too often, (d) is assumed to be the
   case without properly assessing (a), (b) or (c). Frequently,
   the underlying problem to (d) is (a) and/or (b) or (c) (Romiszowski, 1981, pp. 101-119).
2. Analyze the preceding information to assist in the identification of treatment goals. Priortize treatment goals: (i) social
   skills, (ii) peer interaction, etc.
3. Identify the components necessary to achieve the treatment
   goals (e.g., degree of interaction – small/large group activities versus individual activities).
4. Identify a variety of methods/activities to achieve these
   goals.
5. Analyze the activities in relation to prescriptiveness, controls, physical movement, competency, interaction, re-

wards.[1] Activity analysis typically includes the identification of a number of factors: (a) purpose of the prescribed activity, (b) advantages of the activity, and (c) disadvantages of the activity.

6. Identify hard and soft resources. Hard resources are things. Soft resources are people and their skills.
7. Select and modify an activity to meet the goals of the client within the specific circumstances and with the available resources.
8. Implement the activity, modifying it further as necessary to meet the goals of the client and the circumstances (i.e., weather conditions, mood of group).
9. Evaluate the outcome of the activity process in relation to the client's treatment goals.
10. Redesign the activity based on the evaluation results.

These elements of program design and implementation are outlined in Figure 1.

HISTORY OF THERAPEUTIC PROGRAMMING

During the late 1950s to 1960s, much of the child care client population was under twelve years of age and living in some form of residential treatment service. Child care workers were considered paraprofessionals who provided care for clients in much the same way as loving parents (Gilmour-Barrett & Pratt, 1977). Activity programming was used to provide a normalization component and structure in the children's lives (VanderVen, 1972, p. 208) and so included arts and crafts, games, sports, camping and outings.

A major limitation of some of the early programming practices was the tendency to focus on the activity rather than on the treatment process that occurred within the program. Child care workers would select an activity and then try to match it with the clients' goals, sometimes force-fitting one to the other. One could identify benefits in almost any activity if one looked hard enough.

A second limitation of the traditional view of programming involved those child care workers who did not enjoy or feel skilled in arts and crafts, sports, and camping, yet would actively participate

Figure 1

THERAPEUTIC PROGRAMMING CHART

Client Name: Age: Gender:

Client Information:

Level & stage of:

Physical Functioning

Cognitive/Intellectual Functioning

Affective Functioning/Feelings, Emotions

Client interests - skills/hobbies, what does the client
like doing, if anything?

Client's strengths? What does the client see as his/her
strengths? What do you see has his/her strengths?

What is important to the client? Why? (ask
client/observe and provide informed information)

Who is important to the client? Why? (ask and observe)

Life Skills Inventory (summary from Life Skills
inventory chart)

Treatment Goals:
Priorized - long term and short term goals.

Identify Components that would facilitate achieving the
treatment goals.

Activity Analysis

Prescriptiveness?
Controls required?
Physical movement required?
Competency required: - levels?
Amount of competition? Interaction provided by activity
- degree?
Rewards within the activity? Resources required?
Degree of structure required? Modifications necessary to
achieve treatment goals?
Overall advantages?
Overall disadvantages?

Implementation - Process, interactions

Evaluation - To what degree did the program meet the
client's treatment goals? What changes are indicated?

in other activities surrounding their clients' daily lives. The limitation came in the lack of transfer of knowledge and preplanning surrounding therapeutic programming to other aspects of the clients' experience. Programming tended to be seen as a time-filler or a useful activity set apart from the clients' overall treatment.

The client population and treatment settings have now changed and include both children and adolescents, some of whom are living at home or on their own. Front-line workers can be found working in both residential and non-residential settings (such as schools and hospitals) with multiple handicapped, normative delinquent and emotionally disturbed clients (Gilmour-Barrett & Pratt, 1977, pp. 80-81). The range of activities has also changed to fit the age group and the particular client's living environment. Arts and crafts, games and sports make up only one component of the programming spectrum. Any activities (walks, movies, games, life skills) done with a client can be classed as programming, as they are intended to enhance the development of the individual. The purpose of the activity is more clearly focused upon maximizing the movement/process towards the client's treatment goals. Child and youth care work is no longer defined by setting but rather by knowledge and skills which are transferable to a diversity of settings and programs (after school, home care, parent education, and residential programs, to mention a few) (Gilmour-Barrett & Pratt, 1977, p. 86).

THE ELEMENTS OF THERAPEUTIC PROGRAMMING

If your goal is to travel from point A in Ontario to point B in British Columbia in the most inexpensive way, you would probably travel by car—the least expensive method of travel. A map would be used to identify the most direct route to the destination. Applying this analogy to therapeutic programming:

Point A = the starting point—client assessment. Identify the client's intellectual, physical and emotional level of functioning and capabilities compared to the normal level of development.

Point B = treatment goals. Priorize the gaps between the client's level of functioning and normal functioning and identify long-term and short-term goals. If you don't know where you are going, how will you know when you get there?

A map of the route = treatment plan. Select the best route or combination of routes. This will help determine what vehicle (activity program) will be the most viable to reach the identified destination, the treatment goals.

A vehicle = the activity program. The selection of the mode of travel (activity program) should correspond with the selected route (treatment plan) to achieve point B (the treatment goals) (i.e., if time is limited but sightseeing and relaxation are trip goals, then travel by train may be more appropriate than by car or plane).

Activity programming is one of the most widely-used and more useful vehicles for the child and youth care worker, since it fits within the common understanding and experience of most people. There are many different forms and types of programs, each suited to particular treatment goals and developmental stages. For example, a play therapy approach using doll families may be suitable for younger children, but not for most adolescents.

The trip = the process. The trip takes into account such factors as detours, stops, interactions with various people, and other incidents which may occur along the route. Within a therapeutic program, the process includes the interactions and dynamics between the client, other people and the environment.

Cost-benefit = evaluation of the value and comparison suitability of the therapeutic program. Assess the activity process in relation to the treatment goals. Throughout the activity process, treatment goals may become more clearly delineated. Gains or goals that had not been previously identified may surface.

THE ESSENCE OF THERAPEUTIC PROGRAMMING

Not all programming is therapeutic or involves a therapeutic process. For instance, recreation programs can be physically and emotionally beneficial to the participants without being focused upon treatment.

The major distinction between child and youth care workers and recreation specialists is their purpose and use of programming. Child and youth care workers focus upon the treatment process, using programming and activities as a vehicle to meet the clients' treatment goals. Recreation specialists, on the other hand, focus on programming for recreation and leisure. Although treatment is not the primary focus, recreational programs do provide therapeutic benefit.

For example, a group of adolescents playing baseball may be doing so to have fun and fill time. If a baseball coach is employed, it is unlikely that she or he has identified specific personal goals that each player may work towards throughout the game. Within the group of adolescents playing baseball, the identified treatment goals for each individual may vary (e.g., development of hand-eye coordination, peer relationships, sportsmanship, sublimation).[2]

Therapeutic programming consists of any activity that is designed and implemented to enhance the identified treatment goals of the individual client. The focus of therapeutic programming is on the process that occurs within an activity. The actual activity is important only in relation to the process and treatment goals. Therefore, completing an activity or doing something directly related to the activity is important only if it contributes to the treatment goals. The outcome is focused upon interactions and dynamics that occur throughout the process of the activity rather than on the product of the activity alone.

PREPLANNED AND IMPROMPTU PROGRAMS

It is both unrealistic and undesirable to formally plan every program. Impromptu programming can be very effective so long as child and youth care workers continue to focus on their clients' treatment goals. Some preplanned programs may actually be presented as if they are impromptu, although considerable forethought and planning has gone into them. Other programming opportunities just happen; the timing is right and the client either initiates or is receptive to the activity (e.g., "let's go for a walk"). This may be a good relaxed time to talk.

Impromptu programming may seem to have "just happened," but child and youth care workers must be sufficiently informed, skilled and resourceful to be able to facilitate the activity process and steer it toward identified treatment goals. Even when an activity is recreational, workers can still influence the process through their participation, their active intervention, and the environmental structure.

Ideally, both the clients and the child and youth care workers are involved in the preplanning of activities. Some clients will know what their treatment goals are and may be able to readily identify activities that are of interest and that are facilitative of the treatment process. In working with children and adolescents, it is important to encourage their active involvement in the planning and implementation of activities since this will positively affect motivation and investment in actually implementing the activity. It will also help clients develop invaluable life skills such as problem-solving, conflict resolution and organizational abilities, to mention a few. A primary goal for many clients is to develop skills and attitudes that will enable them to take responsibility for their own lives. Think about activities in which *you* have been involved. Was there a difference in your attitude towards an activity if you planned it yourself, or with friends, as compared to something your parents or another adult planned for you?

CHILD AND YOUTH CARE WORKERS' ROLE

"Process" is dynamic and never repeated, even with the same players and similar circumstances. The interactions between clients and workers, clients and other clients, clients and their families, and clients and activities require that child and youth care workers be well-versed in developmental psychology, assessment and formulation, individual and group dynamics, and a repertoire of related activities. The child and youth care worker's capacity to develop open, honest, trusting relationships underlies all other knowledge and skill. The most important tool workers have is themselves — the ability to interact and relate at the client's level of functioning facilitates the development of the relationship. Relationships allow workers to influence their clients' interactions and processes within an activity.

Consider the relationships and conversations that have developed when you have played cards or other table games. Compare this to formal interviews for a job or for admission to a school. In which situation did you feel the most comfortable to just be yourself and express your feelings?

There is a variation in the depth and type of skill and knowledge needed to work with the multiple-handicapped, normative, emotionally disturbed or delinquent client. However, the interactions and processes that occur between clients and their environment within the activity framework remains a primary vehicle for change and development.

Workers who stand on the sidelines and only observe clients participating in activities may be collecting useful information, but they are not actively involved in treatment. This does not necessarily mean that the activity is useless. However, treatment requires that the worker be *involved with the process*, cognizant of the dynamics and influencing the movement toward identified treatment goals. Workers must realize that they can be involved without being obtrusive. This does not always mean movement toward actually completing the activity, although there may be benefits in achieving this, but the purpose of the activity should direct the outcome. The interaction of the individual and the dynamics of the group process that occurs within the activity outweighs the activity itself.

As an example of this process, consider the following situation. A new group, consisting of older adolescents in a day program, had been discussing their sense of disjointedness and lack of group belonging. One day later, three of the group members planned a group collage, 10 feet square, on which all members would imprint their hand and/or footprint and sign their names. Bowls of paint were placed on the tile floor so they could make their marks. During the activity, there was considerable laughter and discussion among the members.

A worker in another area of the building was informed that the group wanted to see her. On the way to the room, she wondered what the problem may be, given that the group had been somewhat splintered and troubled the day before. Upon entering the room, she was immediately invited to sign the collage. Quickly assessing the situation, she joined in the activity, commenting on the great idea. Following more laughter and discussion as to the different colours people used and trying to guess whose handprint or footprint belonged to whom, the group decided where they wanted to hang their masterpiece.

The socializing and the group interactions, supported by the child and youth care worker, enabled the group to move towards cohesion and increased peer co-operation. Had the worker who had been invited responded differently (not wanting to get her hands covered with paint, for instance) or had the group members not interacted so well with each other, the effect on the group and the outcome of the activity may have been quite different. It follows, then, that the value of the product or activity is directly proportional to the process that occurs within the activity. Thus, the focus of programming should be on its use as a *transition tool within the treatment process as a whole*, and not merely on the product of the activity.

CONCLUSION

For an activity to be therapeutic, it must be planned to meet the specific treatment goals of the client in the most effective method possible, given circumstances, hard and soft resources, etc. *The most important aspect of therapeutic programming is the process that occurs within the activity.* The activity is purely a vehicle for the process. From a therapeutic standpoint, it has no other purpose. A solitary activity, such as reading about communication skills, would not help a client develop social skills to the same degree as an activity that encourages group interaction. A highly-competitive team activity requiring particular skills would provide group interaction, but it would not be beneficial to clients if they did not have the necessary skills to be able to play with each other. A lack of the prerequisite skills could result in their being rejected by the team.

To child and youth care workers, therapeutic programs are primarily vehicles used to reach specific destinations — the treatment goals of their clients. Choosing, designing, and implementing effective therapeutic activities, aimed at meeting the treatment goals of each individual, is an integral part of the trip — the transitional tools of the treatment process.

NOTES

1. For an explanation of the dimensions of activity analysis the reader is referred to "Program Activities" (Whittaker, 1969, pp. 103-105).

2. For further information about the adaptation of recreational programs for therapeutic benefit the reader is referred to "Re-Education through Recreation" (Mand, 1983, chapt. 8).

REFERENCES

Gilmour-Barrett, K., & Pratt, S. (1977). A new profession. In J. Shamsie (Ed.). *Experience and experiment* (chapt. 3). Toronto: Crainford Assoc. Ltd.

Mand, C. L. (1983). Re-education through recreation. In L. K. Brendtro & A. E. Ness (Eds.). *Re-educating troubled youth* (pp. 233-254). New York: Aldine.

Ouderkirk, W. (1980). *Programming in residential child care: A training experience for child care workers*. Albany: New York State Dept. of Social Services.

Redl, F., & Wineman, D. (1957). *The aggressive child* (p. 327). Toronto: Collier-Macmillan.

Romiszowski, A. J. (1981). *Designing instructional systems*. New York: Nichols.

VanderVen, K. (1972). Activity programming. In Foster, G. W., VanderVen, K. D., Kroner, E. R., Carbonara, N. T., Cohen, G. M. (Eds.). *Child care work with emotionally disturbed children* (pp. 203-243). Pittsburgh: University of Pittsburgh Press.

Whittaker, J. K. (1969). Program activities. In Treischman, A. E., Whittaker, J. K. & Brendtro, L. K. *The other 23 hours* (pp. 100-119). Chicago: Aldine.

5

Development of a New Approach to Emotionally Deprived Children and Youth

Pierre Gauthier

ABSTRACT. This paper is based on two research and development projects in the reeducation of emotionally disturbed children, which have been simultaneously conducted since 1984 at French and Canadian residential treatment centers for youngsters aged 6 to 16. Their main objective was to elaborate an approach specifically attuned to the psychomotor and affective needs of children clinically described as emotionally deprived.

This chapter is based on reports of two research and development projects aimed at creating a reeducational approach that would specifically answer the psychomotor and affective needs of emotionally deprived children[1] aged 8 to 12. The projects took place respectively at the Institut de rééducation Le Prat, in France, and at the Institut Dominique Savio-Mainbourg, in Montréal, Canada, from September 1984 to June 1987. It involved seven éducateurs, two workers specialized in psychomotricity and three groups of five or six children. Two psychiatrists and three clinical psychologists also participated as consultants. In France the two groups comprised children, éducateurs and psychomotricity specialists while the Canadian project included the same number of children, their parents or substitute parents, three éducateurs and the author.

Pierre Gauthier, in private practice, 10285 De l'esplanade, Montreal, P.Q. H3L 2X9.

This paper gives an overview of the project, describing the syndrome of emotional deprivation in order to derive a set of specifications for an intervention program by child and youth care workers. On the basis of group and individual reactions by children to the program offered (to be found in separate research reports: Gauthier et al., 1986; Gauthier, 1987), applications to child and youth care work are proposed, with reflections on international collaboration.

EMOTIONAL DEPRIVATION AS A REEDUCATION PROBLEM

Emotional deprivation is a behavior syndrome typically found in children who, during their first years of life, lost or never had contact with a stable positive parental figure. It has become relatively easy to diagnose, thanks to extensive work accomplished since the early 1940s by A. Freud and Dorothy Burlingham, J. Bowlby, R. Spitz, M. Ainsworth and many others.

One of the most cogent books on the subject is Michel Lemay's *J'ai mal à ma mère* (1979). After reviewing all major works on ED (see Footnote 1), Lemay concludes that its etiology and prevention have been well documented but efficacious therapeutic intervention with EDC remains largely underdeveloped. Their personality dynamics result in great suffering for themselves and drain the emotional resources of those who intervene, be they parents, surrogate parents, educating personnel or social workers. EDC are constantly referred to institutions where they fall under the "severe" label; they also constitute ever-demanding cases for social workers who try to place them into foster homes or with various community resources.

According to Lemay (1979), the EDC suffers from severe psychic wounds and emits distress signals through a triple language: somatic, affective, cognitive. He or she often adopts a physical posture characterized by an inwardly drawn chest which inhibits breathing. The belly tends to hang out in front, with buttocks protruding backwards, a posture that usually results in lordosis; to compensate, the head is held backwards, pulling on the muscles that control the jaws and causing the mouth to remain slightly open. Legs are rigid, usually underdeveloped, so that ground-feet contact is relatively unreliable (Dytchwald, 1983; Lowen, 1977). The EDC has low consciousness of left and right, top and bottom, as well as position in space (laterality). The child is prone to psychosomatic symptoms: dermatosis, gastric problems that may evolve into ulcers, enuresis often coupled with encopresis, respiratory and sleep difficulties (Lemay, 1979).

Affectively he[2] is forever craving for human warmth and contact. He constantly seeks exclusive attention from almost any adult who manifests acceptance, but shows complete disregard for that person's constraints in time and space or other responsibilities. To peers' expectations he seems impervious, which tends to push him into the role of group scapegoat. Finally he remains unaware of the adults' emotional needs, whether or not the favored person is tired, anxious, aggressive or temporarily distressed.

But while the EDC avidly seeks contact he is overwhelmed by fear of losing it, alternately projecting on the caring adult the image of the all-powerful, loving mother and its reverse, the vengeful "evil sorceress." In that context any manifestation by the caring figure of impatience or the slightest reproach are construed as evidence of total rejection. They provoke in the child (male or female) explosions of anger, with shouts, blows, run away episodes.

At the cognitive level there are important gaps in language development. The child is affected by severe problems of mental representation of his own past or contemporary actions, let alone self-projection into the future. In Piagetian terms, his cognitive performance is typically lacking in several areas: retarded sensori-motor development, a poor, undiversified language which tends to remain at the symbolic level, great difficulty of access to thinking at the concrete operations and abstract levels.

The EDC is a great consumer of health, education and welfare services. But since he tends to reproduce the initial separation, unconsciously provoking rejection in persons most likely to help him, he filters down to "end of the line" care organizations. Typically he has accumulated, over his short life history, a whole series of family, hospital and residential care placements, finding himself, at puberty, with severe psychosocial handicaps; his capacity to learn adult social roles is gravely impaired and institutionalization as psychiatric patient or delinquent is more than likely.

Furthermore, as Lemay observes (1979), ED seems to be transmitted from one generation to the next. Mothers and fathers who were abandoned in their prime years tend to repeat the same kind of behavior with their own children. Hence ED constitutes a basic psychosocial problem that challenges research oriented towards the development of efficient socialization means. Consequently, an adequate approach requires the creation of a social climate where the adult is a stable figure in time and space, emotionally open, able to provide massive doses of affection in a tri-modal form: somatic, affective, cognitive. At the same time the adult figure will focus the child's attention on the latter's internal processes, inviting him to establish a firm human bond while bringing to the fore the excessive demands-rejection circuit into which he tends to become entrapped.

From this brief review of literature and previous experience in child and youth care work with EDC aged 8 to 18, a program was devised according to the following specifications:

1. To develop sensori-motor coordination, verbal ability, self-reliance, trust toward significant others, and initiative, the EDC must find a response to his perennial quest for parental figures. He needs a stable, affectionate family or its nearest equivalent.
2. Parental or surrogate parental figures will communicate with the EDC in an integrated fashion, at the levels of his somatic, affective and cognitive "language." In other words they will mother and father him, accepting his alternating movements between bonding and rejection, regression and maturation.
3. Congruence in educational intervention is of prime importance for the EDC, which means that all caring and teaching personnel must carefully attune their attitudes and modes of behavior.

AN INTEGRATED APPROACH
TO THE EMOTIONALLY DEPRIVED CHILD

To answer these specifications, every weekly session held with the children contained several of the following elements: concentration exercises, non-verbal communication, relaxation, massage, spontaneous play in a specially designed hall and swimming pool, and verbal exchanges about any or all of the afore-mentioned activities.

Concentration exercises consisted of adaptation of zen or yoga meditation techniques (De Smedt, 1979). Non-verbal communication experiences were derived from those often practiced in Gestalt (Perls, Hefferline, & Goodman, 1977, 1979) or bio-energy therapy (Lowen, 1975; Stacke, E., 1983). Therapeutic relaxation of the passive type was first suggested by J. H. Schultz (1960), one of W. Reich's students. His method was adapted by J. Bergès and M. K. Bounes (1974) who practiced in a psychiatric hospital for children for 15 years. Their technique, as explained in their book *La relaxation thérapeutique chez l'enfant*, was mostly used in the project here reported, combined with Korean relaxation (Rishi, 1984).

Massage was used both as a relaxing and non-verbal communication medium, in a climate favoring the child's trust in the adults who accompany him in the sessions. Since the EDC is eager for physical, affectionate but non-sexual contact, sensitive massage was deemed suitable to his expectations. In that form of massage, long pleasurable movements converge on the spinal column where the central nervous system is primarily located, resulting in a general impression of well-being and interconnectedness of all parts of the body. Staff members were instructed to give massage with all the emotional warmth they could feel, and at the same time to be aware of the child's affective state, remaining tuned in to both his verbal and somatic expressions (Stacke, 1985).

Spontaneous play as a therapeutic tool used in a group situation was initially experimented with in Sudbury, Ontario, with neurotic and pre-psychotic adolescents by Girouard (1981), colleague of the author. After extensive briefing and participant observation, Girouard's approach was adapted with various groups of children in residential care. For a group of five to eight children accompanied by three to five professionally trained adults, the typical setting is a large playroom adjacent to a swimming pool where water has been heated to about 85 degrees F. The session starts with either children or adults initiating games, usually of a symbolic nature (simulations of daily life events, adventures with legendary characters, etc.). Adults become one or several of the characters in the ongoing play situation, resorting as little as possible to their status as grown-ups; rather than maintain discipline in an authoritative fashion they influence the unfolding of spontaneously-imagined plots through the characters they impersonate (Girouard, 1981). Within this framework many psychomotor activities were encouraged (Gagnon-Bouchard, Guay-Boisvet, & Harvey, 1984). Body posture and movement were analyzed with reference to the criteria proposed by Dychtwald (1983) and Lowen (1977).

At the end of each session, 10 to 20 minutes were set aside to talk about what happened within the time period. Children could also express their feelings about anything they subjectively defined as "important," or narrate their dreams and fantasies without application of the disciplinary constraints that usually prevailed within their regular units. In leadership of these sessions components, a Jung-inspired attitude prevailed (Jung, 1962, 1976), often combined with guidelines derived from Bettelheim (1977) and Von Frantz (1980).

The program simultaneously took place in France and Canada, from 1984 to 1987, in the September-June period of each year. Its international aspect was primarily due to this author's "discovery," during a prolonged stay at a reeducation center in France, that French éducateurs, more frequently and intensively than their Canadian counterparts, demonstrated affectionate behavior towards the children and youth in their care. For example, hugging a child, taking him or her on one's lap, rocking or kissing on the cheeks were quite common. In turn the children appeared more joyful and showed much affection for "their" éducateurs. In such a context, nobody seemed to fear adult sexual abuse and such behavior was evidently excluded.

On the basis of these spontaneous attitudes, a program was elaborated that would explicitly seek to answer the affective needs of EDC children by applying in adapted forms the new therapeutic approaches developed in the 1960s and 1970s (Gauthier, 1983). In addition an attempt to transcend cultural boundaries would be made by simultaneously implementing the program in France and Canada.

Analysis of group and individual evolution indicates that it obtained largely positive results in both countries. Session contents, emotional attitudes of adult leaders, and their style of leadership provided at least an immediate answer to basic psychomotor, affective and cognitive needs of EDC. Symptomatic traits were greatly reduced in favor of behavior indicative of greater autonomy, improved school performance, mutual give and take in relationships with peers, deeper trust and better continuity in interaction with caring adults. Far from being linear, this evolution was characterized by wide variations between regression to infantile episodes and increasingly long periods of age-congruent behavior.

By the same means, staff reported having concurrently gained insight into their own psychodynamics and those of the youngsters in their charge. As a result of the interaction which developed within group encounters, educating personnel-children relationships were strengthened, with positive consequences in regular life at the units.

Finally, a joint venture involving Canada-France collaboration between professionals and researchers in the field of reeducation has proved quite feasible, with much similarity in the types of behavior manifested on both sides of the Atlantic. The more distant "professional" attitude of the Canadian éducateurs quickly disappeared in favor of a warmer, more demonstrative stance once they allowed themselves to spontaneously answer the affective requests of the children.

APPLICATIONS TO CHILD
AND YOUTH CARE PRACTICE

The work already accomplished within the framework of the project has many implications relative to the therapeutic aspects of reeducation and the training of child and youth care workers. The first requisite is enough time to allow a persistent effort over at least two years. The second is a stable team of adults who are able to feel and show emotional acceptance of the child, irrespective of his behavior or personality traits, and to offer vast amounts of affectionate care. Thirdly, each child needs at least one worker with whom to engage in a long-lasting emotional bonding process.

The approach that has been devised appears necessary on two counts: it offers emotional nurturance to both children and adults, and it creates an environment that is highly conducive to the children's affective maturation. Its proper use requires the development of specific skills by the child and youth care workers:

1. A high consciousness level of their own emotional needs which, in the present state of the art, is best obtained through didactic psychotherapy or group sessions oriented toward human potential growth. For example, all staff who participated in the sessions received between 90 and 300 hours of training in the various approaches adapted to the program.
2. A certain mastery of the following techniques: psychomotricity, relaxation, massage, story telling, role playing, swimming and other pool-related activities such as aquatic yoga.
3. The capacity to accompany both children and adults in gaining insights from the experiences they live through in the various activities making up the proposed integrated approach. From that point of view theories of personality development derived from professional expertise, such as those by Gendreau (1978), Guindon (1982), Lemay (1983), Perls and his associates (Perls et al., 1977, 1979; Perls, 1978) are particularly useful.
4. Above all, intervention with EDC requires, on the part of the child care worker, both the willingness and the emotional capacity to give what at first glance seems to be excessive amounts of nurturance, and where the adult constantly orients the interaction in favor of the child's emotional growth.

Despite many good intentions, few child care workers (or any other caregiver) can do this without intensive self-training under expert guidance. From our experience, we have found the affective requirements of the intervention needed by EDC to be so challenging as to push the well-intentioned but untrained worker into several pitfalls which can be categorized under two headings: loss of emotional balance, possibly leading to unethical behavior, or outright rejection of the child, very often through unconscious fear by the adult of his own emotional upheaval.

From a positive point of view the projects here reported have shown quite clearly that child and youth care workers who have become deeply conscious of their own emotional cravings are best equipped to adequately meet the affective needs of EDC. Such a task constitutes a rather formidable therapeutic and research challenge that can be met by well-trained personnel using novel approaches.

The requisites to professional action have already been specified but more remains to be said from the research point of view. Presently prevailing methods, which emphasize the neutral, evaluative approach by a non-committed observer, appear woefully inadequate. In practice they forbid active involvement by the experienced practitioner who uses his or her intuition "in situ" to develop, reorient, or fine-tune an approach. Insistence on detailed pre-programming with minute by minute advanced timing verges on the ridiculous, or worse, sterilizes clinical creativity. A different type of research seems much more productive, namely the research-and-development scheme where careful examination of clients' characteristics lead to a set of specifications for intervention. From these is elaborated a first prototype which is tested on a very small scale, with corrections made as directed by practice. Then versions two, three, etc. are gradually evolved and tried more and more extensively, with built-in evaluation means, until a reasonably efficient intervention method can be defined within relatively broad variations according to clientele, practitioner, and external circumstances. Such an approach, although unpopular at this time with many research proposal examiners, not only permits but stimulates creativity on the part of professionals interested in developing new methods of intervention to meet hitherto unanswered social rehabilitation needs.

The projects reported here have obtained very encouraging results. However, further development remains to be done about the evolutionary patterns of individual participants, the persistence of their attitudinal change, and their ability to transfer experience from therapeutic sessions to performance in other spheres of their lives, including child-parent interaction. It is hoped further work in new approaches to child and youth care will bring some answers to these questions.

NOTES

1. For easier reading the abbreviation EDC designates the emotionally deprived child, masculine or feminine, in the singular or plural form. ED designates emotional deprivation.

2. The masculine designates both sexes.

REFERENCES

Berges, J., & Bounes, M. (1979). *La relaxation thérapeutique chez l'enfant*. Paris: Masson.

Bettelheim, B. (1977). *The Uses of Enchantment, the Meaning and Importance of Fairy Tales*. New York, NY: Vintage Books.

Bowlby, J. (1973). *Attachment and Loss., Vol II: Separation, Anxiety and Anger*. New York, NY: Basic Books.

De Smedt, M. (1979). *50 Techniques de méditation*. Montréal France/Amérique.

Dychtwald, K. (1983). *L'homme nouveau*. Montréal, Qc: Le Jour.

Gagnon-Bouchard, I., Guay-Boivert, A., & Harvey, G. (1984). *Activités sensorielles et motrices*. Montréal Presses de l'Université du Québec.

Gauthier, P. (1983). Vers une psycho-pédagogie holistique. *Document de travail*, 89, School of Psycho-Education, University of Montreal, Montreal.

Gauthier, P. (1987). Nouvelles formes d'intervention auprès de familles en difficulté. Research report. School of Psycho-Education, University of Montreal, June.

Gauthier, P., Dunoyer, B., Faurie, C., Guillemain, C., Lallet, D., Laurent, S., & Viollet, I. (1986). Approaches psycho-corporelles et ré-éducation d'enfants carencés relationnels. Research report. Institut de rééducation Le Prat, Le Dorat, France, April.

Gendreau, G. (1978). *L'intervention psycho-éducative, solution ou défi?* Paris: Fleurus.

Girouard, P. (1981). Analyse d'une activité fondée sur l'expression dramatique utilisant le conte comme médiation auprès d'un groupe d'enfants mésadaptés socio-affectifs. Unpublished Master's thesis, University of Montreal, Montreal.

Guindon, J. (1982). *Vers l'autonomie psychique*. Paris: Fleurus.

Jacobson, E. (1980). *Savoir relaxer pour combattre le stress*. Montréal Editions de l'homme.

Jung, C. (1976). *La guérison psychologigue*. Genève: Georg et cie.

Jung, C. (1962). *L'homme à la découverte de son âme*. Paris: Payot.

Lapierre, A. (1982). *Fantasmes corporels et pratique psychomotrice en éducation et thérapie: le "manque au corps"*. Paris: Douin.

Lemay, M. (1979). *J'ai mal à ma mère*. Paris: Fleurus.

Lemay, M. (1983). *L'éclosion psychique de l'être humain*. Paris: Fleurus.

Lowen, A. (1975). *La bio-énergie*. Paris: Editions du Jour-Tchou.

Lowen, A. (1977). *Language et lecture du corps*. Québec Editions St-Yves, Part 2.

Masters, R., & Houston, J. *Psy-jeux*. Montréal Le Jour.

Perls, F. S. (1978). *Le moi, la faim et l'agressivité*. Paris: Tchou.

Perls, F., Hefferline, R., & Goodman, P. (1977). *Gestalt thérapie, technique d'épanouissement personnel*. Montréal Stanké.

Perls, F., Hefferline, R., & Goodman, P. (1979). *Gestalt thérapie, vers une technique du self: nouveauté, excitation, croissance*. Montréal Stanké.

Rishi, J.B. (1984). *La relaxation coréenne*. Manosque, France: Convergence (Chemin de Pimayon, 04100 Manosque).

Schultz, J.H. (1960). *Le training autogène, méthode de relaxation par auto-décontraction concentrative, essai pratique et clinique*. Paris: Presses Universitaires de France.

Stacke, B. (1985). *La santé par le massage*. Paris: M.A. Editions.

Stacke, E. (1983). Les apports de la communication no-verbale. *Pratiques corporelles*. 61, pp. 7-12.

Von Frantz, M.-L. (1980). *L'interprétation des contes de fée*. Paris: La Fontaine de Pierre.

6

Youth Workers in the Courts

Shelley F. McMain
Christopher D. Webster

ABSTRACT. Although mental health workers have long played an active and influential role in the provision of services to youth court, they have, as yet, devoted little effort to establishing standards to guide their procedures. As a result, numerous problems arise which to some extent threaten the credibility of youth court workers. The authors draw upon examples from the literature and the experiences of clinicians at the Metropolitan Toronto Forensic Service (MET-FORS) in identifying some of the difficulties associated with current practices. Guidelines are proposed.

This chapter is written for youth workers who are on occasion called upon to supply the courts with information about the mental health status of individuals in their care. It is also intended for child care and youth workers who contribute indirectly to the courts' understanding of a young person through the information they provide to psychiatrists, psychologists, social workers, probation officers and others. Although mental health and youth workers will ordinarily have good intentions in their work, they can nevertheless do youths under their charge grave harm through the provision to court of information that is irrelevant to key legal issues or that is unduly pessimistic. Our point, very generally, is that in the absence of any

Shelley F. McMain is currently completing a PhD in psychology at York University, and was formerly a Research Associate at the Cognitive Therapy Unit, Clarke Institute of Psychiatry. Christopher D. Webster is Director, Department of Psychology, Clarke Institute of Psychiatry, 750 College St., Toronto, Ontario M5T 1R8.

clear guidelines from the law, child and youth workers need, with other professionals, to think about how best to circumscribe their dealings with the court so that they do not go beyond the bounds of their own professional limitations. This matter deserves attention with the growing reliance courts have developed on opinions and reports from mental health professionals (Elwork, 1984).

We review current practices of mental health professionals by drawing upon the literature and examples from actual clinical work of a forensic service, the Metropolitan Toronto Forensic Service (METFORS) (see Turner, 1979; Webster, Menzies & Jackson, 1982). METFORS is a forensic assessment centre which assists the courts with adult and juvenile offenders who are remanded by the courts for psychiatric assessment. Fifty consecutive juvenile assessments were conducted between April 1985 and April 1986. These cases serve as the basis for the following clinical analysis. Suggestions will be offered regarding the conduct of assessments in light of this clinical and literature review. From this analysis we will offer suggestions for conducting assessments and for presenting findings to the court. We center on the preparation of reports rather than on actual verbal testimony since only a small percentage (15-20%) of clinicians are ever called upon to appear in court (Petrella & Poythress, 1983).

UNDERSTANDING THE YOUTH COURT

The role of mental health workers cannot be fully appreciated without an understanding of the system within which they perform their duties. The general philosophical outlook of the youth court determines what role mental health workers play. In this connection it is well to recall that it was not until the turn of the last century that any distinction was made regarding the handling of juveniles and adults in the justice system. In both Canada and the United States special laws came to be developed solely for juveniles. The basis for this change lay in the belief that youths were different from adults by virtue of their "salvageability." The courts assumed a "parens patriae" role with youths in an attempt to rehabilitate them. This rehabilitative philosophy had a major influence over the decisions made in youth court. Sentences were seen as treatment rather than punishment. This goal of treatment led to the development of social services which could support the court's ideologies. Consequently, mental health workers began to play an integral part in this new scheme. As stated by the United States Task Force on Juvenile Delinquency in 1976:

> The goals were to investigate, diagnose, and prescribe treatment, not to adjudicate guilt or fix blame. The individual's background was more important than the facts of a given incident, specific conduct relevant more as symptomatic of a need for the court to bring its helping powers to bear than as a prerequisite to exercise of jurisdiction. Lawyers were unnecessary — adversary tactics were out of place, for the mutual aim of all was not to contest or object but to determine the treatment plan best for the child. The plan was to be devised by the increasingly popular psychologist and psychiatrist; delinquency was thought of almost as disease, to be diagnosed by specialists and the patient kindly but firmly dosed. (cited in Binder, 1983, p.67)

Only in the past decade or so has "due process" for juveniles become a major issue. The picture changed in 1967 in the United States with the Gault decision, while corresponding alterations were made in 1984 in Canada with the introduction of the Young Offenders Act. Juveniles came to be afforded increased legal rights and the courts were restricted in their discretionary power over young offenders. This new outlook meant that young persons had to be cautioned before making statements to the police, they could no longer be given indeterminate sentences and a broader range of dispositions were available to youth court judges. Despite these individual rights becoming incorporated more fully into the juvenile justice system, little has changed regarding the basic rehabilitative philosophy underlying this system (Binder, 1983). In fact, some argue that there is an even stronger emphasis on the emotional needs of young offenders and on matching these needs with appropriate interventions (Binder, 1983). Much of the pressure upon the judicial system to find a solution to the problem of youth crime comes from reports of increases in crime amongst youth.

The law currently allows for great discretion in the recommendation of assessments. With the goal of treatment in mind, judges may order assessments of youth at any stage in the proceedings where such a report may be considered helpful. Typically, issues of concern extend far beyond traditional questions of sanity (Jaffe, Leschied, Sas, & Austin, 1985). Some of the variables which may determine whether a juvenile is referred for assessment include the possible existence of suicidal tendencies, learning disabilities, mental retardation, emotional disorder, impoverished family life, serious psychopathology, or unknown motivation for committing an offence (Curry, 1985). While these may be important variables in the prediction of remand practices, it is likely that the personality of the judge may be equally as important as that of the offender. In addition, pressures upon judges to resolve problems of increasing juvenile crime likely have a great influence over recommendations. The temptation to share decision-making power can be strong in cases where the courts may not know how to dispose of the case. As Curry (1985) notes:

> By and large the counsellors showed little interest in the "diagnostic" aspects of mental health assessments. Faced with large caseloads and pressure to meet sometimes conflicting needs of the adolescents and community, they were primarily interested in what to do for their adolescent clients. (p.41)

The philosophy of the youth court determines not only the focus and methodologies of its mental health consultants but defines the parameters within which consultants must work.

Mental health workers have become increasingly enmeshed with the courts as a direct result of the increased importance placed upon the goal of rehabilitation. Although traditionally assessments were almost exclusively conducted by psychiatrists, other professionals such as psychologists, social workers, and child and youth workers have become considerably involved in this process (Jaffe et al., 1985; Petrella & Poythress, 1983). Despite an increased reliance upon psychologists, psychiatrists, and social workers to supply the courts with clinical information, there lacks any agreed upon standard for the conduct of an assessment.

For the most part, mental health workers are subject to a vague set of criteria. Essentially, they are at liberty to act in an unrestrained fashion when composing reports. Under the Young Offenders Act a broad range of loosely defined criteria serve as a guide to mental health workers. The Act states that youths may be remanded for assessment in any case, ". . . where the court believes a medical, psychological or psychiatric report in respect of the young person might be helpful in making any decision pursuant to this Act" (Young Offenders Act, 1984). Consequently, it was not surprising for us to discover in the METFORS study that psychiatrists exhibited great variability in the issues addressed in their reports to court on behalf of young offenders.

CONDUCTING CLINICAL ASSESSMENTS

The lack of specific standards which define the conduct of assessments has posed a number of problems which have brought mental health professionals into disrepute (Binder, 1983). A large body of literature has been critical of mental health workers who conduct assessments (Poythress & Stock, 1980). In general, criticism has focused on the irrelevance of evidence to legal questions, the worth of legal and moral opinions proposed, the employment of data which are unreliable and invalid, and the use of jargon which is incomprehensible to legal decision makers (Elwork, 1984). One of the strongest criticisms of current clinical assessment practices is the tendency to testify beyond the boundaries of professional expertise. Further, not only are the issues addressed often inappropriate in that they deal with issues outside the realm of professional expertise, but they often violate professional standards.

What seems to exacerbate these problems is the power that forensic reports carry. Recommendations are often fully accepted and implemented, in part, due to the aura of scientific objectivity which they carry (Gass, 1979). A number of studies have documented the high correspondence between recommendations found in reports and court dispositions (Jaffe et al., 1985; Webster, Menzies, Butler, & Turner, 1982). In one study, a review of 616 juveniles assessed at the family court clinic in London, Ontario revealed that in 80% of the cases clinical recommendations were followed by the court (Jaffe et al., 1985). The consistent willingness of judges to abdicate their decision-making power to clinicians is strongly related to the belief that clinicians' assessments are based upon an objective and scientific appraisal of their clients. In addition, it is believed that clinicians offer the hope so necessary if the problem of juvenile crime is to be overcome.

A number of concerns have been raised about clinicians conducting clinical assessments for juvenile court which suggest that the expert witness testimony they provide may be damaging to their client, the young offender. What follows is a critical presentation of these problems and suggestions for clinicians who are called upon by the court for their expertise.

Psychiatric remand procedures are often flawed by a lack of communication between mental health workers and the court. It is not uncommon for mental health workers to be unaware of the reasons that youths are referred for assessment. In our review of 50 juvenile psychiatric remand cases at METFORS, 30% of the cases indicated no information concerning the reason for referral. In another 25% of the cases, information concerning the reason for referral was extremely vague. Notwithstanding this state of affairs, assessments were completed on all 50 youths despite the fact that no attempts were apparently made to clarify the primary issues of interest to the court. Without knowledge of referral questions, it is to be expected that clinicians will address issues different from those that the judges have in mind. Further, clinicians themselves will likely show great variability in the issues which they report. The lack of clarity which defines the process of remand practices serves to render the courts dependent upon mental health workers. A judge's reluctance to assume responsibility for clarifying issues puts pressure upon clinicians to take on an authoritative role.

It is often in actual practice the clinician who chooses the boundaries of the assessment. Perhaps this can be perceived as the court's acknowledgement of respect for the mental health professional. Mental health professionals can expect to receive increased acceptance within the judicial system. Succumbing to the temptation of increased discretionary authority forces the professional to relinquish independence and ". . . develop philosophies and practices that are compatible with legal expectations" (Menzies, 1985, p.476). Information which satisfies legal objectives is not always compatible with clinical objectives in that the ideologies of clinicians may have to be compromised in order to satisfy legal consumers.

Forensic reports have been criticized for being excessively biased (Menzies, 1985). Often, reports focus on deviance while neglecting to elaborate on the positive features of the individual. Examples are apparent in the METFORS reports. An extract, modified slightly to preserve confidentiality, is as follows:

> Mr. B. has been involved in stealing since at least age 13. This has brought him into conflict with the law on a number of occasions, but he states matter of factly that "I usually get away with it." He seldom attended school and freely acknowledges that he was difficult to control in the school setting. He much preferred indulging in drugs to attending school. Mr. B. showed virtually no motivation to change. He was threatening to both co-patients and staff. He is apparently without any moral qualms about his legal activities and I have little doubt that he will continue to pursue them. He is not currently amenable to any psychiatric treatment. He is likely to be a management problem at whatever facility to which he is delivered.

Information is neatly packaged and presented to the court devoid of features other than the negative characteristics of the individual. Consequently, the assessment frequently presents a uniform picture to the court of a "criminal" with few positive attributes. Such descriptions ". . . leave judges with little doubt about the moral inferiority, manipulative character, pathological identity, criminal propensity and dangerousness of the forensic subjects" (Menzies, 1985, p.946). This myopic view of individuals serves only to absolve the mental health professional of responsibility for delinquent youths. Inevitably, it perpetuates the problematic behaviour that brought the individual to the authorities.

Forensic reports often present with more of a legal than clinical tone. This becomes strikingly apparent when one observes the types of recommendations forwarded to the courts. In a review of 50 recommendations made for juveniles who had been remanded for assessment to METFORS, 16% were found to have been recommended for incarceration. Ironically, these recommendations were made regardless of the fact that many of the youth were only at a pretrial stage in their court proceedings. Two further clinical examples are as follows:

> If he is to be convicted of the present charge we believe a custodial sentence would be appropriate as he would appear to be significantly out of control at this time.

> Were he to be found guilty and a period of incarceration recommended, it would be in his best interest to serve his time at an institution where a programme of help may be devised. Such a place is _____.

What is apparent from the above examples is the apparent willingness of clinicians to assume the role of judge and jury. However, it is essential to note that these would-be arbitrators fail to seriously consider the youth's possible innocence. Clinicians appear to be aware in documenting their report that being too presumptuous with respect to their recommendations could be dangerous in that it could be viewed as unethical. Consequently, statements tend to be couched in qualifiers so that they cannot be identified as being overtly biased:

> Prospects for rehabilitation of this young woman are at best poor. Should this young woman, through the peculiarities of our current legal system, be released to the community, it is abundantly clear that others will suffer as a consequence.

Not surprisingly, it has been shown that the involvement of mental health workers in the preparation of presentence reports can lead to more severe dispositions without attendant reductions in levels of recidivism (Morash, 1982). With this in mind, what justification is there for employing mental health workers in juvenile court?

Dismissing the involvement of mental health workers in youth court is tantamount to ignoring the possible relevance of mental illness in understanding a young offender's problems. The positive effect that mental health workers can have in the juvenile system is related to the extent that workers set rules for themselves. Their role must allow for the consideration of legal objectives while simultaneously upholding professional values. Workers should not allow themselves to become agents of the court. Current problems in existing practice will be overcome when mental health workers act in a consistent fashion, collecting information and presenting it according to well-defined guidelines. The following section should be considered by clinicians who are involved in supplying information to the courts on young offenders.

UNDERSTANDING THE REFERRAL QUESTION

Before a proper assessment can be conducted the clinician must have a keen understanding of the reasons why the youth was referred for assessment. This information should, as a matter of routine, be conveyed by the court. In cases where it has not been provided it is necessary for the professional to make contact with the court and obtain the necessary information. Jaffe and Leschied (1986) recommend that in the event that no information is available from the courts, it may be possible to obtain a copy of the transcripts from the court hearing. An assessment can be considered relevant to the extent that it addresses the referral question. Clinicians who persist in extending themselves beyond the referral issue will likely find themselves conveying meaningless or misleading information to the court. Further, they run the risk of overstepping their expertise and compromising their professional integrity. Clinicians must have the referral question(s) clearly in mind before proceeding with their assessment. Information gathering should address the referral question. The more succinct a report is in explaining and clarifying the referral question, the greater is the likelihood that it will influence decisions made in court.

BASING OPINIONS ON RELIABLE
AND VALID STANDARDS

Opinions formulated from assessments and conveyed in reports should reflect a high degree of reliability and validity. Courts rely heavily upon expert witness testimony in making decisions (Jaffe et al., 1985; Webster et al., 1982). It can be highly unethical to allow the court to reach conclusions on fallacious testimony. With respect to the young person, the consequences of poor clinical work can be harsher than in a non-forensic therapeutic setting. Recommendations for a criminal justice disposition rather than a treatment setting can have extremely serious consequences such as restraint and punishment for the individual. In addition, since reports are open to the scrutiny of cross-examination it is important that clinicians be able to defend and explain their work in a manner understood by the judge. Consequently, clinicians should be familiar with the best scientific literature to ensure that thoughtful decisions are made.

BALANCING REPORTS

Clinicians should be cautious not to present a uni-dimensional view of an individual. Rather, they should aim at presenting a global description of the youth. This does not imply that clinicians should engage in writing unrealistic, overly optimistic reports. However, if workers can only convey an attitude of despair toward these youths, what justification is there for their involvement in the justice system? Juvenile court, in large part, has called upon mental health professionals in the hope of receiving suggestions for helping their clients. Where possible, clinicians should do their utmost to offer hopeful alternatives.

SPECIALIZED EDUCATION IN FORENSIC ISSUES

Mental health professionals working in the juvenile justice system should be well informed about legal issues. The forensic setting poses many challenges for clinicians. It is important to be knowledgeable about the legal criteria for evaluating such issues as fitness to stand trial, insanity and criminal responsibility. Furthermore, it is necessary to have an understanding of the various stages of trial proceedings so that only appropriate information will be conveyed to the court at any given stage. A lack of understanding of legal issues has the potential to do a great disservice to the system. Despite the fact that few formal training programs are available to the forensic clinician (Poythress, 1979), it should be a requisite that these persons be prepared to educate themselves in the area of forensic work. Informal educational programs can be organized for clinicians working in forensic settings. Practitioners should appraise their qualifications to conduct an assessment and should, before proceeding, feel confident that they possess a solid grounding in the relevant issues.

ATTENDING TO COUNTER-TRANSFERENCE ISSUES

It is important for clinicians to be sharply attuned to the intense emotions which can be heightened in a forensic setting (Ciccone & Clements, 1984). Working with youths who may be accused of offenses such as murder, rape, and child molesting requires clinicians to attend to negative feelings and deal openly with them. As Ciccone & Clements (1984) note: "This setting requires that the psychiatrist have a high degree of professionalism and pay attention to the burnout syndrome in order to maintain empathy, resist punitive reactions, adjust to fear, and achieve understanding" (p.396). Mental health professionals must maintain objectivity when conducting assessments. Clinicians who are unable to demonstrate empathy and concern for the welfare of the youth risk conveying evidence which is contaminated by personal biases.

REFERENCES

Binder, A. (1983). The juvenile justice system. Juvenile justice and juvenile offenders: An overview. *The Counselling Psychologist, 11*(2), 65-67.

Ciccone, J.R., & Clements, C. (1984). Forensic psychiatry and applied clinical ethics: Theory and practice. *American Journal of Psychiatry, 141*(3), 395-399.

Curry, J.F. (1985). Criteria for evaluating psychological assessments. *Juvenile and Family Court Journal, 36*, 39-41.

Elwork, A. (1984). Psycholegal assessment, diagnosis, and testimony. A new beginning. *Law and Human Behavior, 8*(3-4), 197-203.

Gass, R. (1979). The psychologist as expert witness: Science in the courtroom. *Maryland Law Review, 38*, 539-621.

In re Gault, No. 387, U.S. 1 (1967).

Jaffe, P.G., & Leschied, A.W. (1986, April). *Preparation and execution reports and their recommendations in a format suitable to the needs of the youth courts*. Paper presented at the conference on Young Offenders sponsored by the Alberta Hospital, Edmonton, Alberta.

Jaffe, P.G., Leschied, A.W., Sas, L., & Austin, G.W. (1985). A model for the provision of clinical assessments and service brokerage for young offenders: The London family court clinic. *Canadian Psychology*, *26*(1), 54-61.

Menzies, R.J. (1985). *Doing violence: Psychiatric discretion and the prediction of dangerousness*. Unpublished doctoral dissertation, University of Toronto, Toronto.

Morash, M. (1982). A case study of mental health professionals' input into juvenile court decision making. *Criminal Justice Review*, *7*(1), 48-56.

Petrella, R.C., & Poythress, N.G. (1983). The quality of forensic evaluations: An interdisciplinary study. *Journal of Consulting and Clinical Psychology*, *51*(1), 76-85.

Poythress, N.G. (1979). A proposal for training in forensic psychology. *American Psychologist*, *34*(7), 612-621.

Poythress, N., & Stock, H. (1980). Competency to stand trial: A historical review and some new data. *Journal of Psychiatry and Law*, *8*, 131-146.

Solicitor General Canada, The Young Offenders Act, 1984, c. 110, s. 13.

Turner, R.E. (1979). The development of forensic services in Toronto. *Canadian Journal of Criminology*, *21*, 200-209.

Webster, C.D., Menzies, R.J., & Jackson, M.A. (1982). *Clinical assessment before trial*. Toronto: Butterworth & Co. Ltd.

Webster, C.D., Menzies, R.J., Butler, B.T., & Turner, R.E. (1982). Forensic psychiatric assessment in selected Canadian cities. *Canadian Journal of Psychiatry*, *27*, 455-461.

7

The Therapeutic Potential
of Emergency Shelters

Michael Gershowitz
Alan MacFarlane

ABSTRACT. The emergency shelter is largely ignored in the literature on child and youth care settings. This constitutes a considerable oversight in light of the crucial role that emergency shelters play as the first experience of the child or youth in group care. While shelters share many characteristics common to all group care settings, there are specific differences both regarding the role that shelters play and the treatment opportunities that are possible. The shelter experience is defined and the way that shelters may meet both the client's and their family's needs are presented. It is also suggested that working in a shelter provides a unique challenge for the child care professional.

As their first and often only contact with the social service system, the youth and their family's emergency shelter experience may have a great significance. Youth who come to a shelter come because of a variety of traumatic events and crises that have made a placement out of the home imperative. In these days of budget restraint and ever fewer group care facilities, it is only the most dangerous situations that warrant an out-of-home placement, and so the youth who are placed are almost always those with intense needs for structure, support, and protection. The combination of a new and

Michael Gershowitz, West Island Youth Project. Alan MacFarlane, Program Director, Youth Horizons, and Instructor, Special Care Counselling Department, Vanier College, 821 Blvd. Ste.-Crox, St.-Laurent, Quebec H4L 3X9.

more stable environment, and the opportunity to look at their lives without pressure give the shelter staff a valuable chance to positively impact the lives of their clients. At the same time, shelter staff are continuously challenged by a constantly changing and diverse population who present with a great range of issues in their lives.

This discussion will identify and explore situational and treatment issues specific to emergency shelter programs with an emphasis on how they may be utilized to help the youth and their family begin to deal effectively with their problems. The singular opportunity for skill building and professional growth that shelters offer the child and youth care worker will also be addressed. Despite the possibilities inherent in shelters, very little has been written on the subject. Trzcink (1978) and Ragen (1980) have begun to explore shelter issues and concerns, but a comprehensive evaluation of the therapeutic potential has never been done. It is hoped that this presentation will stimulate further discussion.

EMERGENCY SHELTERS: DEFINITION AND CHARACTERISTICS

While there is no universally accepted definition, most shelters have a great deal in common. "Shelter" suggests that some form of temporary accommodation will be offered. All shelters share a desire to provide a stable environment for youths whose lives have been disrupted by difficult circumstances. This is most often accomplished through the establishment of a highly structured household routine, especially in the first days of placement. Emergency shelters specialize in short-term care; that is, the child's stay is seen as an interim placement. While their length may vary from client to client and from shelter to shelter, stays of less than one month are imperative if the program is to remain open to new referrals. The youth's responsiveness to structure and counseling, the family's openness and capacity for positive change, and, when a return home is not feasible, the availability of an appropriate second-line placement are among the key considerations that will determine the length of stay in a shelter.

Implicit in the term "emergency shelter" is the fact that the client's need for placement is both immediate and urgent. This requires that the shelter be extremely flexible and open with regard to admission criteria. Most shelters consequently have extremely broad admission standards. If the placement is found to be seriously inappropriate, the staff may then ask for the youth to be moved to somewhere that better meets the youth's needs. Thus youth may be accepted who are victims of both sexual or physical abuse, neglect, or a completely chaotic home situation that puts them at serious risk. Runaways, juvenile offenders, and youth with behavioural or emotional problems are also often placed in shelters.

The referral process also distinguishes emergency shelters from longer-term residential units. Typically, youths are referred to shelters by intake social workers who often have little relevant information. Many shelters also accept young people who may be placed by the police, local community groups, family members, or the youth themselves. In such situations, the admitting shelter will often request additional information on the child and family, but may not receive it immediately.

Staffing models may vary considerably, but the professional child care worker model that employs a rotating shift system would seem to have the most potential for this very difficult clientele. The unpredictable conditions of many admissions, diversity of population, and the intensity of the work environment do not recommend a house-parent model for most shelter programs.

THE YOUTH AND THE SHELTER EXPERIENCE

The youth who is placed in an emergency shelter may be experiencing guilt, shame, anger, rejection and a host of other emotions. These feelings are heightened by the absence of his familiar environment, no matter how disturbed, apprehensions with regard to his strange, new living situation and often the lack of support from friends and family.

There is often initial openness on the youth's part, and so observation and comprehensive behavioral assessment may be an important role for the shelter staff at this time. As the youth becomes more comfortable with his new environment, this initial openness may become more guarded, defenses may be more effective, and the youth worker's task is made increasingly difficult.

Another capability of the emergency shelter is as a vehicle for the emotional and behavioral stabilization of the child. Children in care are often victims of chaotic and stressful family dynamics which make normal functioning difficult or impossible. Their removal from the home may have served to exacerbate negative feelings. Shelter programs must therefore be designed to provide living environments which are safe, stable and consistent, and which offer few surprises to the confused youth. As noted above, this may be facilitated by the establishment of a structured daily routine, and complemented by the interventions of warm and caring professionals who will allay the client's fear and anxiety.

The opportunity for effective brief treatment is also offered by emergency shelters. While treatment modalities may vary significantly between programs, most recognise the importance of the therapeutic relationship between child and worker. The intensity of the shelter environment and the child's emotional distress may promote the establishment of a meaningful rapport.

Lastly, emergency shelters may facilitate the child's reintegration into the family unit. Research suggests that with increasing time away from home, and with successive placements, the possibility of the child's successful return home is significantly diminished (Fanshel, 1976). The shelter, with its rapidly gained and intimate knowledge of the child, and acting as a source of information and support to the family, is in an excellent position to ensure that the placement is both brief and effective.

THE FAMILY AND EMERGENCY SHELTER CARE

The placement of one or more of their children in a shelter will almost certainly have a tremendous impact upon the parents' self-image as well as on the general functioning of the family unit. With the removal of the child, confidence in their ability to effectively work through issues on their own, defenses which may have minimized or denied the degree of difficulty, and hopes that the problems will simply go away, are shattered. Concerns regarding the reaction of friends and family may heighten feelings of anger, guilt, inadequacy and self-recrimination. Some parents may relive painful experiences of their youth while dealing with the separation from their child. The delicate balance of family dynamics and structure may also be dramatically altered by the removal of one of the key players.

Because of the stresses precipitated by the youth's placement in shelter care, parents may be especially open to the influence of social work and child care professionals, offering a tremendous opportunity to positively impact upon the family and setting the stage for the child's successful reintegration into the family unit. With time, the impact of the child's absence from the home may diminish. Self-examination may give way to blaming professionals for the family's difficulties. Family structure, altered to account for the continued absence of the child, may resist his eventual return. It is imperative that shelter workers seize the opportunity of the child's placement in their care to constructively engage the family.

What, then, are the goals unique to these initial interactions with families in crisis and how may they be realized? The setting of a positive tone for parent-helper interactions is of primary importance. It may allay parental anxiety and stress, maximize the possibility of their cooperation and involvement, increase confidence in the staff team, and set the stage for beneficial interactions with future professionals.

A recent study on parental feelings following initial meetings with treatment centers found that parents felt unsupported as well as angry, ashamed, and fearful. A majority also believed that they were perceived as failures as parents (Hamilton, 1985). Supportive, nonjudgemental workers who focus on parental strengths rather than on inadequacies are likely to be more successful in establishing a positive tone and constructive rapport with families in crisis. A minimum of professional jargon and the demystification of child care work practices through a detailed explanation of shelter work may also increase parental comfort. Introduction to other parents in similar situations may foster a positive tone by diminishing feelings of isolation.

Extensive parental involvement in the care and treatment of their child throughout his placement is the next major goal of shelter work. Engaging parents, however, may be problematic for a number of reasons. Child care workers may see themselves as the most capable ones to effect positive change in the youths. Parents may be resentful and intimidated by child care professionals or may have unrealistic expectations of them. If the shelter is situated far from the family's home, it may also make parental visits difficult.

Ecologically-based emergency shelters, that is residential programs located in the community which strive to maintain and expand peer, school and other local supports, offer the best opportunity for parental involvement. The presence of the shelter in the neighborhood facilitates frequent family visits, and may allow for the provision of child care support upon the youth's return home. But even in programs which may not be located in the family's community, extensive parental involvement is possible. Child and youth workers should strive to include parents in decisions regarding their child whenever possible. Parental presence at intake, case conferences and staff meetings will make them more meaningful for all concerned.

With the child's first placement in an emergency shelter comes a need for understanding of the family structure which may help explain and guide the treatment of the child's difficulties. Extensive parental involvement offers child care staff an ideal opportunity to observe child-parent interactions and to discern significant treatment issues. Also, it may give workers and parents a chance to learn from each other effective ways of dealing with the child.

Finally, emergency shelter workers are often the first to have the opportunity to educate the family on the social service network which is caring for their child. An understanding of the network will help parents understand their rights and those of their child, and may also give them sufficient information to effectively advocate on their child's behalf.

THE CHALLENGE FOR EMERGENCY SHELTER PROFESSIONALS

As for the child and his family, the shelter offers a unique set of problems and opportunities for the child and youth worker. Since there is little information available on the youth, the worker in a shelter must become proficient at arriving at a speedy and accurate understanding of the complex dynamics of what makes the child "tick." Shelter clients introduced with little or no forewarning give staff little opportunity to prepare the other residents or themselves for the arrival of a new youth. Since there are few, if any, admission criteria for most shelters, the likelihood of the admission of inappropriate clients is great, posing other challenges for the workers.

Shelter clients typically have brief placements. The frequency of admissions and discharges, planned or otherwise, means that each day, each shift, is very different from the one before, making effective planning difficult, unexpected situations likely, and stress at times overwhelming.

The high rate of client turnover also means a tremendous number of families, friends, professionals and community contacts for the child care worker to deal with daily, adding an additional source of stress. Effective control of the unit, largely a function of stability and consistency, is extremely difficult to maintain in such an environment which further frustrates the worker's efforts. The relationships that a child care worker may develop with the clients and that are often considered to be a major source of job satisfaction for many professionals are hampered by their brevity.

Despite these potential drawbacks, emergency shelters offer to both students and beginning workers in the field, in an intense and compressed experience, the chance to learn many of the skills necessary to succeed in the field of child care. Everything that takes place in residential and day treatment settings should also be present in a well-functioning shelter and, while it may take place in a shorter time span, the quality of the learning experience can be even more profound.

The need for structure and routines in a shelter is paramount and the consequences of not being consistent in these areas are immediately apparent. Workers are constantly tested by the diverse and constantly changing clientele to make their structures work, but at the same time keep them flexible enough to meet the needs of a wide range of youth.

Treatment planning may be initiated in the shelter. While it seems true that the more developed treatment plans will usually take place in a second-line residential unit, the effectiveness of brief treatment in a shelter is often underestimated. This means that the workers must recognise treatment issues quickly and implement treatment goals immediately.

Crisis management is a constant issue for most shelters and the shelter teams quickly become expert in defusing and rechanneling crisis situations so that they become a learning situation for the youth. Any personal issues that students or beginning workers have regarding coping with crisis experiences are quickly resolved or the worker will probably not succeed in a shelter work environment.

Relationships both with the children and the rest of the staff are forged under fire. A smoothly functioning shelter team has learned to understand the strengths and weaknesses of each member and has become a well-oiled machine that makes the most of its members, and is able to cope with a great deal of stress.

Relationships with the clients are also surprisingly developed considering the length of time most of the clients are in the shelter. The workers have learned how to make the most of limited interactions. They know what can be accomplished with children under these circumstances and will not attempt more than this. The constant shifting of client populations also means that workers in a shelter become experts at dealing with the issues that always seem to arise around admission and termination.

Lastly, they have the opportunity to work with a wide variety of families under very stressful conditions and this gives shelter staff empathy and understanding for what the families are going through, as well as some ways to help the families begin to function better.

CONCLUSION

We have sought to explore some of the problems that a child's placement in an emergency shelter may pose to his family, the child himself, and to the child care worker. The problems, although numerous and complex, are greatly compensated for by the opportunities they offer.

REFERENCES

Fanshel, D. (1976). Status changes of children in foster care. *Child Welfare, 55,* 143-172.

Hamilton, L. (1985). *Parental involvement in residential centres*. Unpublished Manuscript, Montreal.

Ragen, T. (1980). A shelter care alternative for emotionally disturbed and delinquent or pre-delinquent adolescents. *Residential and Community Child Care Administration, 1*(4), 345-356.

Trzcink, J.J. (1978). Emergency shelter—vital link in protective services. *Social Casework, 59,* 621-625.

8

Competency, Relevance, and Empowerment: A Case for the Restructuring of Children's Programs

Roderick Durkin ˙

ABSTRACT. Children's programs should be restructured so as to provide social systems that vigorously support child and youth care rather than hinder it. Specifically, programs should be reoriented so as to promote normal growth and development, i.e., competency, particularly interpersonal competencies. Programs should be made more relevant to community, rather than institutional, living. Democratizing programs by empowering children and those who care for them will make the programs more effective and appropriate for raising and treating children and youth. Restructuring as a strategy for change is also examined.

Few would dispute the fact that the majority of children in group care in the United States are cared for and have their most salient relationships with child and youth workers who are chronically overstressed, undersupported, and grossly undervalued. Those who care for animals in the zoo are usually better paid than those who care for our children and the elderly. Furthermore, it is extremely doubtful that the resultant stream of "burning out" workers passing through a child's life can adequately achieve the primary goals of child care, namely to cultivate the psychological well-being and to

---

Roderick Durkin is Director, Sage Hill Camp, Inc., Box 57, South Hill Road, Jamaica, VT, U.S.A. 05343.

promote the all-important interpersonal competencies. While one can argue about how damaging such relationships are, few would argue that they can be positive for the developing children entrusted to our care.

Caring for children is difficult under the best of circumstances and is all but precluded in far too many of our children's programs, which are ill-conceived, irrationally organized, and unresponsive to the needs of developing children and their families. The difficulty of our task was driven home to me by a teenager who shared with me his astute observations that we child care workers typically came in energetic, happy, and enjoying the work, while the kids came in angry, depressed, strung out on drugs and in and out of jail or foster homes, etc. After a few years, the kids left feeling better about themselves and life in general, while the child care workers often left drinking heavily, wrecking their cars, flunking out of school, getting divorces, etc.

The prolonged and intimate relationship prerequisite for positive child care is an inherently threatening and exhausting task, rarely accomplished in programs that are specifically structured to support child care work.

In the following sections, this chapter will arque for: (1) promoting competence as a theoretical basis for child care work; (2) restructuring programs so as to make them more relevant for community living; that is, communitize them; (3) restructuring programs to empower child care workers and children alike; that is, to democratize them; and (4) the professionalization and politicization of child care necessary to achieve these long-overdue changes in our children's programs.

THE PROMOTING OF COMPETENCE
AS A RATIONALE FOR CHILD CARE

Promoting the competence of children provides a rational, coherent, and integrated theoretical basis for our work along with commonly accepted means to achieve it.

Allport describes the need for competence by stating that

it would be wrong to say the need for competence is the single and sovereign motive of life. It does, however, come as close as any . . . to summing up the whole biologic story of life. We survive through competencies and we become self-actualized through competency. (1961, p. 214)

The need to become more competent is an innate need particularly strong in developing children and is closely linked to one's environment, which varies greatly in the kind and quality of competencies evoked. A basic question for those of us in child care is what kind of environments are we providing? Are we preparing children for independent and satisfying life in the community, or are we teaching them to be better delinquents, mental patients, and people adapted to institutional living or the streets? From a behaviorist point of view, if the problems that brought a child into care, the solutions to those problems, or the skills adaptive for positive community living do not occur in the programs, how relevant can these programs be for the children?

Most of the children who require professional child care have been harmed psychologically, and will suffer its long-term consequences. A valid approach to treating illness, particularly in children, is to promote health, that is, competency. The more competent persons are, the less disruptive will be their psychopathology and the more likely that they will seek and make use of help in solving their problems. Thus the overriding, twenty-four-hour-a-day, seven-day-a-week concern of group care should be to promote the normal growth and development of children rather than to treat psychopathology. This is not to deny its significance or to trivialize psychopathology but to put it in proper perspective and a bounded, and thus more treatable, context.

A competency-based program focuses on health and normal development and views the child positively, e.g., as a student rather than a patient, and ecologically in the context of family, school, and community, etc. It seeks through developing positive competencies to achieve the more realistic goal of helping the child to become more acceptable and his/her environment more accepting. This is in marked contrast to the more abstract and less feasible goal of "curing" the child. The medical or psychopathology model, with its focus on pathology and dysfunction, stigmatizes the child, abstracts the children from their ecological relationships, in search of intrapsychic causality. This often results in those furthest from the child exercising the most power over the child, reliance on high-priced specialists, and fragmentation of the child's life.

Most of the children requiring professional child care are very troubled and come to us with many unmet infantile needs of dependency and aggression, which they often inappropriately seek to meet in their new relationships with peers and adults. Such efforts are necessarily doomed and often result in a deepening of the cycle of alienation, rejection, hurt, and confusion, and thus ironically perpetuate the very difficulties and hurts the child sought so desperately to mend or avoid.

The connecting link between child care's primary goals of cultivating the psychological and emotional well-being of the child and promoting his or her interpersonal competencies is that most of our emotional needs are met by other people. How others relate to developing children is the mirror they use to define themselves and how they feel about themselves. Thus, by improving a child's interpersonal relationships with peers and adults, we will ensure more ongoing positive feedback which in turn will cultivate their psychological well-being. Child care workers are themselves influential in providing a more positive prototype for future relationships, particularly in comparison to parents in dysfunctional and often destructive families. For many children, what begins as an adjustment reaction to a bad situation may become a maladaptive way of life. In other words, more positive relationships with child care workers, peers, and other adults may prevent the child from maturing "as the twig was bent." Such positive relationships also greatly mitigate the impact of negative experiences. For many troubled children, their first positive, long-term, salient and developmentally significant relationships may be with child and youth care workers.

Interpersonal competencies have their intrapsychic counterparts, such as accurate interpersonal perception, appropriate assertiveness, skills in cooperation, understanding one's feelings, and the ability to communicate with others, etc. There is no better way to enhance self-esteem in developing children than helping them to develop the skills to master the environment, get along well with others, and to succeed in their undertakings.

Children's programs probably took the wrong fork in the road when they chose to misappropriate the interpersonal richness of the milieu to serve the short-term clinical needs of children as determined by specialists in illness. The legacy of this decision includes (1) increasing the risks of iatrogenic illness (i.e., institutionalization) by maximizing the secondary gains of pathology; (2) evoking an adversary relationship between the child and the staff; (3) empowering those furthest and least knowledgeable about the child to make the more far-reaching decisions for the child; (4) disregarding the vital developmental issues; and (5) most important of all, relegating those most influential (developmentally speaking) in the child's life to little more than attendants or guards while costly experts in illness, distant from the child, treat what they view as the acute illness of the child, often disregarding the child's more important long-term developmental needs. Psychopathology is probably better treated in private, and segregated by a barrier of confidentiality. Long-term developmental needs can also be better met in milieux structured to cultivate psychological health and to potentiate opportunities to learn and practice interpersonal competencies, rather than in an unrealistic milieu tailored to support psychopathology.

Restructuring programs as a strategy for change appears to be the quickest and most efficient way to change and improve programs. There is abundant evidence that changing social structures is an effective way to change the nature and quality of interpersonal relationships. Structural changes are generalizable rather than idiosyncratic, and they can be experimented with and studied, i.e., tried out. Restructuring can be based on rational choices that take into account system-wide implications of change. Changing the social structure is probably the most effective way to potentiate the child care worker-child relationship.

THE COMMUNITIZATION
OF CHILDREN'S PROGRAMS

"Communitization" describes a restructuring of children's programs so as to provide a "normalizing" experience, i.e., one that is designed to prepare and equip children for satisfying life in the community.

Deinstitutionalization is better viewed in the context of communitization. Despite the trend away from large institutions isolated from the families and communities of the children, there is and will continue to be a need for ongoing group care programs for those numerous children who either have no one to care for them or whose difficulties are such that they cannot benefit from community living without professional child care. Unlike adults, who have already acquired the skills necessary for independent living, children cannot be deinstitutionalized because, by definition, they must be housed, fed, protected, and most important of all, prepared for adult life.

That large institutions are being phased out is undoubtedly a good thing because the demands of their social systems all but preclude personalized care and the "normalizing" experience that developing children require. It is axiomatic that the more troubled a child is the more he or she requires small, personalized and normalizing programs. Unless, of course, our real purpose is to undermine the potential of retarded children, turn troubled children into chronic mental patients, or to take children in trouble with the law and make them into hardened criminals. If these are our real goals, then our large institutions are indeed well-suited to the task.

There is an ever-growing population of troubled and thus difficult children whose needs cannot be met by their own families or foster care and who require the support and strengths of group care. Professional child care workers are free from the long history of tangles and antagonistic relationships with the child and thus, unlike family members, they can get off to a new start with the child. Group care offers many resources, skills, and the back-up of other workers not available in family living. Very simply, these troubled and all too often throw-away children require professional child care and only can be helped in programs tailored to their unique needs. This is best accomplished in small, diversified programs designed to specifically support quality, developmentally-oriented child care. Many of the children can no longer be coped with, much less helped, by their own or foster care families.

Deinstitutionalization in British Columbia, Canada, was a landmark innovation in child care, which freed the profession from a facility-based definition of child care. Some five hundred child care workers who were "laid off" when large institutions were closed were offered community-based child care work in the schools, group homes, streets, and as family support workers, etc. Unlike most deinstitutionalization programs, which did little more than save money in the short run and obscure society's responsibility for caring for its children, this innovation provided the support in the community prerequisite for children's benefiting from community living.[1] Societies that exercise their authority *in loco parentis* to remove children from their homes should have a commensurate responsibility to provide a better alternative. Most do not.

It is said that if the only tool you have is a hammer, you will treat every problem as if it is a nail. Some examples of innovative community-oriented programs are (1) Childhaven's therapeutic day care program for abused and neglected children and their families; (2) the Sage Hill program which combines and potentiates a positive and brief residential experience with a salient year-round program for teenagers and their families; (3) the Fountain House Club program which provides an integration of housing, transitional employment, and social supports for chronically mentally ill children who often simultaneously age out of children's services and return to the community for which they are ill prepared; and (4) a New Zealand program, where children are placed in group homes according to the social tasks facing them, such as preparing for independent living, reunification with their families, or long-term and out-of-home care. Such a diversity of specialized programs appears to make better use of resources, peer group support, staff, etc.

No profession is better suited or more willing than child and youth care to undertake the long-term custodial and developmentally-oriented care of children, which requires twenty-four-hour-a-day, seven-day-a-week work. Generalists who are competency-oriented, community-based and who can integrate the child's experiences are needed, not specialists in treating acute diseases at a distance and whose work is clearly tailored for their nine-to-five convenience rather than the round-the-clock, long-term needs of developing children.

If we are to restructure our programs so as to be more relevant to the needs of children (no mysteries are involved, for we know perfectly well what is required in terms of facilities, care, supervision, and positive social experiences, etc.), we must anticipate and plan for system-wide implementation of these changes. There should be no programs in which we would not be willing to put our own children.

Almost two hundred years ago, Pinel's moral management of patients was developed. Despite differences in language, it is similar to competency-based milieu therapy programs. While the knowledge is still there, we are yet to achieve the necessary system-wide changes. In addition to maintaining the vested interests of high-priced specialists, i.e., the status quo, traditional programs insulate the staff from the threatening, prolonged, and intimate contact with troubled people. If, as we must, we are to adequately raise the children in our care, we must devise social systems that support us in our work rather than, as so many do now, burden us further in our care of children.

THE DEMOCRATIZATION
OF CHILDREN'S PROGRAMS

Both child care workers and abusive parents share the dilemma of being overstressed, undersupported, and yet held personally accountable for their actions, despite the fact that many of these actions are properties of the systems they function in. Just as redistributing power in the family system, by family therapy, has proved effective, so empowering child care workers and the children they care for will dramatically lessen the tensions and strains which are properties of the social system and will, at long last, provide social structures that are supportive and conducive to providing quality child care.

Inherently, our work is demanding, taxing, and draining under the best of circumstances. However, we rarely work under the best of circumstances; in fact, rather than working in social systems designed to support our work, we typically work in circumstances that add to an already difficult task by (1) evoking an adversary relationship with the children we care for, and (2) burdening us with the double bind of incompatible clinical and child-rearing expectations.

The solution to both of these problems is a democratization of programs by empowering both child care workers and the children themselves. Just as programs will need to be restructured so as to promote competency and a community orientation, so they will have to be restructured in order to empower those who must work, live, and solve their problems together, namely children and their care givers.

It is high time that we ask ourselves, "If what we are doing for children is so good for them, why do they fight us so much?" Typically, we answer that question with "because they don't know what is good for them," or "they are crazy." However, clearly we have reached the limits to which we can coerce, intimidate, threaten, or outright bully children into compliance. Such techniques have failed in the past and more of the same will most likely only be counterproductive and perpetuate the "cops and robbers" game we are trapped into playing. A better alternative is to motivate children to want to do what they need to do. Redirecting our energies to promoting normal growth and development is more likely to be productive. All of us want to become more competent in at least some areas, and this is a good vehicle for establishing cooperative relationships with children. In promoting competence, we don't address "sore spots," stigmatize, or focus on threatening topics. The problem areas are better dealt with in private with a therapist. Once the adversary nature of the relationship is changed, children and workers can become partners and solve the many vexing problems and dilemmas they share in a task-oriented, give-and-take manner which very importantly is rich in opportunities to teach experientially such competencies as assertion, negotiation, compromise, and cooperation.

THE PROFESSIONALIZATION OF CHILD CARE

Just as children must be empowered, so must those directly responsible for their care. Few tasks lend themselves as appropriately as child care to a more egalitarian, management-by-consensus organizational structure. While some say the medical hierarchy has given way to the team concept, that apparently "democratized" version of the illness model amounts to little more than changing chairs on the Titanic. Child care work requires that a myriad of decisions be made on the spot by those familiar with the children and who will be expected to carry them out. Those further from the child should not be making such far-reaching decisions. Programs should be restructured so the child and youth worker is at the hub of the wheel, and experts in psychiatry, social work, education, etc., are used in a more cost efficient and effective consultative manner. Such a structure is better suited to the generalist requirements of caring for children, where the integration of different experiences is as important as the experiences themselves. It only makes sense that those who know the child best and those who have the most salient relationship with the child make decisions with that child that the two of them will have to abide by. The bane of most child care workers is not that of knowing what to do, but how to do it. Working in partnership with the children we care for, we will be able to find the working solutions to our many vexing dilemmas, and this joint problem solving will also help provide the mutual acceptance of these decisions and thus facilitate caring for children.

In many ways, we are very hypocritical in our working with children. We want them to be responsible but are unwilling to take the risks of giving them real responsibility. We want them to be trustworthy but often don't trust them. We want them to feel like they belong, and yet the fact that in the everyday functioning of the programs they are essentially unnecessary is perhaps our cruelist rejection of them. Our programs will go on with or without them. The way our programs are structured, the only salient way the children engage us is by raising hell with us and causing us to fail in achieving our primary goal of preparing them for community living. For the children that is, of course, a most pyrrhic victory. Children and child care workers alike are prisoners of a system that succeeds in bringing out the worst in all of us rather than the best. It is a bitter irony that there are so many needy children and so many good, decent, capable, and hard-working child care workers who are ready, willing, and able to help, and yet the way their relations are structured all too often precludes quality child care.

Programs restructured so that they promote competence rather than emphasize pathology, are relevant for community living rather than institutional life, and empower the children and those who care for them to work as partners rather than as adversaries will support us in our task rather than hinder us. The dangers in such a restructuring are more apparent than real, and the opportunities to make our programs more helpful and relevant to children are vast.

Concurrent with such a restructuring will be the upgrading of the quality of child care, by simultaneously professionalizing, in the best sense of the word, the field, and gaining the political power necessary to restructure children's programs. Amongst the helping professions, child care is unique in that it lacks a clear academic base and that child care skills rely on intangibles such as wisdom, savvy, and interpersonal adroitness. While the skills of child care can be aided by academic understanding, such preparation can never replace the intangibles. In terms of professional training, child care requires a closer integration of experience and knowledge than other professions. A case method of training is perhaps more suited to our needs. Child care workers are generalists and thus need to have a working knowledge of group work, education in the broadest sense, psychology, and life skills, etc. The demands of such comprehensive and in-depth training are great in and of themselves, but they are feasible, as has been demonstrated by the success of the European educateur model of child care. Unfortunately, child care has suffered from a colonialist type of education. We have to go outside our field for training in psychology, social work, etc., but such training often can't help us much in our child care work or prepare us for work outside our field.

The role closest and most relevant to child and youth care work is that of early education "teachers" who provide a comprehensive "education" that is similar to and prepares children for everyday life. This approach is developmentally oriented and seeks to cultivate a child's emotional well-being and competencies, particularly interpersonal competency. Their focus is on the preschool years, but the approach and view of children would, with necessary modifications, also be appropriate for older children and youth.

Clearly, we must demand that we play the game in our ball park, not in those of the other professions. Real career ladders in child care must be established, and the absolute absurdity of non-child care workers, usually specialists in illness, supervising child care workers must be ended.

A risk of increased professionalization is of becoming, like other professions, indifferent to our clients, arrogant, over-intellectualized, and self-serving. Fortunately, those traps, which many in the other professions have fallen into, are less likely to affect us because such demeanor is incompatible with quality and responsive child care. The children we care for do us a great service in that they keep us honest. Hypocrisy, status driving, and indifference can only make the care of children harder.

One of our greatest political strengths is that, unlike the poor, who find it hard to play hard-to-get when they are neither wanted nor necessary, child care workers are indispensable to the programs where we work. Another strength is the fact that most children's programs are not particularly successful, and that by restructuring our programs to promote competencies, making them relevant to community living, and empowering children and those who work directly with them, we can have better programs cheaper. There is abundant dead wood in most programs to more than cover the costs of upgrading child care. With child care workers at the center of the hub, highly priced specialists can be used in a more cost-efficient and cost-effective manner on a consultative basis. It makes no sense that specialists, usually in illness, have so much control and consume so much of the resources in what is preeminently a generalist endeavor, namely the raising of children.

The reallocation of resources to a more optimal system will entail major job disassociations and political struggles, but when threatened with long hours of face-to-face contact with children — days, nights, and weekends — few but child care workers (in spirit and/or in training) will seek to work in our restructured programs.

Our profession must be upgraded to attract talented, competent people suited and willing to work in our restructured programs and to care for the troubled and "throw-away" children that our society produces in great numbers. Rational as our arguments are; desperate as are the short- and long-term costs to society and, more importantly, the needless suffering of our troubled children; and noble as our calling is, make no mistake about it: building the political power necessary to bring about these essential changes is of at least equal importance. Difficult and distasteful as such political struggles may be, we have the right to create social structures that support our work, and we owe it to the children entrusted to our care.

NOTE

1. As innovative and cost-effective as the Family Support Program was, it was eliminated in 1983 in the name of "financial restraint," thereby leaving the Province of British Columbia without either adequate group care or alternative community-based child and youth services.

REFERENCE

Allport, G. (1961). *Pattern and growth in personality*. New York: Holt, Rinehart and Winston.

SECTION 3:
KEY SUPPORT FUNCTIONS IN CHILD AND YOUTH CARE PROGRAMS

Introduction

Although it is of the essence of the child and youth care profession to be based in, or grounded on, direct, day-to-day work with children, a variety of supporting functions are critical to the successful practice of front-line work. In this section, three of these functions, often neglected and misunderstood, and even resented by workers (frequently not without just cause), are examined with a view to suggesting ways in which they can be carried out more effectively.

Mark Krueger, who has been studying the work environment of child and youth care for a number of years, leads off the section by underscoring the challenging and demanding nature of professional teamwork. He provides an overview of the procedures, skills, human conditions, and teaching methods necessary for effective team implementation and functioning. Krueger outlines specific teaching strategies that can be used in helping students (or workers in training sessions) to develop the requisite personal awareness and group skills for constructive teamwork.

Closely linked to the theme of teamwork are two chapters on

supervision in child and youth work. Jack Phelan identifies the most common difficulties encountered by agencies attempting to implement a supervisory system and suggests that, rather than focusing on staff management, child care supervisors need to give priority to the development of worker competence and expertise.

Phelan proposes a systematic evaluation system as a framework for effective supervision, detailing the stages of worker development along with appropriate supervisor responses. He suggests that such an approach can reduce burnout and staff turnover, two of the traditional nemeses of the profession, and can ultimately result in better services to clients.

Carol Ing complements Phelan's stage perspective by offering an analysis of the supervisory process and its key interacting elements of the self (of both the worker and supervisor), role, and communication skills. Further, she draws upon learning styles research in an attempt to provide supervisors and workers with a richer understanding of themselves and each other. A number of examples illustrate some of the problems with traditional approaches and the potential advantages of learning style analysis.

A creative blend of Phelan's developmental stage framework and Ing's suggested application of learning styles research appears to offer a promising package for any supervisor wishing to enhance his or her performance in this vital role.

Finally, the position of the administrator is surely the most underrated component in all of the field of child and youth care. In the early stages of the evolution of the profession, there has been an understandable, and perhaps necessary, preoccupation with the nuts and bolts of direct care practice. Administrators of child care programs have virtually always been drawn from other clinical professions, such as psychiatry or psychology, or from the management sciences, such as public or business administration, or even accounting. All too often there has existed a cold war, or even active hostility, between the clinical child care staff and the program administrator.

Abbey Manburg and Richard Goldman have drawn upon the educational research literature to propose guidelines for effective child and youth care program leadership. With the advent of education and training programs within our field specializing in administration, the child care profession now has a real opportunity to operate at all levels of the service system. Manburg and Goldman make a convincing argument for the acceptance of administrative functions as an integral part of child and youth care practice. We need to understand and welcome our colleagues in child care administration as a sub-group of the profession, not reject them as outsiders (i.e., "they're not *really* child care workers"). Our future may well depend on it.

9

Promoting Professional Teamwork

Mark A. Krueger

ABSTRACT. Teamwork is the most popular method of treatment design and delivery in child and youth care work. In this chapter several of the structural ingredients and human conditions that are needed to implement teams are outlined. A method for teaching teamwork to students and practitioners is also presented.

Interdisciplinary treatment teams are very popular in professional child and youth care. From large institutions to group care facilities to community-based programs, administrators and practitioners are convinced that teams lead to more effective programs for children and youth, and greater satisfaction and commitment among workers (Garner, 1977; Krueger, 1986).

In the midst of this strong support for teams, however, most proponents will also agree that teamwork is a very challenging and demanding process. Extensive practice and training are required to achieve the levels of communication, compromise, constructive criticism, and encouragement which are needed for effective team interaction (Garner, 1982; Krueger, 1982; VanderVen, 1979).

Given the popularity, potential, and challenges of teams, it is clear that team development is an area which deserves considerable professional attention. In this chapter an attempt will be made to briefly describe the procedures, skills, human conditions, and teaching methods that are needed to implement effective teams. The

Mark A. Krueger, Director, Child and Youth Care Learning Center, Division of Outreach and Continuing Education, University of Wisconsin-Milwaukee, P.O. Box 413, Milwaukee, WI 53201.

purposes are to offer a few suggestions for promoting the growth of teams and to encourage further research and study.

DEFINITIONS

- *Team* — A group of individuals assigned to work with a specific group of children and their families. Teams can consist of various combinations of child and youth care workers, social workers, teachers, consultants, administrators, parents and children. Teams normally consist of four to eight members, but they can be as small as two members or larger than eight.
- *Teamwork* — A process in which team members convene on a regular basis to design, discuss plans for implementing and evaluate individual treatment plans, and coordinate activities for an assigned group of children and families.

TEAM POLICIES AND PROCEDURES

Effective team procedures are an essential prerequisite to effective teamwork (Krueger, 1982). Like other major innovations, teams have to be systematically guided into place. Numerous authors have studied teams and the problems that arise when teams do not have a sound structural foundation (Brendtro & Ness, 1983; Garner, 1977, 1982; Krueger, 1982, 1983, 1986; VanderVen, 1979; and Vorrath & Brendtro, 1974). A summary of their recommendations follows:

1. Teams require written definitions, that are consistent with the beliefs and values of team members and the treatment philosophy of a specific agency or program (Krueger, 1982). People have to be aware of how a team is supposed to look and be willing to buy into it, before they can proceed with commitment and dedication.
2. Teams, like the treatment plans team members develop for their clients, require goals and objectives which can be easily and readily evaluated (Krueger, 1982). Team members need to know where they are headed and how they are doing.
3. Team members need clearcut decision-making procedures,

training in teamwork and communication, and meeting schedules that accommodate everyone (Krueger, 1983; Garner, 1982). It is easier for team members to be part of a decision-making process if they know how the process works and are prepared and available to participate.

4. Teams require policies for recognizing the equal or near-equal status of team members (particularly for child and youth care workers) and for minimizing departmental and/or interdisciplinary struggles in order to create an atmosphere in which everyone feels free to contribute (Garner, 1982; Krueger, 1983; Vander Ven, 1979; Vorrath & Brendtro, 1974). People will participate with greater enthusiasm when the opportunities to influence decisions and to grow within the organization are equal.

These and similar management decisions can provide the foundation for creating an environment where team members can interact effectively with one another. Definitions, measurable goals and objectives, a clear course of action, and the opportunity for equal involvement are as necessary to the successful operation of a team as they are to implementing other agency policies. With these procedures in place team members can concentrate their energy on consensus building, compromise and consistent follow through. Without them, team members often spend unnecessary time trying to find a common ground on which to work (Krueger, 1982).

TEAM SKILLS

Teamwork is a sophisticated process which requires considerable skill. Following is a list of some of the skills which are commonly found among effective team members (Krueger, 1986). These, of course, are skills which develop over time and vary according to individuals. It is also worth noting that these skills are similar to the skills required to be an effective child or youth care worker, including the ability to:

— accept and give constructive criticism at team meetings and in day-to-day interactions with colleagues;

— listen as team members disseminate information and show support and interest;

— compromise in order to achieve consensus decisions;

— be assertive in advocating for a specific point of view;

— self-disclose or share feelings about issues which affect children and their families such as chemical dependency, and sexual and physical abuse;

— take calculated risks when it is clear that a course of action is not predetermined by a team or treatment procedure;

— be consistent in implementing team decisions;

— act independently while maintaining the confidence and trust of fellow team members;

— be dependable in following through with team assignments and attending team meetings;

— strive for and display self-awareness in analyzing and formulating solutions to treatment problems;

— constructively express anger at team meetings and in individual interactions with team members;

— give and receive support and encouragement;

— learn from successes and mistakes with team members and in implementing treatment plans;

— articulate observations in informal and formal discussions;

— write descriptive log notes and progress reports;

— study and research issues related to team development.

Finding people with the potential to develop these skills is not an easy task. Thorough screening procedures, often including interviews with existing team members, are required. Nonetheless, it is important to find the right people for the job and to invest resources in their training. Without skills like these it is difficult for even the best intentioned team members to interact effectively.

HUMAN CONDITIONS

If an agency or program has created the necessary structural foundation and has recruited the right people and trained them, then energy can be devoted to teamwork. In order to facilitate an effective process of human interaction, several conditions have to be in place. Some of the conditions that exist within effective teams are:

- *Support*: Team members make a conscious effort to encourage and support one another. This often requires setting aside a designated time to acknowledge accomplishments. For example, team meetings begin with team members complimenting each other for specific accomplishments during the previous week.
- *Resource Sharing*: Team members teach each other in formal training sessions and informal interactions. For example, teachers teach social workers and child care workers basic learning concepts, child care workers teach social workers and teachers group and individual management skills, and social workers help teachers and child care workers understand families.
- *Processing*: Team members take time to discuss and vent their feelings. For example, when team members get upset or frustrated with one another, they discuss their feelings openly before attempting to make a decision. This, of course, is done with the knowledge that feelings left undealt with will undermine the decision-making process, and with consideration for the fact that there is an agenda to complete.
- *Empathy*: Team members are constantly striving to place themselves in each others shoes. Empathy is equally as important to team interactions as it is to interactions with children and youth.
- *Accountability*: Team members supervise and hold one another accountable. Team members give constant formal and informal feedback to one another in order to promote and monitor individual, treatment, and team progress. Standardized tests, oral and written progress reports, record keeping,

group supervision, and individual supervision are just a few of the methods which are used to account for their interactions with themselves and their clients.

The way people interact with one another is the major determinant of effective team functioning. If people are sensitive, supportive and constructively critical of one another, then success is more likely.

TEACHING TEAMWORK

In one study of eight treatment teams, all of the team members felt their training for teamwork was inadequate (Krueger, 1982). Teamwork has to be taught. It cannot be learned simply by doing it. Following are a few suggestions for teaching teamwork.

Teaching Students

Students who plan on entering into child and youth care can be and are being taught teamwork in classrooms. This is usually accomplished by including topics such as communication, listening, positive confrontation, self-awareness, etc. in the direct instruction curriculum.

Teamwork can also be taught by giving class members a chance to experience being on a team. For example, in the author's classroom, class members are assigned to mock teams on which each team member assumes a role such as child care worker, teacher, social worker, administrator, child or parent. Then they are given a case history and asked to begin developing a treatment plan by using their knowledge from previous lessons about techniques and practices in child and youth care. As the class progresses through the semester, the team is periodically called back together to integrate new learning into the treatment plans.

Each time the team meets, team members are asked to reevaluate the progress of their plans, themselves, and the team. They are presented with a series of questions about their treatment plan, such as: "Does the treatment plan reflect your philosophy about treatment?" or "Is your choice of techniques consistent with what we've learned to this point?"

More importantly, however, are the questions that are asked about themselves and the team. For example, they are asked "What are you learning about yourself? Are you a good listener? Are you a leader or a follower? Are you willing to compromise? Are you as assertive as you want to be? Can you communicate your ideas? Have you been supportive of your team members?"

They are also asked: "Is the team making consensus decisions? Is everyone contributing? Are people being open with one another? How are you solving disagreements?"

These questions are followed with the direction, "Try to identify areas in which you'd like to improve and areas in which you have strengths both individually and as a team. Then, the next time we meet, work on these areas."

The goals for classroom exercises such as this are to have each team develop a treatment plan that reflects professional practices and techniques, to have class members develop team skills, and to have them learn about themselves in the process.

Teaching Practitioners

Like students, practitioners can be exposed to an inservice curriculum which addresses team issues and practices. The list of references for this chapter provides one source of information. Excellent books and articles can also be found in other human service fields. These topics can be covered by team consultants, and program trainers and/or supervisors. Another effective method is to have team members teach each other.

Practitioners can also learn from their team experience. The same set of questions which were listed in the previous section can be periodically asked of team members. These questions can then be explored and analyzed together.

SUMMARY

The team approach has tremendous potential. It can promote more effective treatment, and greater satisfaction and commitment among team members. In order to achieve these goals, however, the child and youth care profession will have to encourage the implementation of procedures and the creation of conditions such as those just described. It will also have to play a leadership role in promoting further research and study of teams.

REFERENCES

Brendtro, L., & Ness, A. (1983). *Reeducating troubled youth*. New York: Aldine.

Garner, H. (1977). A trip through bedlam and beyond. *Child Care Quarterly, 6* (3), 167-179.

Garner, H. (1980). Administrative behaviors and effective team functioning. *Residential Group Care, 2* (5).

Garner, H. (1982). *Teamwork in programs for children and youth*. Springfield, Illinois: Charles C. Thomas.

Krueger, M. (1983). *Careless to caring for troubled youth*. Milwaukee: Tall Publishing.

Krueger, M. (1982). Implementation of a team decision-making model among child care workers. Doctoral Thesis, University of Wisconsin-Milwaukee.

Krueger, M. (1986). *Job satisfaction for child and youth care workers*. Washington, DC: Child Welfare League.

VanderVen, K. (1979). Towards maximum effectiveness of a unit team approach: An agenda for team development. *Residential and Community Child Care Administration, 1* (3), 287-297.

Vorrath, H., & Brendtro, L. (1974). *Positive peer culture*. Chicago: Aldine.

10

Child Care Supervision:
The Neglected Skill of Evaluation

Jack Phelan

ABSTRACT. Child care workers can become developmentally stuck in early stages of professional growth and remain para-professionals, concerned with behavior control. This chapter describes an approach to child care supervision in which expectations for staff performance are set on a developmental grid that predicts expertise will increase with experience. Child care supervisors use the evaluation process to create goals with each staff member that are developmentally appropriate.

Agencies that deal with difficult to manage children usually discover that the services they can offer to these children and their families are only effective if the child care work provided by the agency is competently delivered. Social work, psychological treatment, educational remediation and even health care are clearly dependent on a strong, competent child care component to provide a health-facilitating atmosphere that permeates the defense systems of the youth.

Administrators assign the responsibility for delivering competent child care services to the child care supervisor. The individual who becomes a child care supervisor is often hired based on his or her ability as a child care worker. This criterion is criticized because many of the skills needed to be an effective supervisor are very different from those needed in direct work with youth. Newly pro-

---

Jack Phelan, Instructor, Youth Development Program, Grant MacEwan Community College, 7314-29th Avenue, Edmonton, Alberta T6R 2P1.

moted supervisors often describe feeling ill-prepared and very uninformed about supervisory tasks. Child care staff complain about the
incompetence of the new appointee, who until recently was highly
regarded for his or her child care skill. This chapter will argue that it
is quite appropriate to recruit skilled child care workers for supervisory positions. The developmental experience of child care workers
as they strive for competence can provide the framework for a supervisory system that promotes growth, learning, and expanded
professional ability.

THE FUNCTIONS OF SUPERVISION

There are many supervisory tasks that require managerial training. These include personnel issues, budgeting, scheduling and
dealing with adult communication problems. These supervisory
functions are common to most middle management positions and
form a "generic core" that can be learned either within or outside
the agency at workshops or in a school. Child care supervisors who
have a surface view of their role may assume that being capable in
these employee management tasks is all that is required. However,
if a high level of child care skill is the key to an agency's success,
then the development of child care competency is the primary task,
not staff management, thus the role of teacher of child care expertise must become a primary supervisory function. Supervisors who
have not achieved a high level of competence in their own child
care professional development will fall short of the mark on this
function and supervisors with little or no experience as a child care
worker will be unable to make an impact on their child care staff.
The type of teaching that a supervisor does, to be effective, must
rely heavily on practical problem solving, actual demonstration and
using anecdotal material to assist workers in thinking more broadly
and deeply about the roadblocks that youth construct to prevent
change in their dysfunctional behavior.

To become effective teachers of child care expertise, supervisors
must create a system, a framework for providing this teaching that
fits into the daily chaos and "emergency room" atmosphere that
often surrounds the most teachable moments in their interactions
with staff. Supervisors know that they rarely are able to create a

classroom atmosphere with staff, so a good supervisor has to utilize existing contacts to enhance the professional development of the child care staff.

Every supervisory job description includes an obligation to evaluate staff performance and this performance evaluation process can become the fulcrum that the supervisor can use to create professional growth. I will propose a developmental approach to staff evaluation that can be consistently applied on a regular basis to all child care staff. This developmental framework can be clearly stated and understood by both supervisor and staff members and can remain a consistent expectation for all levels of child care experience. A supervisor's effectiveness in implementing this developmental evaluation approach relies heavily on the assumption that the supervisor has himself achieved a high degree of competence and can recognize developmental problems in staff.

The principle underlying this evaluation system is that the professional skills which a child care worker should have, are acquired in a developmental process; that is there are certain abilities that need to be acquired first before the next stage of professional development can be mastered. So there should be tasks and skills that child care staff are required to demonstrate that would be determined by the professional developmental stage they had reached. Simply put, expectations for child care expertise would be based upon the number of years of experience of the child care worker. The evaluation format for a specific child care worker would include goals and performance expectations that would change and become more complex as they acquired experience and expertise in child care work.

This evaluation process would be consistently applied to child care staff across the board and create a measureable level of professional competence that would have minimum levels of performance being raised as experience increased. This expertise requirement would drive the teaching area of the supervisor's job and create the need for skill development discussions.

In order to better understand this evaluation framework, it is important to first look at the current developmental process experienced by most child care workers.

THE PROCESS OF WORKER DEVELOPMENT

The initial experience of beginning child care workers is helpless confusion when confronted with the barrage of behavioral problems encountered in an eight hour period. Sensory overload as well as fear of assault create physically palpable stress that increases during the first few weeks on the job. The hoped for confidence created by being armed with pre-service schooling quickly evaporates and theories about therapeutic intervention get discarded in favor of more pragmatic, immediate, control techniques. Issues like trying not to appear intimidated, confused, or easily manipulated cause new workers to feel incompetent and embarrassed as they walk the gauntlet of testing behaviors dealt out by the youth. New workers find themselves in survival postures where their main task becomes limit setting and rule enforcement in a firm, believeable, and hopefully fair manner.

The break-in period for new child care workers is normally six to eight months, during which time a nervous energy, akin to stomach butterflies, accompanies them to work each day. At some discernable point in the latter half of the first year there is a measurable increase in confidence and comfortability in the setting. Basically, each new worker has now experienced the full spectrum of unusual and aggressive behaviors that the clients have to offer and has observed them being competently managed. Perhaps he or she has personally mastered methods to handle the behavior. Now when he or she sets limits or organizes activities, things run relatively well. The job tasks, and even the clients, become more predictable and order often emerges from the chaos.

This is a crucial point in the new worker's development, because now knowledge of therapeutic approaches, so diligently studied in school, can begin to be utilized. The worker's development as a child care professional is about to commence. All the skills and techniques acquired during the past year merely form the baseline from which to begin to function as a professional. Managing surface behavior, handling aggression, directing the routines and implementing scheduled activities are the child care tasks that can be performed by competent technicians; these skills are learned without formal training and comprise the "on the job" learning which is necessary, but really only provides a context from which treatment can emerge. As Fritz Redl has said, the worker has now created enough time and space to "unpack the medicine" needed to treat these youth (Redl, 1951).

Unfortunately, most child care workers get mired in the phenomena of the daily grind and need some assistance to grow professionally at this point. Many child care workers reach this initial plateau and believe that they have climbed the mountain rather than established a base camp. The result of this misconception is that a worker can spend the next twelve months perfecting skills around limit setting, surface behavior control and daily routine adherence. After eighteen months of this type of child care experience, professional boredom sets in and many potentially good child care workers begin to go look around for new challenges, usually deciding on a career shift into a new discipline and thus exit the child care field. Child care workers with many years of experience who denigrate the striving for professional status of their peers have often stagnated at this point in their development and accurately describe themselves as paraprofessionals.

On the other hand, child care workers who are successful in seeing beyond this limited job description into the complexities of the treatment role, get energized by the nuances and subtle distinctions in behavioral messages communicated by the youth in their care. They begin to respect the clinical expertise and the integration of personality, technical skill and brain power required to be effective in their role. Often the difference between the exiters and the successful professionals is an external influence rather than any special ability or insight. Child care supervisors need to provide a professional road map for staff and become facilitators for staff, helping them to develop more sophisticated approaches in child care practice.

THE CRITICAL ROLE OF SUPERVISION

The child care supervisor's role in this scenario is critical. We have to ask ourselves what the supervisor is doing or is not doing as he participates in the process described above. The supervisor must see himself as a teacher of professional expertise; using crises and impossible behaviors as teaching moments, drawing on his or her own child care experience for anecdotal material. Child care supervisors must develop creative energy rather than anger from staff frustration and train staff to develop better questions to avoid getting blocked by rigid techniques or predictable solutions.

The supervisory interventions described above may seem a bit idealized. I am not suggesting that each and every staff member could profit from such an approach, however, properly trained and developmentally prepared staff can readily fit into this type of supervision.

The next question seems to be, how can a developmental style of supervision be marketed in agencies where theoretical constructs are resisted because they don't seem practical enough? Employee fatigue, ennui, and cynicism are human relations problems that supervisors need to anticipate and their own professional training should include methods to deal with these predictable employee problems. In some ways child care supervisors need to be "master child care workers," with the ability to share expertise and highly developed communication skills with other adults.

Typical problems that supervisors face when attempting to increase the quality of professional expertise of staff include surface behavior control and motivation problems. Staff apathy and professional burnout often create behaviors resembling inexperienced staff performance resulting in punitive responses to difficult-to-manage children and blaming the youth for their inability to improve. New, inexperienced child care workers may lack appropriate professional models to shape their own careers and a grim anger seems to pervade many supervisory sessions. Supervisors are often told they don't share the same frame of reference as the workers, even if they have been recently promoted, and they realize that they have become authority figures to be resisted. It is critical for the inexperienced supervisor to get training and consultation around these issues. Supervisors must have the ability to be clear and directive, particularly in channeling staff performance. Challenging staff and engaging in power struggles are usually counterproductive, as supervisors will recall from their child care days. Supervisory training in dealing with resistance is a must, since common sense approaches often don't work.

SUPERVISION ACROSS THE STAGES
OF STAFF DEVELOPMENT

This proposal for a developmental system of staff evaluation/supervision divides the professional expertise of staff into stages measured in one year increments. This may seem to be an artificial system, but it fits with the author's experience and, pragmatically, it coincides with most agencies' evaluation schedules. The details of each stage can be easily adapted to fit the specific needs of an agency or the level of initial expertise of the worker. The important dynamic is the general framework, with the details under the control of individual supervisors.

Stages of development could be extended well beyond the three listed here, with perhaps six stages being developed for a child care system. The focus here is on using the first three years of professional development to create a method of systematic review of skill development and professional growth. Supervisors should clearly outline the expectations of each stage for individual staff, after determining in what stage the person is presently functioning.

Stage 1 would address the initial year of child care work and the expectations for a new staff member. During this time a staff member would be expected to develop group management skills. He or she would be expected to handle problem behaviors, particularly around agency expectations such as school attendance, vandalism, aggressive impulses, alcohol or drug use and sexual issues. A stage 1 worker would be expected to be able to competently run daily routines; wake-up, meals, chores and bedtime. The professional behaviors that the new worker should develop include becoming comfortable and competent as an adult working with youth, focusing on limit setting and channeling behavior in a positive direction. Role modelling, active involvement in daily living tasks and the ability to put the needs of the youth ahead of one's own feelings are major skills for evaluation by the end of year 1. The emergence of a personal style of interacting with youth that is congruent and not a mere copying of the other staff is another expectation. Verbal counselling skills and treatment planning would not be expected or emphasized during year 1. Treatment planning and preparation of individual goal plans should not be encouraged at all during this stage.

The overall emphasis on surface behavior and the limited view of underlying dynamics often create some poor habits and approaches to treatment planning which are difficult to change later on. At best, taking an observational, auxilliary role in creating treatment plans could be possible. Certainly, the year 1 worker should attend treatment planning meetings and see how more experienced workers create plans for youth.

Child care workers should be rediscovering their preservice training knowledge at the beginning of year 2. As the job requirements become more automatic and the youth become more predictable, the mental energy that is freed up can be used to clinically investigate the finer points of the group dynamics or an individual youth's dysfunction. As stated earlier, if this spare energy is not directed toward increasing professional expertise, it usually turns inward on itself and creates boredom and uneasiness with the "routineness" of the child care role. The supervisor should be assisting the year 2 workers to reinvolve themselves in theories by going to the literature in the field. Expectations should include the development of treatment planning skills, and the use of intervention strategies that go beyond the straightforward, obvious approaches from year 1.

During year 2, the worker should be able to recognize that when a youth doesn't respond well to our intervention strategies, we have to shift our approach, not engage in a power struggle. When common sense approaches, logical motivation systems and skillfully applied punishments don't create the results expected, the year 2 worker should be able to resist the urge to push harder and longer. The clinical judgement to know when to abandon the obvious strategy and dig deeper into one's professional expertise should emerge by the end of year 2. Year 2 staff should be expected to be able to examine ways of improving staff behavior, rather than to focus discussion primarily on poor client behavior in the treatment meetings. The supervisor should expect that treatment plans and case presentations will include developmental information using Erikson and Piaget as well as other developmental theorists. Ego strengths and malfunctions, precise behavior analysis, and indications of psychopathology should be routinely noted. Staff intervention strategies, rather than a listing of behavioral deficits in the youth, should form the major part of the treatment plan. By the end of year 2, child care staff should be able to explain both what they are doing and why they are doing it.

Child care workers in the third year of development should be expected to be able to eliminate the use of punishment as a motivator in their treatment planning. By the end of this year, an awareness of the serious limitations of punishment as an approach with delusional, suspicious, adult fearing youth and the increase in intervention strategies along other lines, should make punishment seem very amateurish and non-productive. Supervisors should expect year 3 workers to be able to diagnose the daily living problems that a youth displays and to put together a context for treatment that has an overall, holistic framework. The child care worker's role as a coordinator of needed services, the professional who has the complete youth and his family in perspective, should be evident in the year 3 worker. At this point, the worker should be able to evaluate the approaches being used, going beyond the year 2 awareness of when something isn't working, and create a spectrum of intervention ideas that are useful. The competent year 3 child care professional should be able to develop new approaches to difficult situations and, in fact, be at the threshold of becoming capable of creating new knowledge in the field. For the worker at the end of year 3, the daily living setting will be taking the shape of a rich research laboratory for the expansion of the knowledge base of child care, a theoretical new frontier. Supervisors should expect that by the end of this stage of development, a worker can competently assist in training year 1 staff. This means that new workers are not given pat answers for "why we do it this way," but that explanations are thorough and not based on "just imitate me."

CONCLUSION

This grid of professional developmental stages can be expanded much further. It is intended as a model to be adapted and revised to fit a supervisor's situation. It can also be used by child care workers who lack supervision to create a framework for their own professional growth. The real problem being addressed is that most workers get caught up in the daily phenomena of dysfunctional behavior and need assistance to get unstuck developmentally. The supervisor must become the external force that assists workers to grow and change as professionals.

Recent literature on the ever present problem of staff burnout confirms earlier findings that the obvious stresses of child care work — salary, hours of work, and children's behavior — are not significant indicators of worker dissatisfaction. As the researchers got beyond these obvious issues, they discovered that quality of supervision, communication with administration, perceived competence of one's supervisor, sense of accomplishment and personal growth are highly correlated with staff turnover. Burnout is caused by a sense of going nowhere and stagnating in professional expertise much more directly than any other issue (Fleischer, 1985).

A final point about the use of the evaluation/supervision format to create change in staff is that it helps to minimize the parental, authority role of the supervisor in his relationships with staff. The supervisor as a teacher and motivator of professional expertise is hopefully encouraging self-directed change in the staff member. Often, supervisors find themselves caught up in the role of managing staff behavior and setting limits. This imposition of external control usually feels quite non-professional for both parties. The evaluation/supervision format described in this chapter parallels the basic helping dynamics cited so often in the literature; one needs to develop self-control and skill development in the client rather than create an imposed external set of motivators (Redl, 1952).

The more clear and objective the framework, the easier it becomes for the client to participate as an informed consumer in the process. The major awareness that develops as a child care worker becomes a skilled professional is that self-control is hindered by strong external control. Supervisory approaches that are focused on management of staff behavior help to create non-therapeutic environments as they actually mirror the external locus of control dynamic that typifies less helpful child-staff relationships (Colyar, 1983).

Supervision should be understood as a process of motivating staff to continue to develop their professional expertise. The overall goal is to provide better service to clients and also to increase worker satisfaction and prevent turnover. Supervisors can use the evaluation process to motivate staff in professional growth and a developmental grid, requiring increased expertise with greater experience, can be a useful fulcrum about which to raise the level of staff performance.

REFERENCES

Colyar, D. (1983). Ten laws of residential treatment: what can go wrong when you're not looking. *Child Care Quarterly, 12,* 136-143.

Fleishcher, B. (1985). Identification of strategies to reduce turnover among child care staff. *Child Care Quarterly, 14,* 130-139.

Redl, F. (1951). *Children who hate.* New York: The Free Press.

Redl, F. (1952). *Controls from within.* New York: The Free Press.

11

The Application
of Learning Style Research
in the Supervisory Process

Carol Ing

ABSTRACT. Effective supervisors must integrate both interpersonal processes and concrete tasks to maximize the learning and growth of their child care workers. By paying attention to learning styles, supervisors can become attuned to their staff's learning processes. Thus, learning styles can help supervisors to individualize supervision and better influence worker's attitudes, development and performance. This chapter describes the nature of learning styles and their application to the supervisory process.

Supervision is a feature of most child care work situations. The intention of supervision is to help the child care worker discharge his or her responsibilities in an effective manner. Ideally, the supervisor will stimulate, enhance, coordinate influence and direct the performance of the child care worker. Supervision is most effective when the supervisor and child care practitioner work together to create and maintain a therapeutic environment that assists in enhancing the growth and development of the children in their care.

Traditional views of supervision have considered only concrete job functions such as planning, coordinating, monitoring and evaluating. Yet, these tasks are only a part of the supervisory process.

Carol Ing, Instructor, Child and Youth Care Program, Lethbridge Community College, 3000 College Drive S., Lethbridge, Alberta, T1K 1L6.

Supervision is a dynamic and complex interaction which involve interpersonal processes such as giving and receiving feedback, communicating role and job expectations, support, leadership and personal influence. Although the concrete tasks of supervision are important, it is through interpersonal processes that the supervisor can create an environment within which child care workers develop their skills and upgrade their performance. Thus, effective supervisors must integrate the interpersonal aspects of supervision with its concrete tasks to maximize the learning and growth of the practitioner.

There are a number of interpersonal factors which can assist or block the performance of supervisory tasks. In this chapter, several of these factors will be identified and briefly described. The concept of learning styles will then be presented as a means of understanding some of the key interpersonal issues involved in supervision. By paying attention to learning styles, supervisors can individualize their work with staff and better influence workers' development and performance. In turn, this will help supervisors better accomplish the concrete tasks associated with their position.

FACTORS WHICH IMPACT
THE SUPERVISORY PROCESS

In a field where conflict, problems, and morale issues are continually arising, it becomes important for the supervisor to be aware of the various factors that influence and have a direct impact on the worker's as well as his or her own attitude and behavior. Figure 1 presents a number of reciprocal relationships which interplay within the supervisory process and highlights the processes involved in supervision. These factors continually interact and impact to influence the behaviors of both the supervisor and the practitioner. They may help or hinder supervision, for they provide the context within which the concrete tasks of supervision are performed.

The supervisory relationship should be seen as a two way process that is both reciprocal and mutual. As shown in Figure 1, there are three main forces which impact the interpersonal processes in supervision: the self, communication skills and role.

FIGURE 1:   FORCES WHICH IMPACT SUPERVISORY PROCESSES

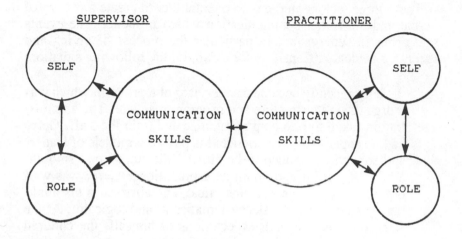

Brief definitions of these factors are as follows:

Self: The self consists of the perceptions, values, attitudes, feelings, past life experiences, education, and learning style that is idiosyncratic to the supervisor or practitioner. For example, a supervisor who believes that practitioners behave responsibly will tend to be trusting and will delegate responsibilities to workers. Similarly, a supervisor who is perceived as credible by the workers is likely to have a positive influence on them.

Communication Skills: interpersonal skills such as genuineness, warmth, empathy, conflict resolution, active listening, etc. are included in communication skills. For example, a supervisor whose style of communication tends to flow in one direction only, especially in the area of decision making, will likely come across as a person who does not listen effectively to practitioners. This in turn tends to cause dissatisfaction and conflict.

Role: includes role conception, role expectations and role performance. How the supervisor views the supervisory role affects the manner in which he or she will define the supervisory role and job functions. For example, new supervisors sometimes try to be "super" supervisors, a situation which can result in problems such as failing to delegate, or making too many changes prematurely.

These three factors merge with one another to create a pattern of verbal and nonverbal communication which influences the events that occur in supervision, in particular the process of giving and receiving feedback. Consider, for example, the following situation:

> Gerry recently became a supervisor of a program which was reorganizing its structure and program mandate. The administration asked him to help reorganize and train the staff. Gerry had no supervisory experience; his past role models of leaders and supervisors tended to be either "dictators" or "smoothers." As a child and youth care practitioner Gerry was well organized, goal-oriented, analytical, and abstract in his thinking. He approached tasks systematically and logically. At the same time he had high expectations of himself, the children and other staff members. His communication style was seen by many as being directive.
>
> In a supervisory session Rick, a feeling-oriented person, was discussing his difficulty in managing one of the children. Gerry presented to Rick a theoretical explanation of behavior problems that Rick found interesting, but not useful, because it had little practical application, and was devoid of personalized feedback. Rick felt inadequate and was hoping that Gerry would observe an incident in which he was having difficulties and that he would be given immediate feedback. Rick came away dissatisfied and frustrated with the supervision he received from Gerry. Gerry, on the other hand, could not understand the need Rick was trying to communicate to him. To better influence Rick's development and performance Gerry needed to take into account Rick as a person and his learning needs.

As seen in Figure 1 and the above example the interpersonal processes are central to supervision. An awareness of the interpersonal processes enables the supervisor to maximize the supervisory process of learning and growth. How the supervisor sees the world and enacts the role of supervision affects the interpersonal processes of giving and receiving feedback. However, the supervisor's communication processes and its consequences will vary from practitioner to practitioner because of the way the different personalities and learning characteristics interact with one another. Therefore, the underlying premise of the chapter is that a supervisor is most effective when he or she takes into consideration not only the professional development and practice skills but the personality and learning style of the practitioner.

Learning styles will be presented in this chapter to illustrate the interactive nature of supervision. The concept of learning styles will now be discussed as a means of enhancing supervision, thereby enabling the supervisor to become flexible and adaptive in the process of giving and receiving feedback.

LEARNING STYLE RESEARCH AND ITS APPLICATION IN SUPERVISION

A major function of the supervisory process is to create a positive climate that will enable the child care practitioner to learn and to develop effective practice skills. By using learning styles in the supervisory process the supervisor is able to communicate interpersonally in a way that will encourage such growth and development. Learning style research has found that people think and learn in different ways (Kolb, 1984; Lawrence, 1982). How people judge, identify, and substantiate information varies from person to person. Learning styles develop over time through personal, professional, and life experiences and are best thought of as an orientation to how a person "translates" his environment (Kolb, 1984). For example, when provided with feedback, some child care practitioners want concrete proof prior to modifying their approach. They seem to express, through their nonverbal and/or verbal communication that "seeing is believing." Other practitioners rely on the use of hunches and when asked about their approach they reply "I had this feeling," or "It seemed appropriate."

Most supervisors use a single approach to supervision in all situations and do not take into consideration individual differences in learning. By being aware of learning styles, the supervisor is able to use a variety of techniques and behaviors best matched to the learning pattern of each staff member, and thereby enhancing the supervisory relationship.

Kolb's Learning Modes

Kolb (1984) identified four basic modes of learning. Each mode represents a process of learning that is a unique combination of perceiving and processing information. Kolb's four basic modes of learning are concrete experience, abstract conceptualization, active experimentation, and reflective observation. Each has developed through an interplay of an individual's education, life experiences, and natural abilities.

1. *Concrete Experience* represents a hands on experience base to learning that relies heavily on feeling-based judgements. Persons with this learning process like, and are good at, interpersonal relationships. They use intuition in problem solving and like to learn from examples, involvement and discussions.

2. *Abstract Conceptualization* indicates an analytical conceptual approach that relies on logical and sequential evaluation. This approach emphasizes thinking rather than doing. Persons with this orientation like systematic planning and learn best from impersonal situations and theory.

3. *Active Experimentation* signifies persons who like to learn by doing and are not deterred by trial and error learning. They are quick to pick up ideas and like to take action quickly. They are risk takers who like to see results but will not follow assignments nor tasks as planned.

4. *Reflective Observation* utilizes a tentative, observational approach that emphasizes understanding rather than practical application. Persons with this learning mode are good at gathering information, reflecting, and analyzing. They learn best from situations that allow time for observation and processing.

In general child care practitioners are unlikely to be seen in these purest forms, although each has a dominant or overt style that is clearly and easily recognized.

Learning Style Profile

Kolb (1984) combined the four learning modes to create four learning styles. It is these learning styles that provide a useful framework for supervising workers. The four learning styles have been placed onto two axes: Concrete — Abstract and Random — Sequential using a combination of Kolb's (1984) and Gregorc's (1979) models of learning styles (see Figure 2).

Kolb's (1984) four learning styles are converger, diverger, assimilator and accommodator. Each of these learning styles represents a method of decision making and problem solving. Gregorc (1979) also developed four similar learning styles but for use in instructional situations. For the purpose of this chapter, Kolb's and Gregorc's learning styles have been selected to illustrate the application of learning styles as a means for supervisors to individualize their work with their staff so they can better accomplish the concrete tasks of supervision.

1. *Converger*: persons with this style have abilities which lie in the area of the application of abstract tasks and ideas. They perform well in situations where there are concrete, orderly presentations and where there is a "right way" to work. These workers are concrete and sequential in their thought and actions. They prefer to work independently and are strong in the area of visualizing concrete tasks and issues.

Fry (1978) and Kolb (1984) found that persons with this style of learning felt that affective and behaviorally-oriented environments hindered their growth. Accordingly, supervisors need to provide a

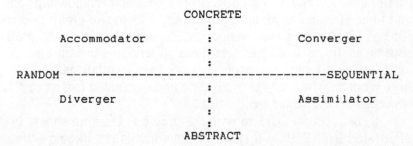

FIGURE 2: LEARNING STYLE PROFILE

cognitive approach in which these workers are provided with an opportunity to work independently. The supervisor should consider the use of case studies and problem-solving approaches with these workers.

Supervisors with this learning style tend to be well organized, and expect their workers to be the same. They have high expectations of their staff members and like instructions to be followed. Yet, at the same time, they support child care staff to master their role as workers, and encourage the staff to think independently. Problems can arise if a supervisor with an overt converger style is supervising a worker with a more random or unstructured learning style. Convergers relate best with other persons who are convergers or assimilators.

2. *Diverger*: The ability of divergent style individuals to learn is enhanced in situations which include such factors as personalized feedback and shared feelings. These workers are creative and do well in situations calling for brainstorming and problem solving. They prefer unstructured environments, and seem to gather information, then reflect on and organize the material.

Therefore, in supervision, child care practitioners who have this style would benefit from a friendly, insightful, and feelings-oriented approach. Because these workers are less structured in their approach to child and youth care, they tend to find that concrete, practical suggestions and goal setting interfere with their learning. Thus supervisory techniques should include: immediate personal feedback, real-life application, discussions and support in organization.

Supervisors with a divergent learning style use a personalized supervisory style which encourages workers to express needs. They usually have excellent awareness of interpersonal relationships and tend to be effective communicators. They like to use group discussions as a method of supervision and expect the workers to profit from these discussions. Because these supervisors use an unstructured feeling-oriented approach, they tend not to relate as well with those workers who are highly concrete and organized (for example, workers with the convergent style).

3. *Accommodator*: Unlike with the previous learning styles, Fry (1978) and Kolb (1984) found that accommodators like an action-

oriented atmosphere. The focus of supervision should be action oriented with practical applications to real life problems. These practitioners thrive on involvement, doing and getting the tasks completed. Like the divergent oriented workers, the accommodators like unstructured situations. However, they differ in that they are less attuned to the nuances or underlying feelings in the atmosphere because they tend to be spontaneous in their action and thinking.

Supervisors should provide ongoing feedback to these workers since they tend to measure their success on how well something worked. Feedback can be offered through small group discussions, peer feedback, and one-to-one supervision. The use of problem-solving processes is an effective approach for these practitioners. The supervisor, however, should not use a "lecture" or "task master" style in supervision since it would not facilitate their learning process.

Supervisors with the accommodator learning style tend to be creative and active as supervisors. Accommodator supervisors encourage child care staff to be active and to apply their learning on the job. They are facilitative supervisors. However, workers with a sequential or observer approach, such as the assimilator or converger, will at times find it difficult to follow the accommodator-style supervisors.

4. *Assimilator*: Finally, assimilators are comfortable in the abstract thinking mode and favor theoretical discussions or analytical approaches. As do convergers, they prefer sequential presentations from which they can analyze and conceptualize the central themes of thought.

Supervisors working with staff members who use an assimilator style of processing information should provide them with the opportunity to reflect and observe child care practice. Kolb (1984, p.200) has stated about such workers that "in task oriented situations when information generation was focused on getting the job done," learning was hindered. In the supervisory sessions these practitioners can relate to theoretical discussions and analysis, and profit from the use of prepared and simulated case discussions. Supervisors should be prepared for "how and why" questions and provide feedback sequentially. Finally, time should be provided to enable the practitioners to analyze and assimilate feedback about their practice.

Supervisors with assimilator learning style are well organized and prepared in their work. They are directive in their communication style and approach to supervision. They relate best with workers who are also assimilators and convergers. They like workers to conceptualize their child care practice and be well organized in both thought and behaviors.

Learning Styles: Their Impact on the Supervisory Process

Each child and youth care practitioner and supervisor has a predominant individual learning style that will impact the supervisory process. The following is an illustration of how learning styles influence the interpersonal processes in supervision:

> Chris is a well-organized supervisor who likes and expects the same degree of organization from his staff. He is highly structured and stresses that the workers be the same with the children. He tends to be a directive and articulate communicator. At times his staff find it difficult to communicate with him because of his concrete, task-oriented and sequential thinking pattern.
>
> Lisa is a child care worker who is energetic, and action-oriented. She, with little planning or thought, tends to jump into projects with both feet. She likes to be creative and experiment; she seems to learn through trial and error. One day, Chris asked Lisa to organize a camping trip for their program. Lisa eagerly began to plan the camping trip, planning activities such as crafts, and preparing lists for mealtimes. When Lisa presented her plan to Chris, he stated that he found the plan lacked both organization and details. For example, he wanted to see clear objectives for the trip, and he was expecting a step by step camping program with clear guidelines and expectations for both the staff and children to follow. He stated that he found Lisa's planning to be disorganized. When he mentioned these points to Lisa she told him that she assumed that such a degree was not needed since the other workers were already

familiar with the program. Lisa was upset with Chris as she felt her efforts had not been recognized. Both Chris and Lisa came away from the session feeling misunderstood by the other.

In the above example both Chris and Lisa were unaware of each other's learning style. If Chris had been aware of Lisa's learning style he would have understood that Lisa was an accommodator and would require support in the area of organization. Her strengths lie in the area of implementation and creativity. Chris would have been more effective if he used her creativity and energy to develop ideas for the trip and supported her in the organization of the plan. To help organize the plan Chris could have provided Lisa with a camping plan outline. In this situation, Chris would have been far more effective by focusing on Lisa's learning style, and approaching her accordingly rather than enforcing his personal learning style on her.

For her part, had Lisa been aware of Chris's learning style, she would have understood Chris's need for organization, instead of becoming upset with Chris when he was providing feedback on her plans. She, therefore, would have been less defensive in her communication with Chris. For Chris and Lisa, becoming aware of their own and each other's learning styles would increase rapport which in turn would enhance their supervisory relationship. Finally, Lisa, through becoming aware of her own learning style and Chris's, would realize a need for developing her own organizational skills.

Because child and youth care is a profession which tends to draw on individuals from a variety of educational and life experiences (Berube, 1984; Ing, 1985), a supervisor must be able to individualize his or her approach when supervising individual practitioners. Friedlander and Ward (1984, p.556) found that a "supervisor's orientation seems to influence his or her style considerably and the supervisor's predominant style, in turn, is predictive of not only a trainee's willingness to work with him but also the trainee's satisfaction with the supervisor." Thus, supervisory sessions which do not recognize a worker's preferred learning style are likely to be less effective and may even be rejected or resisted by the practitioner.

Attention to learning styles in the supervisory process increases the probability of more respectful relationships and productive work and also reduces some of the tension and defensiveness that characterizes many supervisory relationships. As illustrated in the example above, understanding the strengths and limitations of the worker's learning style would enable the supervisor to adjust his approach and build on the worker's strengths, thus creating more positive communication. Through addressing the worker's stylistic differences the supervisor would be able to assess each worker's style, its impact on the supervisory processes, and its effect on their relationship. The supervisor can learn to appreciate the worker's strengths and limitations. Thus, the supervisor learns to accommodate and develop style flexibility, thereby strengthening the process of giving and receiving feedback in supervision.

SUMMARY

Supervision is an interaction between the child and youth care practitioner and supervisor. It is a combination of both task functions and an interpersonal process. The interpersonal aspects of supervision create the context within which the tasks are accomplished. As seen in this chapter, there are a number of dynamic factors which influence the supervisory process. Through becoming aware of learning styles and how these styles influence the supervisory process, a supervisor can individualize supervision, thereby increasing both the quality of supervision and the skill level of the child and youth care practitioner.

REFERENCES

Barnat, M. (1973). Student reactions to supervision: Quests for a contract. *Professional Psychology, 4* 17-22.

Berube, P. (1984). Professionalism of child care: A Canadian perspective. *Journal of Child Care, 2*(10), 1-12.

Boyd, J. (1978). *Counsellor supervision: Approaches, preparation, practices.* Muncie: Accelerated Development.

Carr, J. (1979). *Communicating and relating.* (2nd ed.). Dubuque: Wm. C. Brown.

Cherniss, C., & Egnatious, E. (1971). Styles of clinical supervision in community mental health programs. *Journal of Consulting and Clinical Psychology, 45,* 1195-1196.

Friedlander, M., & Ward, L. (1984). Development and validation of the supervisory styles inventory. *Journal of Counselling Psychology, 31*(4), 541-557.

Fry, R. (1978). *Diagnosing professional learning environments: An observational framework for assessing situational complexity.* Unpublished Ph.D. thesis, Massachusetts Institute of Technology.

Gregorc, A. (1979). Learning/teaching styles: Potent forces behind them. *Educational Leadership.* January, 234-236.

Holloway, E., & Wampold, E. (1983). Patterns of verbal behavior and judgements of satisfaction in the supervision interview. *Journal of Counselling Psychology, 30,* 227-234.

Ing, C. (1985). The acquisition of interviewing skills by child care counsellors: The effects of short-term training. Master's thesis, Nova University.

Johnson, L. (1986). *Social work practice: A journalist's approach.* (2nd ed.). Boston: Allyn and Bacon, 181.

Kadushin, A. (1976). *Supervision in social work.* New York: Columbia University Press.

Kolb, D. (1984). *Experiential learning: Experiences as the source of learning and development.* Englewood Cliffs: Prentice Hall, Inc.

Lawerence, G. (1982). Personality structure and learning style: Use of the Myer-Briggs type indicator. In *National Conference: Student Learning Styles and Brain Behavior.* Reston: National Association of Secondary School Principals.

Loganbill, C., Hardy, E., & Delworth, U. (1982). Supervision: A conceptual model. *The Counselling Psychologist, 10*(1), 3-42.

Phillips, J. (1985). *Improving supervisor's effectiveness.* San Francisco: Jossey-Bass Publishers.

Rosenblatt, A., & Mayer, J. (1975). Objectionable supervisory styles: Student's views. *Social Work,* 184-189.

Rowe, W., & Shields, R. (1985). A supervisory model for child care. *Child Care Quarterly, 14*(4), 262-272.

Shulman, L. (1982). *Skills of supervision and staff management.* Itasca: F.E. Peacock Publishers, Inc.

Siegel, A. (1980). Employee attitude survey reveals some clear messages for managers and supervisors. *Management.* Spring, 13-15.

Tittnich, E. (1986). Training that takes place: Adult learning and adult teaching are the key. In K. VanderVen & E. Tittnich (Eds.) *Children in Contemporary Society.* New York: Haworth Press, pp. 47-55.

12

The Role of the Administrator in Effective Program Delivery

Abbey Manburg
Richard Goldman

ABSTRACT. Although the child and youth care field has experienced enormous growth in the past 10 years, the general direction of this growth has ignored the role of the administrator in the development and maintenance of quality programs. This chapter argues for recognition of the administrator's role as key to quality and presents recommendations to support the professional preparation and training of administrators.

The field of child and youth care has experienced an unprecedented level of growth in recent years. The creation of provincial and state organizations, the dramatic increase in the frequency (to say nothing of the quality) of conferences, books, articles, monographs, and journals speaks eloquently of the growth in professional status of those involved in child and youth care today. This level of activity, which surely represents only the most visible expression of a powerful and long awaited movement, is even more remarkable because it occurs at a time of general budgetary cutbacks in Canada and the United States, and the apparent shift from favor of social programs that tends to accompany the election of conservative governments.

Abbey Manburg, Director, Master's Program for Child and Youth Care Administrators, and Richard Goldman, Dean, Center for the Advancement of Education, Nova University, 3301 College Avenue, Fort Lauderdale, FL 33314.

As we recognize the activity of the child and youth care field, it is important to note too that this activity seems to focus primarily on line workers to the exclusion of others who have responsibility for children and youth in care. To some extent, this focus, and the resulting exclusion, is understandable. Line workers themselves have been systematically excluded from the tight circle of professionals whose decisions impact on the lives of children and youth in care. The current emphasis on line workers represents an act of affirmation by the entire field. It is a communal statement of strength and a long overdue recognition of the importance of line workers and the centrality of their contributions to the quality of care.

This new emphasis on the line worker is important too because the lack of professional recognition that has characterized the field created a situation where the segments of our societies with the greatest need were served by individuals who, as a group, were inadequately prepared and poorly paid for their work.

While acknowledging the fact that this movement has been appropriate to the developmental level of the field, as well as a powerful force for its professionalization, it is time to begin a more thorough examination of its emphases and focuses to determine whether important groups have been excluded from the process. This chapter will examine the role of the administrator in program design and delivery and argue for a new emphasis on this critical subgroup within the field of child and youth care.

LEADERSHIP ISSUES

A critical element of a profession is its ability to develop its own knowledge base (Etzioni, 1969). Child and youth care is at the pioneering stage of this knowledge explosion through the publications and journals aimed at the professionals in the field. A profession to which child and youth care is often compared regarding goals, working conditions, and salaries, is the field of education. While education as a field has not developed the knowledge base of the professions that it aspires to emulate, law and medicine, it has undergone an explosion of research in the last ten years regarding such issues as how children learn, what are appropriate environments for learning, and how the work environment should be improved for the professionals working in the environment on a day-to-day basis. These issues and other substantive questions form the foundation of the school improvement research and its accompanying literature. A common element is at the base of the many studies conducted under the umbrella of the school improvement research focus: given the broad array of complex variables in the school environment, one variable tends to stand out in all of the studies — the primary importance of the principal's performance as it relates to all of the behavioral outcomes in the school.

A typical focus of the research on the principal compares two schools with similar attributes (e.g., inner-city, history of staff turnover, high dropout rates). Researchers have found in study after study that the variable associated with success or failure is the quality of leadership. In this chapter, we want to identify the primary competencies of the successful school administrator and suggest that effective child and youth care administrators can adapt and adopt the competencies to their work environments. We are not suggesting, of course, that schools and the child and youth care environments are identical settings. They are not. It is obvious that the child and youth care facility is more complex in the services offered, the severity of the problems presented and the hours of operation. While differences exist, similarities of the two environments are obvious: focus on helping the client, working with inadequate financial resources, difficulty in identifying if objectives have been met, and lack of public recognition. Many of the assumptions underlying the effective principal were adapted from the literature on leadership in business and industry (Peters & Waterman, 1984). Since the transition of the findings on effective leadership from business to educational administration and supervision has proved to be beneficial, it may be a safe assumption to conclude that the transition of findings from the school to child and youth care environments is feasible. This conclusion is based on the numerous common elements across the two institutions.

KEY LEADERSHIP BEHAVIORS

Each leadership behavior described below is based on the findings of the school improvement literature. The behavior, and its accompanying examples, use "child and youth care administrator" in place of the "school principal."

1. The child and youth care administrator must establish a long range plan (2 to 4 years) (Cass, 1985). The plan should be a vision for the future with links to the present. All elements of the program should relate directly to the plan (evaluation, supervision and new program elements). The plan is not a rigid set of commandments, but can and must be adapted to evolving changes in society and the needs of the organization.

2. The child and youth care administrator must develop yearly goals and objectives (Cass, 1985; Manasse, 1984) which relate to the long range plan. The goals and objectives must be shared with all constituents (providers, board, children, general public) so that there is commitment to the direction and focus of the program.

3. The child and youth care administrator must establish a reward system that recognizes the performance of all persons in the organization who contribute towards the attainment of the goals and objectives (De Bevoise, 1984). The reward system should be individualized to accommodate the wide array of skills of those in the organization (Manasse, 1984).

4. The child and youth care administrator must develop a governance structure which involves all staff in policy development (Cass, 1985). This involvement can range from the creation of specific policy to the opportunity to critique a policy. The involvement in the governance process leads to a joint "ownership" or commitment to the organization.

5. The child and youth care administrator must create a supervisory system that is based on direct observation of the staff person combined with a conference which follows the observation (Acheson, 1985; Cogan, 1974). The focus of this "clinical supervision" is on those behaviors which will help the staff attain the competencies related to the organization's goals and objectives. Since most administrators lack the requisite skills needed for the observation and conference, training programs should be designed for administrators (Goldman & Manburg, 1986).

Inherent in the supervisory process is the need for the administrator to have a close, direct relationship with all staff within the organization. An outgrowth of this relationship is the ability to be aware of the resources needed by the staff to perform effectively. Hand-in-hand with the awareness of the resources needed is the ability to provide the resources (Keedy & Achilles, 1982).

6. The child and youth care administrator must be responsible for designing a safe and orderly environment for all persons involved in the organization. Maslow (1974) stated that the need for safety is a prerequisite for meeting all of the higher level goals for the organization and those involved in the organization.

As a child and youth care administrator, what do the above behaviors say to me? The position is a complex one, and after reading the above, may be even more complex than I perceived. I could look at the six behaviors and evaluate my performance for each of the behaviors—perhaps a satisfactory beginning. At the same time I realize that the behaviors are not discreet, but interact with one another in multi-dimensional ways. As part of my development, I could design my unique Individualized Development Plan based on the six behaviors described and others which I feel are implicit in my leadership role. Since administration tends to be a lonely role, I could develop a support group with other administrators with the goal of assisting one another with Individualized Development Plans. In combination with one or more of the above ideas, I could write a short position paper on leadership and management which could be shared with my staff or board. Or, I could. . . .

A message in this chapter is the need to be aware of the pivotal nature of the administrator's position. This awareness should lead to *a* plan (not *the* plan prescribed by an outsider) for the organization's continuous growth which is based on the best available literature on leadership and management. The plan should not be a clone of an IBM approach or the local school's approach, but should be a coherent document adapting the best and most appropriate ideas from other organizations.

LEADERSHIP DEVELOPMENT

The pattern of administrative staffing in child and youth care programs, not unlike other areas of social service, is characterized by a system of promotion as reward; reward for loyalty, seniority, availability, etc. Administrative competence, technical or clinical knowledge, capacity for leadership, and ability to supervise others are often secondary considerations in decisions regarding promotion of staff.

This pattern creates a situation in which the leaders of programs, those individuals who are in positions to establish policy, create initiatives, analyze needs, advocate on the public level, and monitor the day-to-day activities of subordinates and the general progress of the agency or program are not, in all cases, people with the greatest competence and ability, those whose efforts will lead to the high test level of success.

Following are recommendations geared toward the professional development of current administrators and the preparation for those who will serve in this capacity in the future.

1. Inservice Training

An ongoing system of continuing education is characteristic of any healthy profession. While colleges and universities have traditionally assumed this responsibility, it is up to the profession itself to organize training if it does not come from traditional quarters. Large agencies are in a position to move into this area on their own. Where this is not possible, agencies of various sizes can work together to create and implement models of inservice training.

2. Degree Programs

An examination of the child and youth care programs offered by colleges and universities will indicate that there are few opportunities for the study of administrative and supervisory issues which lead to an undergraduate or graduate degree. While the number of degree programs in child and youth care is increasing, there are few examples of programs created specifically for the administrator.

3. Organization and Conferences

In the last 10 years the field of child and youth care has witnessed an explosion in professional organizations. Provincial, state, national and international conferences abound. This is, naturally, a good indicator of healthy growth and is welcomed by all. Along with this growth, however, it would be appropriate to see the development of organizations, or groupings within current organizations, of administrators and managers. While some fear that this will fragment a group which has only just begun to reap the rewards of coalescing, the act of separating the larger group to meet more effectively the needs of the members of the subgroups is surely a sign of professional maturity.

Further, when this is accomplished skillfully, it serves to energize and strengthen the larger group as well.

4. Journal Articles and Newsletters

A number of publications have appeared in recent years which attempt to present a real-world view of child and youth care. Often written by working professionals, the articles are consistent with the editorial policy of avoiding the ivory tower syndrome by presenting material of immediate value to the line worker. These new publications are echoed by existing journals which recently have begun to print articles that represent more accurately the child and youth care field. These developments, too, are important indicators of growth. It would be appropriate at this point in the development of the profession to see the central role of the administrator reflected in the selection of journal articles. The development of publications and newsletters specifically for administrators is also recommended.

5. Certificate Programs

As mentioned above, promotion to an administrative position is not always tied to ability, experience, or training. It is recommended that provinces and states develop credentialing systems tied to training and demonstration of competence which could then be used as a tool for promotion and hiring.

CONCLUSION

The unprecedented level of growth of the child and youth care field in recent years has focused attention on the line worker as the critical locus of contact between the agency or program and the client in care. Although this direction is, for the most part, appropriate and, thus far, has been quite successful, it has generally ig-

nored the role of the administrator in the development and maintenance of programs.

This chapter has (a) argued for recognition of the administrator's
role as key to quality, and (b) presented recommendations for action
which, if implemented, would bolster the preparation, ongoing
training and, therefore, the effectiveness of practicing administrators. Far from fragmenting the field, it is believed that the entire
field of child and youth care (and the clients served by professionals
who work in this field) is strengthened by attention to the natural
subgroups of professionals within.

REFERENCES

Acheson, K. (1985). The principal's role in instructional leadership. *Oregon School Study Council Bulletin, 28*, 1.
Cass, M. A. (1985). Exploring horizons: The implication of experiential learning sourcebook. Durham, New Hampshire (ERIC Document Reproduction Service No. ED 261829).
Cogan, M. (1974). *Clinical supervision*. Boston, MA: Houghton-Mifflin Company.
De Bevoise, W. (1984). Synthesis of research on the principal as instructional leader. *Educational Leadership, 41*, 14.
Etzioni, A. (1969). *The semi-professions and their organization*. New York: Collier Macmillan Publishers.
Goldman, R., & A. Manburg (1986). Relationships among child care professionals: A model of collaborative supervision. *Journal of Child Care, 2*, 53.
Keedy, J., & C. Achilles (1982). Principal norm setting as a component of effective schools. Paper presented at a meeting of the Southern Regional Council on Educational Administration. (ERIC Document Reproduction Service No. ED 227545).
Manasse, L. A. (1984). Principals as leaders of high-performing systems. *Educational Leadership, 41*, 42.
Maslow, A. (1974). Integrating humanism and behaviorism: toward performance. *Personnel and Guidance Journal, 52*, 513.
Peters, T., & R. Waterman (1984). *In search of excellence*. New York: Warner.

SECTION 4:
DEVELOPING PROFESSIONALISM

Introduction

Although, in a very real way, each of the preceding chapters has been dealing with aspects of the future of the profession of child and youth care, the perspectives in this section address the issues and structure of professionalism *per se*. Whatever one's personal view on whether we are an "emerging profession," "a para-profession," "a semi-profession," or "a profession at an early stage of development," it is clear that we have, to borrow a phrase from Robert Frost, many "promises to keep, and miles to go before we sleep" (or even take a moment to rest!).

Carol Kelly opens the discussion with a review of the criteria traditionally used to define a profession and seeks to assess contemporary child and youth care in light of them. She then defines and explores what she sees as the essential tasks yet to be completed in order for child and youth care to be recognized as a profession. As well, she draws upon the insights of several futurists to sketch a picture of the future we can expect to have a hand in creating.

In the next article, Douglas Powell questions the appropriateness of the conventional model of professionalism for child care. In addition to two areas that need to be addressed, namely developing our research-based knowledge and defining a collective stance on our core competencies, we must come to terms with the necessity to relate more closely and collaboratively with parents. Such a relationship with parents runs contrary to the conventional view of professionalism and, Powell maintains, nothing less than a social-political revaluation of our work is necessary in order to achieve the improvements in the field that we desire. In short, although Powell focuses on the care of children in early childhood programs, by implication he is arguing that all child and youth care workers must become more politically active and astute.

Mary Lyon and Patricia Canning argue the case for the professional status of day care, addressing a number of the same issues raised in the previous three chapters from a day care perspective. Lyon and Canning particularly emphasize the role of professional education and the responsibility of academic programs to raise the profile of social and political issues in the training curriculum. They also suggest that skills in such areas as public relations, lobbying, collective bargaining, unionizing, and developing and running professional associations must be taught so that graduates enter the field convinced of the importance of their role and well-prepared to affect the decisions and policies upon which their work depends.

This section concludes with Peter Gabor's provocative and sobering case analysis of media impact on the visibility and perceived credibility of the child care profession in society at large. There can be no doubt of the powerful influence of the media, and reputable newspapers in particular, on the consciousness and decision making of politicians, public leaders, and the lay public as a whole.

Whether or not media coverage of child and youth care issues everywhere in North America is as negative as that documented in Alberta by Gabor, none of us can afford to neglect its key role in influencing the future development of the profession. Not only must we work to achieve positive developments in the field, we also need to ensure that these are well communicated to the media, and thus to the public at large.

13

Professionalizing Child and Youth Care: An Overview

Carol S. Kelly

ABSTRACT. This chapter proposes that in order to professionalize child and youth care, we must begin with criteria accepted for professional recognition and develop into a unique profession based upon our own well-founded criteria. This chapter presents a brief historical perspective of professions, an assessment of the current situation, and a delineation of tasks essential to professionalize child and youth care.

AN HISTORICAL PERSPECTIVE

The origins of professions can be traced to magic of primitive cultures, ancient religions, and medicine. During the Renaissance, the clergy, law, and medicine emerged as professions. Prestige and education set professions apart from other occupations. There was a prevailing assumption that service to people was intrinsic to the professions. Professionals became powerful political and economic forces. Universities became the primary social institutions for educating professionals. Governments established legal controls and there was general agreement that all professions have the following characteristics: (1) Formal education. (2) An organized body of knowledge with theoretical underpinnings and minimum competencies. (3) Research activity. (4) A code of ethics regulating the pro-

Carol S. Kelly, Associate Professor, Interdisciplinary Major in Child Development, School of Communication and Professional Studies, California State University, 18111 Nordnolf Street, Northridge, CA 91330.

fession. (5) A professional culture or association supporting a long term commitment to the occupation. (6) Autonomy and self regulation. (7) A clientele which recognizes the authority and integrity of the profession (Cullen, 1978; Moore, 1970; Vollmer, 1966).

These characteristics became the criteria for achieving professional status. Recently the criteria have been questioned by persons within and outside the professions.

Historically, child care has been viewed as women's responsibility and the value of caring for children has been "humanitarian." Rewards have been intrinsic only; thus, power, prestige, or money have not been of particular concern. Only with the social changes of the last decade have the myths about child care been examined seriously. The reasons typically stated for seeking professional status — low pay, no or few fringe benefits, undesirable working conditions, lack of opportunity for career advancement, and low status — can be traced to traditional women's roles. The deeply rooted attitudes and values related to caring for children and the social-political-economic manifestations may be our greatest challenge in professionalizing child care.

There are some basic assumptions which are important. The tasks before us are many, diverse, and complex. Professionalizing child care is a *process* in which the work is not linear so that tasks can be pursued simultaneously. The tasks are interrelated and/or overlap. Significant progress will occur only when child care personnel from all realms work together to use multiple talents and abilities. Communication is the key to professionalizing child care. (See Figure 1.) We must communicate among ourselves, with parents, the general public, other helping professions, and those in the legal-judicial system.

AN ASSESSMENT OF THE CURRENT STATUS OF CHILD AND YOUTH CARE IN THE PROCESS OF PROFESSIONALIZING

While we need to establish our own criteria to professionalize child and youth care, it will be useful to begin with an assessment of where child care stands in relation to the traditional characteristics of a profession. This assessment is followed by a brief discussion of

COMMUNICATION

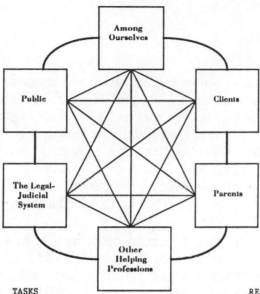

TASKS
Formal education expanded
Body of knowledge articulated
Research expanded
Code of ethics developed
Professional associations strengthened
Self regulation formalized
Public acceptance increased
Model(s) for child and youth care
      professionalized

RESOURCES
Child and youth care experts
Parents and public
Other helping professions
Legal-Judicial system

TOOLS
Media
Advocacy
Literature

PROCESS
Problems identified; solutions found
Issues identified; resolutions proposed
New ideas generated
Esprit de corps generated
Alliances formed
Stronger professional identity

BENEFITS
Clients better served
People educated
Advocacy strengthened
Increased knowledge
Research data
Long term planning
Power, prestige, and status

Figure 1 Professionalizing Child Care: An Overview

the contemporary situation in the professionalizing of child and youth care.

Formal Education

Formal education, continuing education and inservice education are standard characteristics of any profession. Education results in expertise which others do not possess. A bachelor degree level of formal education is usually accepted as minimal to be considered professional. There are college and university programs throughout Canada and the United States which offer bachelor and master degrees in child care. Titles of such programs include child care, child development, child study, early childhood education, and youth care.

Articulating child care education curriculum is in a formative stage. The Conference-Research Sequence in Child Care Education provided an opportunity for dialogue among persons from a variety of practices and academic settings regarding child care education. "Principles and Guidelines for Child Care Personnel Preparation Programs" is a product which provides a foundation for establishing core generic curriculum across educational programs (Vander-Ven, Mattingly, & Morris, 1982). Agreement that curriculum is generic and that human growth and development serves as the core of child care was a significant outcome.

Body of Knowledge

All professions have a body of knowledge which is essential to provide services to clients. VanderVen proposes that a framework for our knowledge base needs to come "from the particular perspective of child care and its defined content and form of service" (VanderVen, 1980, p.4). She further proposes that an internally consistent system which reflects generic dimensions of the field and includes theoretical underpinnings of the field is necessary (Vander-Ven, 1980, p.4).

Research

Research is an essential component of all professions since it evaluates current knowledge and practices and generates new knowledge and questions. Expanded research activity is another encouraging sign of professionalization. There are many questions to be answered. We cannot cling to traditional methodologies and research designs. Qualitative research methods and designs which are appropriate for child and youth care need to be developed and employed. An ecological perspective is necessary (Bronfenbrenner, 1977; Porter, 1980; Powell, 1986).

Code of Ethics

A code of ethics to guide practice is an essential component of professions. There have been codes of ethics developed by some organizations concerned with child care and while such documents are important to the specific groups served, it is necessary to develop a code of ethics which encompasses all child care. Mattingly suggests that the American Association for the Advancement of Science's AAAS Professional Ethics Project is an excellent resource (VanderVen, Mattingly, & Morris, 1982).

Professional Organizations

There is a growing professional culture among those providing child care. There are over eighty national organizations and associations concerned with children and youth in the U.S.A. and Canada (Porter, VanderVen, & Mattingly, 1980/81, pp. 76-82). These organizations are vital in moving child care toward professionalization. Conferences, workshops, publications, efforts to develop self regulation by certification and accreditation, and advocacy are among the contributions made by professional organizations and associations. Child care encompasses the spectrum of age-stages, multiple settings, and a variety of functions and while there are specializations, what is increasingly clear is that there is much more in common than there is different. If we are to achieve professional status, we must work together toward the common good of children and youth through diverse professional organizations which span the various aspects of the entire child and youth care field.

Self-Regulation

Traditionally, professions are self-regulating. There are internal structures and procedures which determine membership requirements, ethical guidelines, continuing education, and so forth. In the last several years, efforts to certify and accredit have been made by several organizations including the Association for the Care of Children's Health, the National Association for the Education of Young Children, and the National Organization of Child Care Workers Association. These are important actions toward self regulation. It is essential that coordination and cooperation strengthen child care. It is desirable that licensing and legally mandated aspects of caring for children be coordinated with certification and that child care personnel provide pertinent input into legislation.

Public Acceptance of Authority

Being professional requires that the public accept the authority and integrity of those who offer the service. The reality is that most people now view child care as something anyone can do. The reasons for this wide spread view are complex. Educating others requires clear articulation of what our professional expertise is and why and how we make a significant difference in the lives of children and youth. Efforts to inform parents, the public, and other professionals are increasing. Media can be one of our most effective means of gaining public acceptance, and there has been national coverage of many areas related to child care. For example, the Today Show featured a debate on infant care during the spring of 1987. Marion Wright Edelman, Director of the National Children's Defense Fund was profiled in the March 23, 1987, issue of *Newsweek*, *Fortune* featured a cover story, "Executive Guilt: Who's Taking Care of the Children?" (February 16, 1987). *Trendletter* identified child care as a business showing great opportunities (February, 1987). On February 12, 1987, the *Wall Street Journal* commented upon the low salaries of child care personnel. Local and regional public relations and positive publicity are increasingly effective in gaining public acceptance and understanding of the field of child care. Increased efforts are necessary, especially in being able to state clearly what makes us experts and why and how we contribute significantly to the lives of children.

Long Term Commitment to the Field

Existing conditions in child care which deter long-term commitments are well known by those in the field: low salaries, no or few fringe benefits, few career advancement opportunities, difficult working conditions, and low status. These circumstances greatly affect the quality of child care as persons leave the field and unqualified persons are hired. Yet, there are encouraging signs. Career options are increasing for those in child care, including supervisory and administrative positions. Social changes have provided opportunities to create careers. Among new careers developed are therapeutic companions, child advocates, children's program directors at shelters for battered women, child care specialists in schools, and positions in the media. Generic foundations allow career changes for child care workers which include moving into indirect services. All of these factors should contribute to less rapid turnover of workers in the field and more employment stability over longer periods.

TASKS TO BE COMPLETED
TO PROFESSIONALIZE CHILD CARE

While there has been progress in professionalizing child care, much remains to be done. A brief overview of essential tasks for child care to be recognized as a profession is presented below.

Educational opportunities which will prepare competent child care personnel need to be expanded just as continuing education and inservice training need to be further developed. Efforts to identify our body of knowledge, develop self regulation, and research need concerted attention. Development of a code of ethics is a task requiring completion. Inquiry into how we "fit" with other helping professions is desirable. We must establish our own identity, not merely assume we should follow the traditional professional model. Cullen's (1978) empirical study concluded that autonomy, power, and prestige associated with being professional stem from occupational complexity rather than technique. He proposes that social scientists need to study process and the relationship of variables. This challenge may be a productive project for researchers in child care.

A major task we need to address is communication among ourselves. Effective use of technology makes it feasible to readily share information. A variety of communication vehicles are available: journals, books, newsletters, conferences, telecommunication, and computers in addition to informal sharing, supporting, and collaboration. Alliances with parents, the public, other professionals, and those within the legal-judicial system need to be established to work together for and with children. Regional, national, and international clearinghouses could greatly facilitate communication and regional, national, and international task forces could complete essential tasks for the development of the profession.

Continued competence in advocacy at the local, state, national, and international levels is a challenging task. Advocacy is a relatively new endeavor for child care personnel, since the past altruistic orientation of child care did not include advocating for children and adolescents. There are now models and literature from which to draw. The National Children's Defense Fund has become a strong voice for children at the national level. California Children's Lobby employs a lobbiest at the state level. At the local level the San Fernando Valley Child Care Consortium and the Guardian ad Litum (advocates for children in court proceedings) are model child advocacy programs. Courses in Child Advocacy need to be a part of professional preparation as advocacy will enhance our endeavors to professionalize.

We are a visual culture. Media is probably the most powerful tool we have to educate and advocate. We must use the media effectively in order to professionalize child care. Child and youth care experts need to work with private and public television networks at local, regional, and national levels. Child care personnel should have input into home videos as well as educational and entertainment media.

Funding will continue to be a serious problem. Being knowledgeable about funding from both the public and private sector and how we can influence decisions would serve us well. Literature such as Kamerman and Kahn's (1987) *Child Care: Facing the Hard Choices*, government publications as well as advocacy, business, and marketing literature can provide valuable information. The private sector provides sources with which alliances to benefit all can be formed. For example, Scott Products donates five cents for each "Helping Hands" paper product purchased to medical research and help for special needs children.

Professionalizing requires top quality literature be developed by those in the field. We must also learn from literature which has implications for child and youth care. For example, we need to study the literature on the future and use it as one data source for professionalizing child and youth care. Naisbitt (1984) makes the poignant point that planning is worthless unless there is first a vision. We are challenged to create our own well-founded ideas of what we want and need to serve children and youth. Our vision today profoundly influences tomorrow's realities. What an exciting challenge to accept in professionalizing child and youth care!

SUMMARY

This chapter has presented a brief historical overview of professions, assessed the current status of the professionalization process, and identified tasks to be done. We are living during a major transition in our society. This historical moment provides a rare opportunity to influence the changes which are occurring. Child care is worthy of respect, power, and prestige. Initial efforts to professionalize in the last decade have been a major first step in our development. Our challenge is to mature as we continue our journey in the process of professionalizing child care.

REFERENCES

Beckwith, B. (1986). *Beyond tomorrow. A rational utopia*. Palo Alto: Beckwith Press.

Bronfenbrenner, U. (1979). *The ecology of human development: Experiments by nature and design*. Cambridge: Harvard University Press.

Casale, A. M. (October, 1986). *U.S.A. today: Tracking tomorrow's trends. What we think about our lives and our future*. Kansas City, Mo.: Andrews, McMeel, and Parkes.

Cullen, J. B. (1978). *The structure of professionalism*. N.Y.: Petrocelli Books, Inc.

Child Care Information Exchange. (May, 1987). Exchange Press, Inc. Issue Number 55.

Denholm, C., Ferguson, R., & Pence, A. (Eds). (1987). *Professional child and youth care: The Canadian perspective*. Vancouver: University of British Columbia Press.

Kamerman, S. B., & Kahn, A. J. (1987). *Child care: Facing the hard choices*. Dover, Mass.: Auburn Publishing House.

Moore, W. (1970). *The professions: Roles and rules*. New York: Russell Sage Foundation.

Naisbitt, J. (1984). *Megatrends*. N.Y.: Warner Books, Inc.

Oxford Analytic. (1986). *America in perspective: Major trends in the United States through 1990's*. Boston: Houghton Mifflin.

Porter, C. J., VanderVen, K., & Mattingly, M. A. (Eds.). (November, 1980. June, 1981). *Perspectives on educating for child and youth care practice. Outcome of the Initial Conference of the Conference-Research Sequence in Child Care Education*. NIMH Grant #T 24 MH 15869.

Porter, C. J. (1980). "The case for inductive inquiry in the child care profession." A paper prepared for the Conference-Research Sequence in Child Care Education. NIMH Grant #5 T 24 MH 15869-02.

VanderVen, K. (1980) "The nature of professional education: Implications for child care." Paper supported by the Conference-Research Sequence in Child Care Education. NIMH Grant #5 T 24 MH 15869-02.

VanderVen, K., Mattingly, M. A., & Morris (Eds). (1982). Principles and guidelines for child care personnel preparation. *Child Care Quarterly, 11*, 221-244.

Vollmer, H. M., & Mills, D. L. (Eds). (1966). *Professionalization*. N.J.: Prentice Hall.

14

Professionalism and the Child Care Field: What Model?

Douglas R. Powell

ABSTRACT. This chapter argues that the conventional model of professionalism is of limited use to the child care field due to problems in generating a widely recognized technical data base for child care practices, and inherent conflicts in maintaining close relations with parent-clients. The child care field needs to modify the conventional paradigm of professionalism so as to emphasize the field's historical role as child advocates and long-standing interest in collaborative ties with parents.

A critical question in efforts to improve the professional status of child care workers is whether the conventional model of professionalism is appropriate for the field. Increasingly the dominant perspective on professionalism, which characterizes such well-established professions as medicine, law and divinity, is viewed as a needed paradigm for upgrading the status of child care workers. As dissatisfaction with the conditions of child care work fuels growing movement toward enhanced professional status, it is essential to examine whether the conventional model of professionalism is feasible and desirable in the child care field.

This essay argues that the conventional model of professionalism is of limited use to the child care field. Two areas are particularly

Douglas R. Powell, Professor, Child Development and Family Studies, Purdue University, West Lafayette, IN 47907.

[Ed. Note: In this article, the author uses the term "child care" to refer to the care of children in early childhood programs.]

problematic in an application of the model to the work of child care: (1) the knowledge base of child care practices; and (2) relations between child care workers (programs) and families.

THE PROCESSES AND APPEAL
OF PROFESSIONALISM

In moving toward increased professional status, an occupational group needs to develop and claim rights to a body of knowledge that serves as the profession's technological base. An attribute of a high-status profession is considerable protection from lay interference. Professional autonomy and detachment from clients are key characteristics. It is the professional, not the client, who defines the presenting problem and prescribes the remedy (Hughes, 1971). Professionals often view these freedoms as a necessary precondition for the proper performance of work (Freidson, 1972).

Current interest in this model of professionalism is seen in fields closely related to child care. In the teaching field, for instance, there are several influential reports arguing for practices to transform teaching from an occupation to a profession. A task force assembled by the Carnegie Corporation of New York issued a report in May, 1986 titled "A Nation Prepared: Teachers for the 21st Century." The task force noted the conditions under which teachers work are "increasingly intolerable," and, among other strategies, called for teachers to function as professionals who enjoy a high degree of autonomy in carrying out their work. The report suggested a national system of certifying teachers, an elimination of undergraduate education programs, a diversification of teaching staffs, and partnership rather than hierarchical systems of school administration. Similar strategies focused on teacher education have been recommended by the Holmes Group, a loosely formed consortium of education deans in the U.S.

It is understandable why this model would be appealing to the child care field. The low salaries, minimal or no fringe benefits, long working hours, and limited career ladder make it difficult to attract and sustain good workers in child care. These conditions are inexcusable and must be changed. Whether traditional approaches to professionalism are an appropriate way to bring about improved work conditions is questionable.

The autonomy element of the conventional model of professionalism may be especially welcome by many in the child care field because it carries the illusion of solving a major "gray" area: relations with parents. Years ago Willard Waller (1932) suggested that parents and teachers are "natural enemies" because each maintains a distinctive relationship with the child. Recent work has pointed to distant relations and some tension between parents and child care workers (Powell, 1978; Kontos & Wells, 1986). A national survey of child care workers at all job levels (teachers, administrators, specialists) found relationships with parents to be the greatest area of ethical concern among early childhood educators (Feeney & Sysko, 1986). Increased professionalism may be viewed as a way to establish greater autonomy from parents, thereby reducing the number and magnitude of perceived problems created by lay (parent) involvement.

THE KNOWLEDGE BASE OF CHILD CARE

For the child care field, a major stumbling block in pursuing the conventional model of professionalism is the perceived lack of a unique body of knowledge and skills regarding child care practices. Wilensky (1964) has suggested the first step in establishing a profession is to create a vocabulary that is not familiar to most everyone. On the surface, the work of child care *is* familiar to everyone, especially parents (Joffe, 1977). The widespread notion that instinctual abilities and a "love of children" are adequate preparation for the care of children negates the argument that the field is a profession with a unique technological base.

In fact, effective work with young children *does* require a distinctive set of information and skills. There is a growing body of research literature pointing to a relationship between the academic preparation of a child care worker and child behavior. The National Day Care Study, for instance, found greater increases in day care center children's scores on the Preschool Inventory in classrooms where the lead teacher had specialized training in early education and child development (Ruopp, Travers, Glantz, & Coelen, 1979).

In part, then, the problem of a perceived lack of a unique data base for child care work is a matter of inadequate public understanding. Child care practices that appear to the lay person as familiar and ordinary no doubt reflect a command of special knowledge and skills.

Until recently, the field has done a poor job of collectively determining and articulating the core components and practices of quality child care. For years individuals have set forth theoretical frameworks and operational prescriptions for good child care through textbooks, conference presentations, program demonstration models, and other dissemination vehicles. Collective decisions about essential ingredients of quality practice have occurred only recently. Prime examples are the position statement of the National Association for the Education of Young Children (NAEYC) on developmentally appropriate practice with young children, and the establishment of a national accreditation system for early childhood programs.

The data base of these positions is a mix of research findings and the clinical wisdom of practitioners. Even though there is a healthy and relatively long tradition of research in child development and early childhood education, the empirical yield does not permit a solid foundation for defining a body of knowledge for child care practices. To date, research on developmental processes has produced primarily equivocal findings, and research on programs is inconclusive regarding the conditions under which certain practices are beneficial (Powell, 1986).

In sum, the conventional perspective on professionalism poses three problems regarding the knowledge base of the child care field: (1) many child care practices do not give the *appearance* of work requiring specialized information and skills; (2) until recently the field has not offered a *collective* stance on core competencies required of child care workers; and (3) research is limited in providing a strong technical data base for the field.

The second and third problems are major but not insurmountable. The second problem can be remedied through the field's acceptance of, and adherence to, a sound set of principles and guidelines for good child care practice. A key challenge will be to develop a set of principles specific enough to be useful but broad enough to incorporate diverse theoretical frameworks operating in the field. Whether NAEYC's efforts in this regard will be successful remains to be seen. The third problem, the limited research base, inhibits but does not prevent claims of a unique base of knowledge and skills. Fields such as psychotherapy have managed to attain respectable professional standing with a research knowledge base that is equivalent to and perhaps weaker than research on child development and program practices. Moreover, research regarding young children and program operations has a rich tradition and an increasingly sophisticated set of methodologies. Over time, empirical data are likely to be of greater use to the field.

The *appearances* problem is the most difficult to address and by far is more salient than the other two problems. To argue that child care work is physically demanding, and in need of tremendous personal stamina, can be readily observed and verified by the lay public. But this argument does not create a view of child care as work in need of special interpersonal and cognitive abilities. Whether the appearances problem can be solved is not clear. Certainly some curricula may appear more rigorous to the lay outsider than other approaches. For example, several years ago an early childhood educator remarked to me she preferred to use the highly didactic DISTAR curriculum in her classroom partly because it gave parents the impression she was doing more than babysitting.

RELATIONS WITH PARENTS

The importance of close professional-parent relations has been central to notions of good child care for many years. Popular textbooks in early childhood education, for instance, strongly recommend close working relations between parents and child care programs (e.g., Hess & Croft, 1981). Key leaders have argued that quality child care functions as an extended family to parents and children (e.g., Caldwell, 1985). The annual meeting of the National Association for the Education of Young Children typically includes a significant number of presentations on strategies for involving families in child care programs. Moreover, standards of good practice set forth by the NAEYC national accreditation project call for parent involvement as a component of quality programming. Also, the Child Development Associate, a competency-based credential for child care practitioners, emphasizes worker sensitivity to family child-rearing values.

Underlying these principles is a long-standing belief that children's experiences in a child care program are enhanced when there is close coordination and communication between home and center. A child's socialization experiences are thought to be improved when major socialization agents adhere to similar values and practices (Lippitt, 1968). An individual's ability to function effectively in a new setting may be facilitated by supportive linkages between settings (Bronfenbrenner, 1979).

The conventional perspective on professionalism is at odds with this long-standing principle of quality child care. It places the professional in a superior role, as the dispenser of expert information and an autonomous judge of what the child needs. Brickman and his colleagues (1983) have referred to this as the medical model of helping. Individuals see themselves, and are seen by others, as uninformed or misinformed. Within this model, in order to become properly informed, lay persons need experts who have been trained to recognize what the problem is and to provide needed service or treatment. The major deficiency of the medical model is that it fosters dependency. The more parents feel they know very little about child development and parenting, the more they feel dependent on the experts in the field. Once people are made to feel dependent on others, they may lose the ability to do something they once did very well.

In reality, employment of the conventional view of professionalism will not remedy most of the parent-professional tensions many child care workers find to be difficult. Most potential or actual conflicts are of an ethical or value nature. Possession of scientific wisdom will not resolve these issues. Consider, for instance, the matter of sex role socialization. Parental objection to boys playing with dolls at a preschool program cannot be remedied satisfactorily by the professional asserting scientific or moral authority. Values, not expert knowledge, are at issue.

THE CHILD CARE FIELD IN CONTEXT

Our field's current interest in the professional status issue is motivated largely by survival needs. Salaries and other conditions of the workplace are causing serious problems in terms of recruitment and retention of staff, as well as overall morale. Our field does not like to speak publicly of negative effects on children, but psychological if not physical harm is difficult to avoid when overworked, undertrained people are put in charge of too many children. So far in this chapter I have attempted to suggest it may not be feasible for the child care field to use the conventional model of professionalism to enhance its status. I also have pointed to a potentially undesirable social distance from parents that a traditional approach to professionalism would entail.

What are we to do? As a beginning step, we need to remember the social-political context of services to young children. The status of work with young children is directly related to the history of women in our culture. Work with young children has been seen as women's work. It has been a socially acceptable, "genteel" job that should be above material concerns (Beatty, 1985).

Historically, work with children has been viewed as a "calling," an important humanitarian contribution to the betterment of society. Intrinsic rewards, not financial benefits, have been viewed as the source of job satisfaction. Elizabeth Peabody equated kindergarten teaching with the ministry. Compared to earlier times, it appears these factors are less important in decisions to enter the child care field. Today my experience has been that undergraduate majors in child development and early education show greater interest in corporate day care (with the erroneous assumption the salaries are higher) than in work with children in poor neighborhoods. Just a decade ago the latter was considered a desireable, if not fashionable, pursuit. In spite of these recent trends, however, the field continues to adhere to benevolent spirit, serving a model of self-sacrifice for the good of society. This ethos makes it difficult for the field to talk about money, especially salaries.

The status of the field, then, is connected to important social forces and values. We cannot isolate the professionalism issue from this larger context. To argue for higher pay conflicts with the benevolent character of the field. Yet the "doing good" culture of our field must undergo modification if we are to attract and sustain high-calibre workers. Advocacy for change in the social forces that impinge in the state of our field (e.g., status of women in society; limited societal investment in children) may be a better route to enhance our standing than a narrow emphasis on professionalism. This does not mean we should abandon efforts to formulate and monitor standards of good practice. But these efforts alone are unlikely to result in desired improvements in a field whose status is a function of external as well as internal forces.

Our field needs to modify the conventional model of professionalism in a way that strengthens the child care worker's role as an advocate for children and for social change. The professional preparation of child care workers needs to include serious examination of the social and political forces that influence our field. Without an examination of this context, new members to the field may well assume the low pay and status are a statement about their level of skill and competency. Skills in advocacy should be seen as an integral part of child care work. Strict adherence to the conventional model of professionalism runs the risk of abandoning our historical role as spokespeople for the needs and rights of children, especially those from low-income families (Silin, 1985).

Our field also needs to foster collaborative relations with parents. Collaborative rather than hierarchical relations with families should be an inherent component of professionalism. Such relations can contribute to the advocacy role our field must pursue. Strong coalitions can result from joint efforts of parents and child care professionals working toward an external cause. At the same time, collaborative ties with parents can serve as an empowering force for families as well as child care workers. When we approach parents in a collaborative role, both parent and worker share resources; both are viewed as possessing resources and needs. Both can experience growth and change through the relationship. This departs dramatically from the traditional expert role, where it is assumed the helper is resourceful, not deficient. In this model, it is the helpee who has deficiencies. The helper gives to the helpee; there is not a sharing of resources. After all, what resources of any significance does the helpee possess? Change is to occur in the helpee, not the helper; the influence flows one way, from the helper to the helpee. Collaborative, empowering roles emphasize joint action (see Tyler, Pargament, & Gatz, 1983). The professional role is one of enabling families to assume control over their lives and to take an active part in their communities, including the child care program.

Movement toward this model of professionalism is not easy. The traditional view is dominant; fee-charging professions such as medicine, law and psychotherapy command a pedestal position. For reasons outlined herein, we cannot adopt this perspective. What is more, the anticipated benefits of pursuing an alternative model of collaboration are considerably greater. Increased professionalism *is* a pressing need in our field. The task before us is to draw upon our pioneering spirit and humanitarian traditions to carve out an alternative view of what it means to be a professional in our increasingly segmented society.

REFERENCES

Beatty, B. (1985). Historical effects of female dominance in early childhood education. Paper presented at the annual meeting of the American Educational Research Association, Chicago.

Brickman, P., Rabinowitz, V.C., Karuza, J., Coates, D., Cohn, E., & Kidder, L. (1982). Models of helping and coping. *American Psychologist, 37*, 368-382.

Bronfenbrenner, U. (1979). *The ecology of human development: Experiments by nature and design.* Cambridge, MA: Harvard University Press.

Caldwell, B. (1985). What is quality child care? In B. Caldwell and A. Hilliard, *What is quality child care?* (pp. 1-16). Washington, D.C.: National Association for the Education of Young Children.

Feeney, S., & Sysko, L. (1986). Professional ethics in early childhood education: Survey results. *Young Children, 42*, 15-22.

Freidson, E. (1972). *The profession of medicine.* New York: Dodds Mead.

Hess, R., & Croft, J. (1981). *Teachers of young children.* Boston: Houghton Mifflin.

Hughes, E.C. (1971). *The sociological eye: Selected papers.* Chicago: Aldine, Inc.

Joffe, C. (1977). *Friendly introducers: Childcare professionals and family life.* Berkeley, CA: University of California Press.

Kontos, S., & Wells, L. (1986). Attitudes of caregivers and the day care experiences of families. *Early Childhood Research Quarterly, 1*, 47-67.

Lippitt, R. (1968). Improving the socialization process. In J. Clausen (Ed.), *Socialization and society* (pp. 321-374). Boston: Little Brown.

Powell, D. (1978). The interpersonal relationship between parents and caregivers in day care settings. *American Journal of Orthopsychiatry, 48*, 680-689.

Powell, D. (1986). Research in review: Effects of program models and teaching practices. *Young Children, 41*, 60-67.

Ruopp, R., Travers, J., Glantz, F., & Coelen, C. (1979). *Children at the center*. Cambridge, MA: Abt Associates.

Silin, J. (1985). Authority as knowledge: A problem of professionalism. *Young Children, 40*, 41-46.

Tyler, F. B., Pargament, K.I., & Gatz, M. (1983). The resource collaborator role: A model for interactions involving psychologists. *American Psychologist, 38*, 388-398.

Waller, W. (1932). *Sociology of teaching*. New York: John Wiley and Sons.

Wilensky, H. (1964). The professionalization of everyone? *American Journal of Sociology, 70*, 138-156.

15

Professionalizing Day Care

Mary E. Lyon
Patricia M. Canning

ABSTRACT. Comparisons with other occupations, which may be seen as entailing similar levels of responsibility and training, indicate clearly that day care providers do not have comparable professional status. Reasons for this relate to two general areas: public perception of the value and nature of the work; and the lack of a clear identity within the profession. The situation will only improve if those entering the field are aware of the issues and prepared to address them. Training programs have a crucial role to play in this regard.

The criteria which define the "professions" and differentiate them from other occupations have become less clear-cut as new areas of knowledge and occupation have developed, and increasingly more groups have aspired to the profession label. At the same time, the role and value of professional status has been increasingly questioned. The traditional view of the established professions (i.e., medicine, law and the church) has seen them as vocations in which groups who have mastered high levels of specialized knowledge and skill accept the responsibility of "professing" this knowledge and skill in order to contribute positively to the welfare of individuals and society. In return, the "professors" are afforded high status and/or recompense by society. Recent sociological study

Mary E. Lyon, Director, and Patricia M. Canning, Associate Professor, Child Study Program, Mount Saint Vincent University, 166 Bedford Highway, Halifax, Nova Scotia B3M 2J6.

of professions and employment has prompted this view to be challenged by the assertion that professions, far from being guarantees of altruistic good practice, are monopolistic, patriarchal, elitist self-interest groups whose very status and differentiation from the individuals they serve militate strongly against optimum practice.

At the present time day care has little or no professional status although it can be argued that as an occupation and a service it meets many of the criteria defining a profession (Ade, 1982). There is a clearly defined knowledge base which underlies day care practice and practitioners require education and training in order to acquire and apply this knowledge. Day care provides a service to the community for which there is widespread demand. Professional associations have begun to develop codes of ethics as well as methods of self-regulation through certification. However, there is no (or at best, marginal) legal regulation or recognition of the profession and very little community recognition of the occupation as having professional status (Powell, 1982).

Other human service occupations which can be seen as comparable to child and youth care and day care — nursing, social work and teaching — have all aspired to increase their professional status during this century. The degree to which they can be considered to have achieved that status depends on the absolute criteria used to define a profession (Lembright, 1983). There is no question that these groups have striven to raise entrance qualifications, to define codes of ethics and practice, and in many cases to widen the knowledge base by research. The view that they are not full professions stems from the fact that they do not meet fully other criteria of self-regulation, community recognition, authority over clients, and occupational culture.

It can be argued that the greater professionalization of these occupations has not necessarily been in the best interests of the services provided and that this should not be the route for child and youth care (Eisikovits & Beker, 1983; Maier, 1983). On the other hand it is obvious that no significant improvements in the standards of care for large numbers of young children will be possible in the absence of steps to improve the status and concomitantly the conditions of employment of those providing the care.

Nursing and teaching began to become recognized as having

more professional status after, not before, they had achieved better working conditions and increased salaries. These were a result of unionization, not professionalization. In spite of this there are those who continue to argue that unions have no place in professions, that professions are by nature altruistic and that by unionizing they lose this essential characteristic. Unionization and professionalization are not mutually exclusive. It can be argued that unionization by ensuring better pay and better working conditions actually serves to enhance the service being provided. Indeed, it appears, at least in some less recognized "professions," that the former is necessary for the latter to occur.

DAY CARE IS NOT A PROFESSION

There are a number of factors which have influenced the status of day care both as a service and a profession. Any moves to improve this status will need to be based on a clear understanding of these factors, and somewhat paradoxically, of the potential negative effects of changing them. These factors relate to two general areas, the perception of society as to the value and nature of the work and the lack of a clear identity for the profession.

THE VALUE OF THE TASK

Child and youth care traditionally has been viewed as a crisis management, safety net service to provide for "unfortunate" children whose families cannot, or for children and young people in need of protection for their own or society's sake. Historically, day care has been viewed in the same light; that is, as a necessary but not necessarily good thing, as a service provided as a safety net for families with no other choice. Until very recently it was assumed that most women would and should stay at home and care for their children and that the home was the only good environment for young children.

A fundamental hindrance to the development of day care services and the status of those who work in it is that the care of children is still almost exclusively a woman's responsibility. While women, either through choice or economic necessity, have continued to work outside the home in increasing numbers since World War II, it is only recently that public concern has been directed at day care. Even when children are cared for outside the home in groups the care givers are still women and the work consequently continues to be a low status, low paying, and poorly recognized occupation.

The recent Task Force and Special Parliamentary Committee on Child Care in Canada exposed the mismatch of the perceptions that day care is a minority or pathological need, and that it is always the second best option, with the reality of the situation. Day care quite evidently is not a minority or pathological need. Changing patterns of family life and wider social changes mean that many families need or would benefit from a high quality system of day care as they do from health care and public education. By 1984, 52 percent of mothers with a child under three, 57 percent of mothers with a child aged three to five and 64 percent of mothers with children aged six to fifteen were employed outside the home (Statistics Canada, 1984). More than half of all women work outside the home and they do so in spite of the fact that day care services are so inadequate, not because they are so readily available.

As day care is increasingly required by children and families, regardless of economic and social circumstances, it is gaining wider respectability. There is, however, still concern that "day care" is not a positive developmental environment for children. "Pre-school education" on the other hand, even full-day programs, especially if associated with explicit social and educational goals, is viewed predominantly positively. This dichotomy stems from the different historical roots of the two services. Thus, day care has been viewed as a substitute for a poor home, or as an unfortunate short term necessity, while pre-school education has been seen as a beneficial addition to a good home. However, quite clearly it is impossible to separate the care and education functions of any environment for young children.

There is a considerable body of evidence from research which allows us to be confident that good day care is not detrimental to children's development (Esbenson, 1985). It is obvious to those within the field at least, that good day care seeks to provide the benefits of a good home and pre-school education. If the reality is different, it is because resources are inadequate to the task and not because day care is always inherently a poor substitute. Training programs make no distinction in the preparation of those who work in part-time pre-schools and day cares, nor do professional organizations or provincial government legislation. One of the most pressing responsibilities of all concerned with day care is to convince society and governments that day care can be an appropriate developmental environment for children, but that low quality, poorly funded care provided by inadequately funded, nonprofessional caregivers can never be.

THE NATURE OF THE TASK

The very existence of the traditional professions has relied on a body of esoteric knowledge that those within have, and those without do not. Most people will accept that doctors need specialized training in medicine, lawyers in law, teachers in subject matter and how to teach it, and nurses in health and patient care. The position of day care is quite different. The common view is that, whatever else people may or may not know, the one thing everyone knows about, especially every woman, is young children and how to look after them. This is not necessarily the case for other areas of child care. It may be more easily accepted that those who work in residential or special care, social service agencies, or the juvenile justice system require specialized knowledge and training than it is that those who look after groups of pre-schoolers require similar preparation.

Stevenson (1981) makes the point that attempts to get nursing recognized as a profession with a scientific knowledge base were adversely affected by the relationship of the task to traditional nurturing and mothering. Hearn (1982) discusses how the professionalization of the other service professions has been associated with their being brought into the public service domain and removed from the home, their defeminization, and their separation of professional and client. Both of these aspects have relevance for day care. On the one hand, there is the need to emphasize the value of the rapidly expanding knowledge base in child development and the application of this to programs for young children. On the other hand, separation of professional and client and the devaluation of traditional nurturing can only be detrimental to the service provided to parents and children, and any moves towards professional status must be made with full awareness of this.

This is not a philosophical or ethical stance. Empirical evidence on the effectiveness and value of programs for young children shows clearly that they have lasting positive effects on children only if parents are involved as integral members of the team or partners in the task, and not as clients for whom services are provided by experts (Bronfenbrenner, 1979). Indeed, this is true not only for day care but for all other professions. Teachers now recognize, and parents demand, that parents are involved in children's education. Hospitals encourage parents to care for hospitalized children and become involved in their treatment. Not only must parents not be relegated to the role of "consumer" of "expert services," but also the traditional function of parenting must not be undervalued as the base of the professional role in day care.

An issue of increasing concern, and one which underscores the need for professional status for day care providers, is that of the development of early education programs in the public school system. The concern is that these are a result more of falling school rolls and strong teacher's unions than real commitment to the concept of appropriate developmental experiences for younger children. Child care and early education are different from schooling. Elementary teachers are not prepared to meet the needs of the very young. The danger is that teachers are recognized as "professionals" providing an essential service (i.e., teaching children), while day care workers are not.

The urgency to socialize day care professionals to define their role, not as a teacher who directs and instructs, but as a caregiver supporting and responsive to all the needs of children, is underscored by recent findings (Haskins, 1985; Logue, Krause Eheart, & Miles, 1986; Schweinhart, Weikart, & Larner, 1986). Taken together, these findings indicate that teachers with specialized training in early childhood focused on cognitive development to the detriment of other aspects of development. This does not appear to be because educators do not emphasize promoting the development of the whole child (Almy, 1982; Caldwell, 1984; Clarke-Stewart, 1977; Hendrick, 1986; Leavitt & Krause Eheart, 1985). It more likely occurs as a result of the lack of identity as a "caregiver" and an identification, perhaps an unconscious one, with the more established and valued profession of "teaching." Day care needs to be recognized as an equal profession in its own right to prevent its potential and inappropriate replacement by "education."

THE IDENTITY OF THE PROFESSION

Professional Affiliations

The lack of clear identity is reflected in the lack of a single clear title for those who work in day care. They are referred to, and refer to themselves, as day care workers or staff, child care workers, day care teachers, pre-school teachers or early childhood educators, regardless of the type of center in which they work. It may seem trivial to consider titles as important to status but they undoubtedly have symbolic signficance and indicate recognition or lack of it by others.

Administrative Structure

Administratively, day care usually comes under the aegis of Departments of Social Services or Human and Community Services. Day care legislation defines minimum standards for facilities offering care. These standards are mainly concerned with safety and health standards. Until recently, little or no attention was given to developmental and educational aspects of the care environment. Standards for educational and training qualifications for staff have begun to be included, however, requirements are minimal and far below the standard required by teachers in schools, nurses or social workers.

Training

A prerequisite to entering a profession is a lengthy education, largely theoretical, but with a practical component as well. This education is usually given in a post-secondary education institution and more often than not within a university. Currently, extensive preparation for day care providers is available at community colleges and universities. And there is a growing consensus on what the body of knowledge essential to developing a child and youth care professional is (VanderVen, Mattingly, & Morris, 1982).

University departments which offer training themselves reflect the lack of a unified identity in the field. In North America training programs may be situated either within Departments of Education, Family Studies, Child Care, or be independent and separate departments. Training is undertaken in conjunction with other human service professions, often in the same department, and is designed to be of equivalent standard to the degrees required by teachers and social workers. This seems quite logical to those providing and receiving the training who accept that the knowledge base and level of skill required by these occupations is comparable. The difference is, of course, that this is not the accepted perception of society as a whole, and graduates go on to work in a society which offers day care staff very different status and rewards in terms of hours of work, conditions of employment, and salaries from those offered to these other professions.

The Interdisciplinary Nature of the Knowledge Base

The specialized knowledge base needed by those who will provide optimum environments for young children must be drawn from an array of disciplines including child development, education, child and youth care, health, and social work. This variety of perspectives is a positive and essential feature of training. Nevertheless, it complicates the establishment of clear professional recognition as, traditionally, professions have been identified by the discrete and specialized knowledge possessed by their members which conveys upon them the unique right to practice their profession. However, the realization that narrow specialist knowledge is insufficient for the effective practice of all the human professions has become increasingly accepted. For example, medicine is recognizing the role of psychological and social factors in health care practice and accepting that doctors need more than a narrow focus on diseases and medical interventions (Bar-Om, 1986).

IMPLICATIONS FOR TRAINING
AND TRAINING PROGRAMS

Clearly, there can be no real improvement in the provision of day care services without significant upgrading of the status and recognition of those working in the field. Such changes will only be brought about if those within the field are convinced they are necessary, understand the difficulties to be faced as well as the issues involved, and know how they can influence public opinion and policy. The role of programs which prepare graduates to work in day care is crucial. In many ways, the state of professional practice is a measure of the success of the educational system and educators must accept some of the responsibility for the failure of day care to progress further than it has.

Many educators have been concerned with the care of children to the exclusion, or downplay, of the larger environment providing that care. We need only to examine university and community college calendars to see the predominance of courses relating to direct care of children (e.g., methods of teaching young children, curriculum in early childhood programs, play and development, art, and music) compared to the almost total exclusion of courses addressing larger social and political issues (e.g., political studies, social policy, women's studies). The inward looking attitude reflected in these curricula must be replaced. Just as our knowledge of child development has expanded in recent years by the adoption of an ecological approach (Bronfenbrenner, 1979), the profession of day care would benefit by the adoption of that model by training institutions. Training must address child development and care, the caregiver's role and professional identity, and the larger social and political processes and institutions which affect, and are affected by, day care. Only by adopting an ecological model will all aspects important to a profession be addressed and understood, and only then can a "profession" develop.

The period of professional education is crucial to the development of a sense of professional identity in new members. Academically based training programs must be well attuned to the profession and they must be willing to allow a place in the curriculum for courses which have not been considered germane to the training of day care providers. Students must be given the opportunity to develop a "meta-awareness" of the field they are entering. They must be fully aware of the status of the "profession," the reasons for and issues associated with this status, and the relationship of the field to the position of the other human service professions. They must be fully aware of what it means to be a professional, and the potential dangers associated with professionalization. The process of socialization is vital to developing and maintaining the ideology of the profession. An analysis of professionalization can have a refreshing effect on the understanding of empirical realities implicated in professional socialization. It helps to highlight sources of variations between attitudinal and structural elements in occupations undergoing professionalization.

In addition to the professional socialization of students, educators must also attempt to socialize them politically. While these two aspects are not mutually exclusive, we cannot afford to assume that if we address one the other will occur automatically. Political socialization may be more important in the education of day care providers than some other developing professions since most providers are, and current student enrollments indicate that they will continue to be, women who are known to be less politically socialized and less represented in the political process than men (Maghami, 1976; Riccards, 1973).

Students must identify themselves as professionals and be fully convinced of the value of their work to society, if they are to view themselves as warranting higher recompense and better conditions. They also must be politically astute and aware of the means of accomplishing these objectives. The issues in day care are contentious as in other human service professions, but discussion of the merits and drawbacks, and the appropriateness and the means of public relations and lobbying techniques, collective bargaining, unionization, and professional association must be included in the training process. Obviously, students must come to their own political and professional decisions, but they need the knowledge and awareness to be able to come to informed ones.

Graduates need to be fully convinced of the importance of their role in order to convince others. They need also to know how decisions and policy are made and how mechanisms and structures in society affect, and can be affected by, them. Above all graduates need to understand that only they as practitioners in the field can raise their own status in society. If graduates are not prepared to address these issues they cannot effectively do the job for which they have been prepared.

REFERENCES

Ade, W. (1982). Professionalization and its implications for the field of early childhood education. *Young Children, 37* (3), 25-32.

Almy, M. (1982). Day care and early childhood education. In E. F. Zigler & E. W. Gordon (Eds.), *Day Care: Scientific and social policy issues* (pp. 476-496). Boston, MA: Auburn House.

Bar-Om, J. (1986). Professional models versus patient models in rehabilitation after heart attack. *Human Relations, 39* (10), 917-932.

Bronfenbrenner, U. (1979). *The ecology of human development*. Cambridge, MA: Harvard University Press.

Caldwell, B. (1984). What is quality child care? *Young Children, 39* (3), 3-12.

Clarke-Stewart, K. A. (1977). *Child care in the family: A review of research and some propositions for policy*. New York: Academic Press.

Esbenson, S. (1985). Good day care makes a difference: A review of the research findings on the effects of daycare on children, families and communities. Report submitted to the Task Force on Child Care. Ottawa. Status of Women.

Eisikovits, Z., & Beker, J. (1983). Beyond professionalism: The child and youth care worker as craftsman. Also, Rejoinder. *Child Care Quarterly, 12* (2), 93-112, 119-120.

Haskins, R. (1985). Public school aggression among children with varying day care experiences. *Child Development, 56* (3), 689-703.

Hearn, H. (1982). Notes on patriarchy, professionalisation and the service professions. *Sociology, 16* (2), 184-202.

Hendrick, J. (1986). *Total learning: Curriculum for the young child (2nd ed.)*. Columbus, OH: Merrill.

Leavitt, R., & Krause Eheart, B. (1985). *Toddlers day care: A guide to responsive caregiving*. Lexington, MA: Lexington Books.

Lembright, M. (1983). Why nursing is not a profession. *Free Enquiry in Creative Sociology, 11* (1), 59-64.

Logue, M. E., Krause Eheart, B., & Miles, J. (April, 1986). The influence of training and choice on teacher behavior in toddler day care. Paper presented at the Fifth Biennial International Conference on Infant Studies, Los Angeles.

Maier, H. W. (1983). Should child and youth care go to the craft or the professional route? *Child Care Quarterly, 12* (3), 113-118.

Maghami, F.G. (1976). Political knowledge among youth: Some notes on public opinion formation. *Canadian Journal of Political Science, 7*, 334-340.

Powell, D. (1982). The role of research in the development of the child care profession. *Child Care Quarterly*, *11* (1), 4-11.

Riccards, M.P. (1973). *The making of the American citizenry: An introduction to political socialization*. New York: Chandler.

Schweinhart, L. J., Weikart, D. P., & Larner, M. B. (1986). Consequences of three preschool curriculum models through age 15. *Early Childhood Resarch Quarterly*, *1*, 15-45.

Statistics Canada, The Labour Force, (Ottawa: December 1984).

Stevenson, J. (1981). The nursing profession: From the past into the future. *National Forum*, *4*, 9-10.

VanderVen, K., Mattingly, M., & Morris, M. (1982). Principles and guidelines for child care personnel preparation programs. *Child Care Quarterly*, *11*, 221-244.

16

Developing the Child and Youth Care Profession Through Effective Use of the Media

Peter Gabor

ABSTRACT. Although child care workers have created many of the structures, such as associations, conferences and journals, that are required for attaining professional status, they have been less successful in winning recognition for the professional status of child care from political decision makers and the general public. The news media are an important means of informing and influencing these groups. This chapter explains how the media work and presents data which suggest that child care workers have not been effective in getting their message across. Strategies for winning public recognition for the profession through more effective use of the news media are then suggested.

During the last fifteen years child care workers have invested much effort and energy into developing their profession. These efforts have met with considerable success, primarily in the creation of child care workers' associations, the establishment of new training programs, conferences and journals, and in obtaining better working conditions and more career opportunities. More importantly, there is now a stronger sense of professional identity shared

Peter Gabor, Associate Professor, Faculty of Social Welfare, University of Calgary, Lethbridge Division, 4401 University Drive, Lethbridge, Alberta T1K 3M4.

The assistance of Ms. Laurie Cargo, Research Assistant, in collecting the data used for analysis in this paper is gratefully acknowledged.

by child care workers. Unfortunately, progress towards obtaining recognition for, and acceptance of, child care as a profession in society at large has been less encouraging. Even a casual survey will reveal major problems confronting the profession:

1. Child care is often not recognized as a profession by other professionals or by the general public;
2. Even when child care is recognized as a profession, it is the least important and least influential of social services professions;
3. Child care is misunderstood; the profession has not been able to convey an accurate description of its services and role to the general public, to other professionals, or to government leaders;
4. Child care has not been able to influence child welfare policies and programs or the development of the child care profession in society at large.

Clearly, these are very important obstacles to be overcome before child care can claim a place as a full-fledged profession. Most advances in the field have related to practice methods and the development of professional organizations. These are, for the most part, internal developments in the sense that they are changes in arrangements within the child care field. The problems listed above are located, primarily, outside of the field. To effectively address these problems, child care workers must begin to turn their attention to the greater community and skillfully present an accurate description of their work and an effective case for its importance in children's services. This task becomes all the more important in the current political and economic climate which limits further growth in the social services. Child care must compete with other professions for support and resources and, unless it can overcome some of the problems listed above, it is not likely to do so successfully.

A range of activities and strategies may be useful in developing the profession in the greater community. A particularly important approach involves the news media, whose impact on the development of social policy has been well documented (see, for example, Siegel, 1983). The media transform events of the day into public issues and concerns and, thus, help create the agenda for political action. The way child care work is portrayed in the media will influence how well the profession will be understood and the degree of public support it will have. These, in turn, will have serious implications for how successfully child care can influence government decision makers and, hence, for the future prospects of the profession.

This chapter will briefly describe the role of the news media in the development of social policy, legislation and programs. The current image of child care, as a profession, will be explored and illustrated using examples from newspapers and problems and concerns arising from this image will be identified. Finally, it will be argued that child care workers must learn to use the media effectively to promote the development of the profession. Relevant strategies to do so will also be suggested.

THE INFLUENCE OF THE NEWS MEDIA

In recent years, the influence of the news media in North American society has become self-evident. The media impact all aspects of our lives from fashion to culture to politics. While few would argue that the media play a key role in our social processes, how the media operate and how their influence is exerted is less well understood.

Indeed, many people accept the view that the news media are unbiased mirrors which reflect society as it exists. The media themselves promote this view as exemplified by the motto of *The New York Times*. "All the news that's fit to print" implies that the paper will include all newsworthy events in its coverage. This, of course, is an impossible objective because on any given day far more events will occur locally, not to mention elsewhere in the world, than can be included in any newspaper. For example, the criminal activities of the day alone could fill the pages of any large city newspaper. Clearly, this does not happen; some crimes are reported while a great majority are ignored. Also, not all possible things are reported about events which do make it into the paper. Conceivably, a crime story could describe the crime, the victim, the circumstances and the investigation at considerable length. However, many articles are quite short, thus aspects of the event are selected for presentation. The point is that the news media are not mirrors but rather select, filter and shape the news that are presented. An understanding of how the news media are structured and organized provides an insight into the process of the selection and shaping of the news.

Selection: Shaping the News

First and foremost, the news media are businesses and operate under the same constraints as do other businesses. There is an ever-present impetus to maximize profits and, in part, this is achieved by controlling costs. Thus news departments are often understaffed and overworked so that reporters cannot cover all possible newsworthy occurrences.

Each of the media have their own formats (Altheide & Snow, 1979), the requirements of which also influence the coverage. For example, television will be more likely to use a story where video footage is available. Ongoing, slowly developing events do not lend themselves to this format as well as dramatic sudden occurrences. Generally, media formats favor the concrete and tangible, thus "Group home opens in community" may become a news item while "Changes in life skills program increase its effectiveness" will be unlikely to make it into the line-up.

Because of space and time limitations there is also an emphasis on simplifying stories and including only the basic facts, a process which may remove a report from its context (Snow, 1983). This process does not serve to educate the public about social services, which tends to be a complex field that can best be understood in full context.

News coverage also tends to favor the unusual or sensational. On the one hand, such events will likely be concrete and tangible, lending themselves better to coverage while, on the other hand, such reports will also help to increase circulation or audience and thus enhance profitability. The impact of this tendency is that over a period of time, coverage of many issues will likely be unbalanced, leading to distorted perceptions on the part of the population. As an example, in recent years coverage has often been given to situations where single able-bodied persons have obtained welfare assistance.

At the same time, little coverage has been provided regarding the vast majority of recipients who have genuinely been in need and have been helped by such payments. A result of this process is that many people in the general population believe that there is extensive abuse of welfare assistance and consequently support for this social service has declined.

Further imbalance in coverage occurs because the media hold a political and economic bias favoring business (Snow, 1983). This is understandable because the media themselves are big businesses. A free enterprise, pro-business ideology, however, is quite incompatible with socialistic beliefs on which social services are based. The result is social services coverage which emphasizes shortcomings and inefficiencies in the system. As well, it has been observed that the media provide more exposure, legitimacy and approval to the ideas, values and interests of powerful individuals and groups (Altheide, 1985), thus displaying a pro-establishment, status quo bias. This would tend to place at a disadvantage aspiring and developing groups such as child care.

All events and occurrences are not equal. Some become news and some do not. The events and interactions of the day are not transformed into news through a random process of selection and shaping. Rather the structure, organization and formats of the media exert a strong influence on the process with the result that certain patterns and biases emerge.

Having examined how the media create news reports, it will also be instructive, for purposes of this chapter, to consider the influence of the media. Several sources of media power have been identified (Siegel, 1983) and the most relevant of these will be briefly outlined.

Influence: Shaping the Public

Most obviously, the media provide basic information about many aspects of life. Media reports are the main source of information in our society. Thus the media fulfill an educational role in the sense that many people learn about aspects of our increasingly complex society through media reports. Many people rely heavily on the news to form their opinions and conclusions about a range of matters. By providing information and education, the media impact the development of public opinion, which, in turn, influences political and bureaucratic decision makers.

A second important source of power arises from the media's agenda-setting function (Litz, 1982). As has been discussed, the media selectively transmit news. The issues that are chosen receive public attention. Cumulative attention to an issue raises its visibility and increases the likelihood that it will receive political priority and action. Thus, by emphasizing some issues and neglecting others, the media play an important role in establishing the public agenda.

Finally, the media provide political linkage between some segments of the public and the government (Siegel, 1983). Some groups in society have direct access to the government. For example, members of the legal profession often have former colleagues who occupy senior government positions. It is possible for members of such groups to hear about programs and policies from, and raise issues and concerns directly with, government leaders. Many other groups, such as child care workers, seldom have direct access and communicate with the government primarily through the media. Information about public affairs is transmitted from the government through press releases and news reports, while at the same time public officials scrutinize the media to discern public opinion and concerns.

HOW THE MEDIA PORTRAY CHILD CARE WORK

In this section, the current image of child care, as portrayed by newspapers, will be described. Two major Canadian newspapers were selected and the coverage they accorded to child care under direct circumstances was examined. The methodological approach was an informal content analysis; the intent was to take a first look at how child care is depicted in the print media.

The first newspaper selected was the *Globe and Mail*, a Toronto newspaper with national circulation in Canada. A two year period, August 1984 to August 1986, was selected and all articles containing a mention of child care work or workers were included in the study. The period to be reviewed was selected to provide current information, while the length of the period was established with the objective of yielding an adequate number of articles.

The findings, as summarized in Table 1, reveal much about the visibility and current image of child care in society.

Most striking is the fact that over a two year period there were only 33 child care related articles in the paper studied. This represents an average of one article every three weeks. Nor did the articles all focus on child care exclusively or primarily. Because the criterion for including an article in the study was that child care should be mentioned at least once, many of the 33 articles were in fact not primarily about child care, although child care work or workers were mentioned. For example, one article described a demonstration against the erosion of Medicare coverage and one of the spokespersons of the group was identified as a former child care worker. Significantly, only six articles could be found during the entire two year period in which child care was the central topic of the story.

How child care work is described was examined next. Of all the articles only 2 contained clear descriptions of what child care workers do, while another 8 provided a vague picture and 4 provided what were judged to be inaccurate descriptions. The analysis also revealed that 7 articles were based on a case of mistaken identity and were not about child care at all but about child welfare protection workers mistakenly identified as child care workers. As well, only 7 articles described or implied that child care was a profession while 5 indicated or suggested that child care was not a profession.

Articles containing direct quotations by child care workers were then selected from the total coverage and examined to determine how the profession is presented by its own members. Only 4 articles were found which contained quotes by child care workers. Three of these described various aspects of practice, while one contained a comment about child welfare policy developments. No remarks or comments about child care as a profession were quoted during the two year period.

Finally, each article was categorized according to whether it described positive or negative developments. An example of the former is a story describing the use of phototherapy in child care, while a report detailing a strike by child care workers is typical of

Table 1: Articles Mentioning Child Care Work or Workers

Globe and Mail
August 1984 – August 1986

CATEGORY	NUMBER *
Type of Article	
News	30
Editorial	1
Letter	1
Miscellaneous	1
Relevance of Child Care	
Central to story	6
Incidental to story	19
Child Care Identity	
Correct	14
Mistaken	7
Child Care Work Description	
Clear	2
Vague	8
Inaccurate	4
CCW Role Description	
Professional	7
Not professional	5
Ambiguous	12
Article Context	
Positive	7
Negative	15
Neutral	11
Comment by Child Care Workers on	
Practice	3
Policy	1
Profession	0

* The total number of articles was 33. Within most categories, the totals do not reach 33 as not all categories were applicable or relevant to each story.

the latter. During the period studied, negative articles outnumbered positive ones 15 to 7. Thus, when child care work or workers are mentioned in an article, it is likely to be within the context of a negative story.

If the data presented above suggest that child care normally receives little attention from the media, it should not be assumed that child care is never in the public eye. Occasionally, child care becomes involved in a controversy or scandal and receives intensive exposure for a brief period of time. The second analysis relates to just such an event, "The Peace River Dogfood Incident" as covered by the *Edmonton Journal*, the major newspaper in the province of Alberta.

The Northern Regional Treatment Residence, actually a six-bed group home, was located in a small town in northwestern Alberta and was operated under contract from the provincial government by two women who had previously worked in child care positions but who had no formal training in child care. They staffed the home with the assistance of a mechanic and his wife. The program also received consultation from a local psychologist.

Over a period of time, a number of bizarre behavioral programs were designed by the psychologist and implemented by the residential staff. Among the most outrageous was the program drawn up for a six-year-old boy who liked to eat food left out for the dog. Under the direction of the psychologist, center staff began to lace the dogfood with Tabasco sauce to discourage the child from eating it. Other extreme programs included attempting to teach a child not to wet the bed by forcing him to urinate into his own bed prior to going to sleep and forcing another child to stand over a sink overnight, hands in dishwater, to teach him to attend to his dishwashing chores more promptly.

After a few months, the mechanic and his wife resigned and informed the press of the practices in the home. The *Edmonton Journal* covered the scandal and subsequent developments extensively—a total of 56 articles were printed in less than a month in early 1980. Because of the apparent public uproar and the demands of the *Edmonton Journal* the government was forced to agree to a number of investigations relating to the incident and to child welfare practices generally.

Several aspects of the coverage are worth noting. First, and perhaps most important, the paper used the term "child care" extensively in its coverage. Child care became a generic label for child welfare, child protection, formal therapy, as well as group care. In fact, there had been no trained child care workers involved in the situation but almost every story spoke of scandals and problems in child care and of unacceptable child care practices. There were four banner headlines related to this incident, three of which reported various investigations into "child care." An example is the headline, "Major Child Care Probe."

As the episode progressed there was speculation in the press about similar malpractices occurring elsewhere in the province, and at one point an editorial asserted that there were "serious questions about the status of child care practices in use in Alberta's child care facilities" (*Edmonton Journal*, March 11, 1980). In fact there were no current events which would suggest such a thing. Even though no trained child care workers had been involved in the dogfood incident, the coverage left a negative impression about all Alberta child care workers.

As well, it is instructive to review the comments and suggestions made by various professionals which were reported in the coverage. Although child care was in the headlines, psychologists were the most frequently quoted professional group, followed by psychiatrists.

The psychologists condemned the practices and indicated that this episode underlined the need for more training programs for psychologists, including at the doctoral level. Moreover, they suggested that a greater degree of control over group care programs should be exercised by qualified professionals. One psychologist, who conducted one of the investigations into the incident, was quoted as saying that the child care staff had enough experience to work with the children but not to offer treatment. In his view treatment should only be carried out by a psychologist.

Psychiatrists' comments were similar. They condemned the practices and advocated a more extensive presence for psychiatrists and other medical doctors in group care programs. Although social workers were not prominently mentioned in the newspaper coverage, a letter from a social worker was also printed. This letter suggested that more trained social workers and protection of the social work title would help to improve the quality of child welfare services.

Finally, we come to comments by child care workers. Although child care was prominently implicated in the scandal, only one comment by a child care worker was reported during the entire month. The worker was quoted as making a case for higher salaries for child care workers in order to attract and retain higher quality people.

DISCUSSION

In view of how the news media are structured and organized it would be expected that child care, a young profession short on status, legitimacy and power, would normally receive very little coverage. Because of the media's bias for the sensational, the coverage that child care does receive is likely to be in connection with problems, concerns, and unusual occurrences. When problems arise, members of more established professions will be called on to explain and comment and their interpretation of events will be congruent with the interests of their own group, but will often be contrary to the interests of child care. Further, it can be predicted that the media will be unlikely to accord much attention to less tangible but complex matters such as the role of the child care worker and how child care work relates to other professions. The coverage described above is consistent with these expectations.

Over two years, the *Globe and Mail* provided very little coverage to child care, particularly if only those articles dealing primarily with child care are considered. There were more articles reporting problems than positive developments and very little information was provided regarding the nature of child care work itself. Not only was little information provided, but several of the articles described child care inaccurately. A person unfamiliar with child care would not likely learn much about the work or the profession by reading the *Globe and Mail*.

In effect, child care workers do not actively work to explain their profession to the public or promote its interests. They are passive recipients of media coverage and do not try to influence it. This can be contrasted to the efforts of other professions such as psychology, medicine, law, nursing and teaching. While collecting data for this study we noticed numerous articles relating to each of these professions. Members of these groups seem to make it a practice to use the media to describe practice developments or innovations, to comment on legislation and to promote the interests of their own group.

The reporting of the "Peace River Dogfood Incident" was devastating and damaging to child care in Alberta. Although no trained child care workers had been involved, the coverage repeatedly connected child care with the outrageous practices that had taken place in the group home. Moreover, the impression had been left that such occurrences were probably common in other programs where child care workers were employed. More importantly for child care, various professionals who commented on the incident promoted an old medical model concept of group care with the suggestion that child care workers should confine themselves to providing custodial care while other professionals design and implement treatment.

Child care workers did not join the public debate that ensued and were not asked to comment on the situation or to suggest remedies. Other, more established professions did comment extensively. Psychology, for example, took the opportunity to place before the public the need for higher education for psychologists and advocated a tighter system of licensing. It would obviously have been desirable for child care workers and leaders to comment on various aspects of the case. At the very least, the record regarding the fact that no trained child care workers had been involved in the situation could have been set straight. Child care could also have emphasized that this was not a "child care" crisis but a "child welfare" crisis. The suggestions regarding medical models of group care also needed to be challenged. And finally, this would also have been an ideal opportunity to make a strong case for establishing minimum required qualifications for child care workers and for the expansion of child care education.

The consequences of the type of coverage accorded to child care by both papers are clear. Over a period of time the public, as well as key decision makers, will develop a distorted and negative perception of child care. For the most part, they will hear of child care only when problems arise. Because there will be little information presented in the media about the nature of modern child care work and its benefits, the public and government will have only the vaguest understanding of child care work and practices. In fact, much of that understanding will be based on misleading impressions that child care work entails, primarily, caregiving functions and not remedial work. This view will continue to be reinforced by the more established professions, who do find opportunities in the media to put their views before the public. If child care continues to passively accept this type of media coverage, it is unlikely that it can gain the credibility and support required to make major advances in professional status.

OBTAINING POSITIVE COVERAGE FOR CHILD CARE

The purpose of the foregoing presentation is not to critique the news media, but rather to explain how they work. The media prepare and present news according to their own imperatives. The coverage child care has received can be understood in the context of media structures and organization. The main point of this discussion is that child care should not expect to receive positive or helpful coverage merely by being a deserving profession. Rather, the coverage which has been described in this paper is what child care can typically expect unless it begins to work towards presenting itself more effectively in the media. A number of strategies are available to achieve more positive coverage.

Obtaining positive coverage involves at least two specific goals. It is important both to increase the frequency of articles relating to child care and to try to ensure that such coverage reflects positively on the profession. To achieve these goals requires a change in approach towards the media. It is not sufficient to stay away from the media with the attitude that "no news is good news," but rather, child care workers should seek out opportunities to present their profession and explain their work to the public through the media.

As explained above, the news media usually will not actively seek out stories detailing positive but modest developments. This, however, does not mean that they will not communicate such information to their audience. Indeed, they often welcome such information, particularly if it is presented in a format that is ready to be published or to be presented (Brawley, 1983). For example, a child care worker could prepare an article detailing how a new community support program works and present it to the reporter covering social services for the local daily. Similarly, child care workers can bring to the attention of the media issues and concerns relating to the profession or to children. Such approaches require child care workers to actively seek out and contact reporters. Not all efforts will result in a story but, at the very least, reporters will become educated about child care issues through the process, making it more likely that future coverage will be thoughtful and knowledgeable. Ultimately, such efforts will result in key concerns being placed before the public, thus promoting child care issues to a higher place on the public agenda.

A campaign to inform and educate the public about child care should be considered as a long-term proposition involving the efforts of many child care workers. To be successful, it is important that such efforts should not be confined to times when major problems have arisen. It is much easier to present a case at a time when things are going well. Moreover, many child care workers need to contribute to such efforts, describing their work, outlining program developments and commenting on professional issues. Although child care workers' associations should become more active in this area as well, it is suggested that individual child care workers who have or could learn the skills needed to approach the media should consider it their professional responsibility to do so. The profession should support such efforts by providing courses and workshops on working with the media at conferences and within the curricula of educational programs.

Cumulatively such activities could have many benefits for child care. The public and government leaders can learn about child care work and its place within children's services. The profession can develop increased credibility if it is sometimes connected with positive developments. Child care workers' concerns can gain higher visibility and obtain more priority on the public agenda. Generally, a stronger base of public support can develop for child care. Such support, in turn, is indispensable if child care hopes to advance its professional interests in society.

CONCLUSIONS

News is not an objective entity; rather, the making of news is a social process. To date, child care workers have not participated in this process and consequently the coverage they have received has not, on the balance, been helpful to the profession. Further growth of the profession in society at large may well depend on the ability of child care workers to generate public support and create credibility for their work. One important way of obtaining such support is by working through the media to explain their work and to present their cares to the public and to decision makers.

REFERENCES

Altheide, D. L. (1985). *Media power*. Beverly Hills: Sage.

Altheide, D. L., & Snow, R. P. (1979). *Media logic*. Beverly Hills: Sage.

Brawley, E. A. (1983). *Mass media and human services: Getting the message across*. Beverly Hills: Sage.

Edmonton Journal. (1980). March 6 - April 3. Edmonton: Southam.

Globe and Mail. (1984 - 1986). August 23, 1984 - August 26, 1986. Toronto: Thompson.

Litz, E. T. (1982). *Media cues: Setting the legislative policy agenda*. Unpublished doctoral dissertation. Tallahassee: The Florida State University.

Siegel, A. (1983). *Politics and media in Canada*. Toronto: McGraw-Hill Ryerson.

Snow, R. P. (1983). *Creating media culture*. Beverly Hills: Sage.

SECTION 5:
CURRENT ISSUES
IN EDUCATION AND TRAINING

Introduction

This section contains a selection of chapters that will be of interest to students, practitioners and instructors (both trainers and academics) alike. In recent years, at a number of child and youth care conferences, the call has been heard for more programs that will strengthen the educational foundation upon which any profession must stand. The chapters which follow address a variety of significant issues and present innovative developments in child care education and training.

Raymond Peterson, Steve Young and Jamie Tillman lead off the section by tackling the question of what is *core* to the profession, and how we can ensure that this core is properly taught, understood, and integrated into practice. They identify ethics as being at the heart of caring, and they grapple with the three-fold task of (a) trying to define ethics, (b) coming to terms with the fact that "caring," a seemingly everyday and natural process, lies alongside "science" at the center of our profession, and (c) learning to apply ethics in the processes of our work and our training programs.

The authors present us with a way they have found "to preserve care as the core identity of both the field and of individual practitioners" and to develop a training program which itself "embodies the central ethics of caring."

In the following chapter, "Worlds Apart?", Alan Pence argues that the apparent opposition of "research" and "clinical practice," characteristic of much writing and discussion within the profession, is the product of an illusion. He aptly compares the task of the child and youth care practitioner to straddling two trotting circus horses. If one believes that the rider (i.e., the worker) is having to hold the two steeds (i.e., research and practice) together by force of might, the feat appears to demand a Colossus of Rhodes! However, as Pence points out, when one realizes that it is the rhythmic gaits (i.e., the process common to research and practice) of the horses that makes the team a unified whole, the apparently rare feat becomes an attainable goal for all practitioners. The results of Pence's experience with incorporating this concept in the academic coursework are also described.

Next, Michael Demers addresses the question of the adequacy of a purely competency-based approach to education and training. Demers maintains that students (and by implication, all workers), must become aware of the assumptions they hold about themselves and their world, and not simply develop competency in tasks. Drawing upon some recent literature in the adult education field, he sketches the outline of what he terms "a process of perspective transformation." Demers cautions that this process can be a frustrating and painful one, but stresses that it must be faced if the child and youth worker is to possess the critical awareness necessary for engaging children and families across a variety of settings and in a variety of roles.

In their chapter, Carol Stuart and Mary Lynne Gokiert draw upon their experiences in delivering a college-based child care program to Native Indian students in suggesting cross-cultural and ethical issues relevant to any training efforts involving students from different cultures. They believe that programs offered to culturally different groups must be of an equivalent standard to those offered to any student; at the same time, such programs need to recognize the different values, customs, and perspectives of the special group, and the unique problems they may be called upon to face in their own communities. Specific suggestions are made for handling cultural biases and making changes to the child care curriculum.

Continuing the theme of adapting educational programs to meet the needs of certain learners, Roy Ferguson provides a comprehensive overview of the rapidly developing phenomenon of distance education. He details how in recent years part-time students have come to outnumber their full-time counterparts as a result of social, technological, and economic changes in North American society. Child and youth care programs across the continent are coming together to form a Child Care Educators and Trainers Cooperative to facilitate the efficient development and exchange of quality curriculum materials. This is a significant step forward to be welcomed by all members of the profession.

Concluding the section on current issues in education and training, Sharon Moscrip and Adrien Brown focus on the transition from "gown to town." Having themselves moved into child and youth care positions from degree programs, both are eminently qualified to present the tensions and frustrations, as well as the joys and opportunities, of this critical time in a professional's career. Lessons learned regarding the issues of "readiness to practice," "defining the child care role," "supervision," and "agency structures" along with a list of practical coping strategies make this chapter *must* reading for anyone about to undergo this transition.

17

Applied Ethics:
Educating Professional Child and Youth Workers in Competent Caring Through Self Apprenticeship Training

Raymond W. Peterson
Steve E. Young
Jamie S. Tillman

ABSTRACT. Applied ethics are introduced as a means of preserving caring as the core of professional child and youth work. The Self Apprenticeship Training approach (Peterson, 1978) is discussed as a methodology for developing competency in applied ethics.

INTRODUCTION

Ask any member of the emerging profession of child and youth work if ethics are important and the answer is likely to be an emphatic, "Yes!" Question the person more closely to define and articulate the important ethics of the field, and you may encounter some hesitancy. But press the person further still to discuss how ethics apply to the dilemmas and ambiguities of the day-to-day

Raymond W. Peterson, Mental Health Specialist, 2463 NW Quimby, Portland, OR 97210. Steve E. Young and Jamie S. Tillman are affiliated with Western Oregon State College.

An earlier version of this chapter was presented by the authors at the Symposium on the Ethics and Practice of Care in Private and Public Places, the Annual Conference of the American Association for the Advancement of Science, Vancouver, British Columbia, June 1986.

work—the tasks and interpersonal relationships in which the worker is continually engaged—and you may find that such description is difficult indeed.

Ethics are important to the human service professions; in fact, a formalized code of ethics is one of their hallmarks. In the field of child and youth work, many have called for the development of a code of ethics, of standards for certification, and for programs of training and higher education as a means to assist the field in its transition to full status as a profession in its own right (Courtioux, Jones, Kalcher, Steinhauser, Tuggener, & Waaldijk, 1985; Pinniger, 1987; VanderVen, Mattingly, & Morris, 1982).

Although the child and youth work profession does not yet have a universally agreed upon code, the profession's core ethic is that of care, and its central purpose is the promotion of service which is caring, healthy, and life-affirming for children, youth, and families. Unfortunately, in the process of professionalization there is a paradoxical tendency to relegate care to a secondary status. The question becomes, how do we preserve caring as the core identity of both the profession and of its practitioners? To press this point further, how can we assist practitioners in applying the ethics of caring within the context of the day-to-day work? If the child and youth work profession is to seriously address these questions, it must develop means which not only inculcate new members in the caring identity, but which also continually revitalize and renew the code of ethics for all its members.

This chapter proposes a partial solution by conceptualizing the competent practice of ethicality as "applied ethics." Generally speaking, applied ethics are actions guided by the ethic of care. Applied ethics constitute the action point where the domains of a static code of ethics overlap with the professional's personally practiced value system. In the higher educational setting, applied ethics can be taught through experiential learning approaches which model, within the classroom, the tasks and relationships which occur in actual child care work settings. The Self Apprenticeship Training approach (Peterson, 1978; Peterson & Maciejewski, 1988) illustrates educational processes which foster ethics of care and enhance the competent application of ethics.

THE FUNCTION OF ETHICS IN THE EVOLUTION
OF PROFESSIONALIZATION

As Cullen (1978) observes, the development of professionalism within the field emerges from three associated phenomena: an increase in scientific and technical knowledge, evolution of value systems fostering growth of knowledge and the application of this knowledge toward valued ends, and a growth in individual and collective power to influence the environment toward achieving desired ends. The Latin root meaning of power is "posse," meaning "to be able." Power is defined as "the ability to act, . . . the capacity of producing or undergoing an effect" (Webster's New Collegiate Dictionary, 1982, p. 468). The ability to act, to respond creatively to changing social conditions, and, most importantly, to address the pressing needs of young people and families is critical to the development of professional potency. Such power is shown, for example, in the ability to create and shape new services, to advocate for and raise awareness of clinical, social, and political concerns, and to provide leadership in addressing collective interests. This type of power is generally productive and life-affirming, yet it is also vulnerable to destructive influences.

The emergence of increased power through the processes of professionalization evokes a need for some means to ensure that this power is expressed legitimately—hence, the function of ethics. Social ethics are, in essence, the manner of synchronizing society's collective interests with interests of the individual. For a social ethic to be viable, it must foster mutual, reciprocal relationships between individuals and the larger community. Professional ethics are one form of social ethics. Professional ethics guide the expression of power so that our actions remain congruent with our collective values, codes of conduct, and social commitments, thereby ensuring we remain in alignment with our professed goal—that is, competent caring as the core and the foundation of the practice.

Values refer to what is held to be of worth, that which is cherished, nurtured, and cultivated; as such, our values guide the direction, process, and results of our work. The purpose of professional ethics is largely to make explicit the substance of our values, that we might more clearly and directly choose how we cultivate and express them in practice. To the degree we cherish our young people, we will seek ways, collectively and individually, to support their well-being. In terms of professionalization, this means committing ourselves to the application of ethics in our practice. However, the subject of professional ethics raises a number of difficult issues.

ETHICS REQUIRE REVITALIZATION

The first issue is that, once codified, ethics require ongoing revitalization if they are to guide the professional's actual behavior. A code of ethics has some basic limitations. The development of a code of ethics by a professional association does not necessarily mean the occupational group's values are the same as those expressed in the code, nor does it "mean that . . . the code works as proclaimed" (Cullen, 1978, p. 66). Consequently, the establishment of a code of ethics does not by itself ensure its acceptance and application by the association's membership. For practitioner endorsement and application to occur, individuals must engage in a process of identification with and personalization of the code of ethics, so that it becomes relevant, understood, and expressed, rather than remaining an abstract, external list of rules and principles.

Similarly, the professional association itself must create its code of ethics in a manner such that there is shared recognition and support of the values embodied in the code. Collectively-held values allow members of a profession to hold colleagues accountable and, even more importantly, provide mutual support towards maximizing the excellence and integrity with which those values are applied in practice. The alternative to this process of personalizing ethics, for either the individual or the group, is a dead code — one that lacks the personal relevance and commitment necessary to influence professional behavior and attitudes.

A problem which must be addressed soon after the founding members and original leadership of an association have identified and codified their ethics is the tendency for the code to begin to lose its vitality and to die. Ethics can be said to be alive only to the degree they are embraced, used, and depended on to provide purpose, guidance, direction, sanction, and parameters. What keeps a profession's ethics working as an influential force in its practice? One factor is that new members come to identify with the ethics of the profession as they enter it. However, more is necessary. Just as early members personally claimed their collective values and standards of practice, a process is needed through which all members (new and old) discover and rediscover, integrate, and bring life to their code of ethics (Corey, Corey & Callahan, 1984). It is this process which must be kept alive.

ETHICS OF CARING ARE DIFFICULT TO DEFINE

A second difficulty regarding ethics relates directly to the core of child and youth work, that is, to caring (Maier, 1987; Peterson, 1981). The nature of caring is that it is value-infused and, essentially, the action of expressing humanistic values. Hence, the ethics of caring demand the integration of values and action in practice. Yet for most practitioners, values, although they are a vital and central theme, remain by their nature largely undefined and difficult to articulate. The first implication of this is that the core or heart of the practice is also one of the most difficult aspects of it to define or measure. A second implication has been noted elsewhere:

> Although caring is the hallmark of our profession, . . . the capacity to love and care are like the attributes of wisdom, intuition, creativity or sensitivity . . . [and] the population of educated professionals and the population of laymen would probably not differ significantly in the distribution of these attributes. (Peterson, 1981, p. 5)

These factors have caused us to shy away from using "care" as the defining element of the profession. Consequently, in the development of the field, the focus has been on what is more easily articulated, that being the "science" of the field, specifically, its theory and methodology.

The problem is that ethics are only partially defined by theory and methodology. Regarding theory, Hall (1977) has stated, "All theoretical models are incomplete . . . By definition, they are abstractions and therefore leave things out" (p. 14). Much of what is left out in defining theoretical models and the technology of the practice is the "art" of the practice. The teaching of the science by itself is insufficient to teach the competent application of the ethics of caring. This leads us to the conclusion that our education and training programs are crippled to the extent that science and content are emphasized over the art and process which characterize the practice.

A legitimizing aspect of a profession is task-required competence, or professed expertise. However, the danger exists that, in the effort to identify its expertise in order to affirm and claim legitimacy as a profession, the field may emphasize and over-identify with forms of specialization and methodology which are not clearly and strongly rooted in values of caring. In fact, such an orientation may foster an interpersonal "distance" which is actually counter to these values.

An over-emphasis on method may foster an attitude of "doing this *to* them" which undermines the atmosphere of mutuality and the attitude of "*with* them" that is essential to care (Maier, 1987). When our professional identity is associated with the technology, methodology, or theoretical knowledge of the practice to the exclusion of the values of caring or their relegation to a lesser status, we begin to dissociate ourselves from the core of the practice. To the extent this is typified in professionals' relationships with their clients, the true legitimacy of the profession is violated.

ETHICS ARE ONLY PARTIALLY DESCRIBED IN TERMS OF LIMITS

A third difficulty in the utilization of ethics relates to regulation, limit-setting, boundary-making, and other forms of control and structure. Clearly, these forms can be expressions of values in the service of providing protection and guidance. However, compliance with rules and regulations alone is insufficient to ensure quality service. What is out of focus when we concentrate primarily on form is process. The dynamics of our practice are much like a dance. While dance involves structure, it is also process-oriented, being creative, spontaneous, interactive, evolving, intimate, and expressive. Inherent in the practice of child and youth care are processes of relational interaction and reciprocity which are difficult to measure.

The integrating link between form and process is the articulated ethics of caring which guide action. To the extent our education and training programs emphasize form over process, this link is broken and the manner in which ethics are applied in practice tends to be overlooked. Unfortunately, certain trends (such as increased demands for accountability) exacerbate the division between form and process, between science and art, because these demands focus on the quantifiable aspects as opposed to the difficult-to-measure, relational and evolving phenomena. A dilemma of professionalization is that not only must we affirm the importance of both form and process, but we must also integrate the two with balance. This is a challenge which must be addressed if ethics are to be competently applied to the "nitty-gritty" action required by the practice.

APPLIED ETHICS

Thus far, we have discussed the function of ethics in the development of the profession and have identified some of the very difficult, if common, issues which complicate or impede applying the ethics of caring in our work. Applying ethics requires child and youth workers to identify and state their own practice values, to embrace and personalize a standing code of ethics, and to utilize this frame of reference in the work-place. It is the latter step, of course, which is the most difficult one. It is, therefore, useful to distinguish between a code of ethics that is merely acknowledged, understood, and agreed to and what is here termed applied ethics.

Applied ethics are internalized values which are consciously clarified and personally embraced, and which direct one's decisions and actions. The use of applied ethics is an ongoing process which fosters congruence between our values of caring and our action (Kitchener, 1985). As such, applied ethics demand the practitioner's personal engagement in considering the complexities, multiple perspectives and flux encountered in real life child caring and treatment.

For instance, a practitioner working directly in the milieu setting must grapple with a number of ethical issues when confronted by a problem such as a child's failure to comply with program rules. One common ethical intention is to work within the values of the child rather than impose one's own value system on the child. A second ethic is to treat each child as an individual, without imposing conformity for conformity's sake but rather allowing individuality and supporting each child's capacity for self-determination. A third ethic is to respect the child's differences which reflect the cultural practices of the child's family of origin. Each of these ethics may routinely conflict with the needs of the group, the rules of the agency, the norms of the immediate community, and the personal values of the practitioner. Thus, applied ethics involves the process of coming to grips with the meeting and overlapping of these domains in the real world of milieu practice. In this context, the practitioner can not be simply an objective observer; rather, he or she must participate actively. In order for an ethics-based frame of reference to guide what the practitioner actually does on a moment-to-moment basis in the life context of the child, the practitioner must develop certain qualities: an attitude of discovery, a sense of mutuality, and active, personal engagement.

The discovery attitude is characterized by a seasoned humility. It functions to refresh and revitalize one's ethics and to hold the "expert" role in check by preserving an open-minded perspective that there is always more to learn. The attitude of discovery contains elements of anticipation and curiosity as well as the tension of the unknown (acknowledgement of the uncertainty and unpredictability of the work). When this attitude is carried into the work, it becomes necessary to call upon one's principles and values to provide direction and creative approaches. Thus, rote, routinized practice is minimized. A discovery attitude also fosters recognition of the relational, situational and ecological contexts of the event at hand (whether with client, colleague, supervisor, or the public), as well as recognition of the underlying values and beliefs of the client, a recognition which is necessary to the effective application of ethics in practice.

The second fundamental quality of an applied ethics-based practice is the ability of the practitioner to create a sense of mutuality with the client which would include shared human experience and a co-authored agenda for change. The perspective of mutuality promotes a cooperative approach wherein values, purpose, and motivation (i.e., ethics) emerge as the foundation and substance of the helping interaction.

The third quality, active, personal engagement, is at the heart of applied ethics. The concept of alive, personal engagement is used to highlight the interactional and person-to-person nature of child and youth work. This work is touch-intensive, both physically and emotionally. The term "applied" suggests the expectation of full, active, personal engagement; it is comparable to "applied research," where an identified problem spurs experimentation with the goal of producing solutions applicable to real world problems. This contrasts with "pure research" which awaits a practical application. Applied ethics then are to "pure ethics" (static rules of conduct such as a code of ethics) what applied research is to pure research. Pure ethics offer potential for application, while applied ethics describe an ongoing process wherein practitioners engage their personal values, beliefs, and professional ethics and integrate these into the actual tasks of the practice. It is through active, personal engagement that the practitioner brings vitality to that amalgam of personal and professional values in action called applied ethics.

The fusion of the attitude of discovery, the sense of mutuality, and active, personal engagement (the process of applying ethics) produces what could be called the "creative caring response." Applied ethics are the answer to the challenge raised at the beginning of this paper — that of the need to preserve caring as the core identity of both the profession and of its practitioners. Creative caring enriches both client and practitioner. The process of applying ethics appears to engender or enhance in the practitioner the qualities of autonomy, interdependence, flexibility, adaptability, savvy (intelligence born out of experience), cautious or reflective spontaneity and responsiveness, personal and professional potency, and, most vitally, the infusion and guidance of values in sensitive, efficient, and competent, active caring.

TEACHING APPLIED ETHICS THROUGH SELF APPRENTICESHIP TRAINING

Professional training which emphasizes competence and knowledge to the exclusion of training in applied ethics is incomplete (Welfel & Lipsitz, 1984). Programs preparing advanced practition-

ers and graduate students have special responsibility for instilling
emerging professionals with the ethics of their particular discipline.

Two programs for training professional child and youth care
practitioners utilize the Self Apprenticeship Training (SAT) approach to teach applied ethics. The graduate program in Clinical
Child and Youth Work (Western Oregon State College, Monmouth,
Oregon) accomplishes this in a series of seven core courses; the
Child Care, Treatment and Assessment Advanced Certificate program (Marylhurst College, Marylhurst, Oregon) utilizes the SAT
approach in an intensive, 12-credit-hour training program.

Self Apprenticeship Training incorporates the dynamics of applied ethics: it is discovery-oriented, fosters a deep sense of mutuality, and encourages active, personal engagement during the learning process, both in and out of the academic setting. The SAT
system attempts to overcome problems which arise when the educational approach differs significantly from the desired educational
outcome. It fosters congruence between the form of the teaching
and the process of learning, thereby facilitating creative, caring outcomes and equipping student practitioners to actually and successfully work with clients. SAT integrates what may otherwise remain
dichotomous aspects of the field—the art with the science, the theory with the practice. Such an approach to professional training can
thereby reduce the translation problem between the training techniques modeled in the classroom and the therapeutic approaches
applied in practice.

The SAT system's overall goal is to use modeling and teaching
methods in the classroom which mirror those behaviors and values
that effective practitioners use in work settings and, further, to fashion assignments directly involving student practitioners in relevant
experiences mirroring those of their clients. As students study their
own lives, they individually and cooperatively discover and design
concepts, theories, and techniques. With systematic application of
their discoveries to their own lives, students work towards personal
integration of the material. Out of this active personal engagement,
students gain respect for the teaching power of life's experiences
and an attitude of humble but systematic discovery. Thus, SAT
strongly complements more traditional teaching approaches.

SELF APPRENTICESHIP TRAINING

Briefly stated, SAT is the disciplined apprenticeship of practitioners to themselves as their own mentors; it is a structured system for learning how to learn from themselves, their clients, and the personal and professional contexts of which they are a part. (For a more detailed explanation of the aesthetics of teaching using the SAT approach, see Peterson & Maciejewski, 1988.) The approach of SAT was derived from an understanding of the nature of the work required in child and youth care. The foundation of treatment is the practitioner's capacity to create therapeutic relationships, to facilitate growth, and to orchestrate health-supporting changes in children's ecosystems (Peterson, 1978). Toward this end, SAT focuses on developing the practitioner's capacity to utilize the self as the primary "tool of the trade."

Traditional educational approaches often do not use teaching methods which sufficiently enhance "on-line" clinical judgement, empathy, teamwork, independence, and leadership. The SAT system stresses innovation exploration and leadership through action-research orientation, by encouraging students' initiative and skill in creating models, concepts, and techniques derived from experience in personal life and professional practice. Through structured learning, the "findings" from action research are related directly to the varied situations and complex treatment dilemmas encountered in the work-place.

With the SAT approach, students develop the capacity to use themselves as the primary tool of the practice, both in formulating diagnostic judgments and in orchestrating and tailoring the moment-to-moment interventions and interactions of the therapeutic milieu. Much of the learning is interactive, both in and out of the class setting, and requires the development of teamwork capabilities and interdependence. This process mirrors the team orientation of child and youth work.

Instruction from the established literature and traditional methodology should figure prominently in clinical training. However, training sources such as these, which are primarily external, do not necessarily foster attitudes of caring, empathy, independent thought, and creativity. Such attitudes are promoted through practitioners' apprenticeship of themselves to themselves in the context of real life experience.

In the SAT approach, the instructor assumes the varied roles of trainer, actor, mentor, student, facilitator, therapist-model, and peer, orchestrating learning experiences rather than singularly imposing information on the student. Although certainly an expert in the field, the instructor is most importantly a facilitator and guide for the interactive, multi-method teaching (Peterson, 1978) and learning process.

In addition to the SAT system, a number of common experiential teaching techniques may be useful in teaching applied ethics. These include clinical, case simulations and analysis; video-tape training with clinical dilemmas and critical incidents (Beker, 1972); structured role play; genogram self-assessment of family and ethnic background; and structured exercises in values clarification.

The merits of the Self Apprenticeship Training approach are at least fourfold. First, SAT ensures teaching approaches are not only practice-oriented, but are personally relevant in a way that evokes questions about the student practitioner's values, morals, and ethics, from which awareness and clarification can occur (Peterson & Maciejewski, 1988). Secondly, SAT enables students to experience a multiplicity of life-coping strategies and different perspectives from which to interpret experience. Discovering multiple perspectives and value systems relating to varying contexts and experience provides an appreciation for the variations in meaning which clients give to their own experiences. Thirdly, practitioners are encouraged to develop a humble and empathic perspective from which to appraise the values of the clients, thus furthering mutuality. Fourthly, as practitioners develop awareness of their roles as parent figures to children and moral agents to families, they become more able to suspend judgment and to practice vigilance in their decisions to withhold or employ their own value systems as a very conscious part of the treatment process.

Thus, the SAT approach functions as an equalizer between practitioner and client, protecting the student from losing touch with the realities and actual life-coping predicaments of clients, as well as from assuming a superior role or attitude, a tendency that can occur with increasing amounts of education. So, rather than increasing the distance between practitioner and client, the educational experience becomes a context for deepening the creative, caring response through an appreciation of the human condition and the capacity to build rapport with persons very different from the individual child and youth worker. This is particularly important when the ethnic or cultural background of the practitioner differs from that of the child or family. The need to foster in student practitioners a capacity to balance therapeutic distance with true empathy highlights the importance of teaching applied ethics.

There are four primary benefits to students in learning through the SAT approach. First, SAT requires that new skills or concepts be applied and tested in the child and youth worker's life before they are used in practice with clients. In this manner, students are provided with a rich understanding of each therapeutic modality's effect, as well as with an impetus to expand their own personal theories of human change and development. Central to the meaning of applied ethics is the commitment to ensure that action is in accord with personal values. Experiencing treatment techniques and concepts through personal application facilitates just such an integration. Opportunities to explore and confront their own life views, beliefs, and coping strategies enable student practitioners to appraise, internalize, and integrate their values with professional ethics.

Secondly, personal involvement with the "tools of the trade" enhances students' sensitivity to the subtleties of the art of the practice, and fosters a well-grounded clarity and ownership regarding their own particular caring and treatment approaches. This becomes an important experience of an ongoing, maturing, professional identity.

Thirdly, as the wise man said, "The real learning begins when the training ends." The SAT approach is aimed at giving students a head start on developing their sense of professional potency and competence. Professional potency increases not only with sharpened effectiveness but also through the deepened confidence which comes from understanding why one is effective, what one's limits are, and when one needs to ask for help or turn to new sources of knowledge and methodology.

Finally, the SAT approach strengthens character and personality, reinforcing the foundation of inner strength (that is, professional potency) requisite to serious and conscientious upholding of the child and youth worker's first admonition, "Above all do no harm." In the endeavor to carry this out, the dilemmas and ambiguities of day-to-day practice confront the need for an integration of the child and youth worker's personality, personal values, and professional ethics. SAT balances a curriculum of theory, methodology, and ethical code with a practicum of experience based in the personal and professional life contexts. Soundly developmental, individually-planned and implemented, and grounded in an understanding of the requirements and challenges of the field, Self Apprenticeship Training prepares advanced child and youth workers not only to articulate, but also to apply their personal and professional ethics of caring.

CONCLUSION

Practicing caring in child and youth work is seldom easy. Unremitting pressures to make choices in the best interests of children, youth, and families exist side-by-side with the constraints of reduced resources and expectations to do ever more through an already over-taxed service system. The work calls for great technical expertise, clinical judgement, management ability, and therapeutic skill, as well as qualities of dedication, leadership, and ethicality. The field seeks to assure these competencies through professionalization. A code of ethics is not only essential to this process, but may be essential to the survival of the profession's very identity over time.

Caring is the creative, life-giving core of that code. If our profession is to escape being static, then our code of ethics must be frequently renewed and revitalized throughout the field. Otherwise, in the process of professionalization, the paradoxical tendency to relegate care to a secondary status will persist.

The teaching of applied ethics through the Self Apprenticeship Training approach addresses this challenge. It integrates the science and art of child and youth work through a systematic and structured learning system. A disciplined apprenticeship to self helps students gain competency in applying the ethics of care to the complex tasks and interpersonal relationships of the work. SAT also provides students with a life-long means of learning and of revitalizing their ethics.

The technology exists for programs training advanced child and youth workers to augment their traditional educational approaches with training in applied ethics. Further, these programs must do so if they are to fulfill their mandate to instill in student practitioners the ethics of the profession—that is, the ethics of care. For, although care may be a nearly universal human intention, it is not an inherently-enduring, professional competency. Caring is both the gift and the grail of the profession of child and youth work.

REFERENCES

Beker, J. (1972). *Critical incidents in child care: A case book for child care workers*. New York: Behavioral Publications.

Corey, G., Corey, M. S., & Callahan, P. (1984). *Issues and ethics in the helping professions*. Monterey, CA: Brooks/Cole.

Courtioux, M., Jones, H. D., Kalcher, J., Steinhauser, W., Tuggener, H., & Waaldijk, K. (1985). *The socialpedagogue in Europe—Living with others as a profession*. Zurich: F.I.C.E. (Federation Internationale Des Communautes Educatives) with support of UNESCO.

Cullen, J. B. (1978). *The structure of professionalism: A quantitative examination*. New York: Petroceli Books, Inc.

Hall, E. T. (1977). *Beyond culture*. New York: Anchor Press/Doubleday and Company, Inc.

Kitchener, K. S. (1985). Ethical principles and ethical decisions in student affairs. In H. J. Canon & R. D. Brown (Eds.), *Applied ethics: Tools for practitioner* (pp. 17-29). San Francisco: Jossey-Bass.

Maier, H. (1987). *Developmental group care of children and youth: Concepts and practice*. New York: The Haworth Press.

Peterson, R. W. (1974). *Toward an integration of behaviorism and humanism in psychotherapy: An introduction to the "action-focused choice-building technique system."* Unpublished manuscript. Western Washington State University, Psychology Department, Bellingham, Washington.

Peterson, R. W. (1978). The child care worker as a child life specialist and systems interventionist: A model of multi-method child care training. *Child Care Work in Focus, 2* (2 & 3), 10-16.

Peterson, R. W. (1981). The focus, content and progress of professionalization in the child-development youth-work practice: Reflections from the child-care worker's perspective. *Child Care Work in Focus, 4* (2), 2-6.

Peterson, R. W., & Maciejewski, G. (1988). The aesthetics of teaching through self apprenticeship training: An application of Gregory Bateson's epistemological analysis to graduate education for child, family, and youth care practitioners. *Journal of Child and Youth Care Work*, Vol. IV.

Pinniger, M. (1987). *Practitioner standards: A contribution to professionalism*. Unpublished master's thesis, Western Oregon State College, Monmouth, Oregon.

VanderVen, K., Mattingly, M., & Morris, M. (1982). Principles and guidelines for child care personnel preparation programs. *Child Care Quarterly, 1* (3), 221-243.

Webster's new collegiate dictionary. (1982). Springfield, MA: Merriam-Webster.

Welfel, E. R., & Lipsitz, N. E. (1984). The ethical behavior of professional psychologists: A critical analysis of the research. *Counseling Psychologist, 12* (3), 31-43.

18

Worlds Apart?
Integrating Research and Practice
in Professional Child and Youth
Care Training

Alan R. Pence

ABSTRACT. Research and clinical practice in professional child and youth care are often depicted as two dissimilar "worlds" within the profession. This paper argues that such perceived dissimilarity is principally a function of focusing on *dissimilar* aspects of the two undertakings: research *product* and clinical *process*. It is further argued that if one focuses on certain fundamental *processes* of child and youth care research and the *processes* of child and youth care practice, the two become quite similar and highly complementary. Indeed, skills in the one enhance abilities in the other.

Questions surrounding child and youth care practice and child and youth care research periodically percolate to the surface during this, the formative period of the profession. The most recent intensive activity in this regard was the special issue of *Child Care Quarterly* in the Spring of 1982. (This issue includes articles by: Powell; Garduque & Peters; Shelly, Porter, Strauss & Johnson; Alejandro-Wright; and Webster.) The issue, totally devoted to "Research Issues in Child Care," indicated, in the words of the issue Editor, the late Carol Porter (1982) that there were definitely "signs of life" in what had at times been a rather barren field of inquiry.

Alan R. Pence, Associate Professor, School of Child and Youth Care, University of Victoria, P.O. Box 1700, Victoria, B.C. V8W 2Y2.

THE "TWO WORLDS" IMAGE
OF RESEARCH AND PRACTICE

The image of research and child and youth care that emerges from several of the seven articles in the special issue is largely one of "two worlds" of child care: the world of the researchers and the world of the practitioners (Garduque & Peters, 1982; Strauss & Johnson, 1982). This two-worlds image is not unique to this set of child care articles, (for example, see Pence, 1983) nor to the child and youth care field alone. Educators, therapists and other frontline practitioners have generated similar questions of dichotomy and similar models of "transcendence" often discussed under the rubric of the research-practitioner (Minor, 1981; Howard, 1985).

Accompanying the two world image one generally finds a "bridging" theme either within the same article (Garduque & Peters, 1982) or in an accompanying article (Powell, 1982; Shelly, 1982). Implicit in the bridging notion is the idea of separation — unique identities. The role of the bridge in such articles or sets of articles is rather like the role of a circus rider standing astride two horses while racing around the ring. Our attention is drawn to the difficult bridging function in dealing with two dissimilar beasts. In many ways separateness is accentuated through the use of a bridge and any thoughts of ultimate accommodation, or merging, between the two elements are kept at bay.

The supposition of this article is that the two-worlds scenario is neither a necessary, nor a particularly useful, image in relating child and youth care practice and child and youth care research — particularly in the context of an undergraduate training program. The thesis proposed here is that the two-worlds conceptualization is a function of a *dissimilar focus* on different aspects of research and practice rather than problematic differences between the two activities per se. The dissimilar elements of the two-worlds scenario are: research *product* and child care *practice*.

The world of research is often perceived (and presented) as encompassing the distant and enshrouded summits of the Ivory Tower of Academia. It is the *pronouncements* of researchers, the final *products* of the research endeavor, their reports and articles that are most often passed down to those labouring in the frontlines. The *activity* of research: of planning, of data collection, of site visits, is often so obscured in the magical writing of tables and statistics that a worker in the field is forced to consider only the distilled punch-line, the conclusions; and too often these more intelligible parts of a report or research article are couched in either so narrow or so cir-cumspect terms, that the reader emerges from the experience rein-forced in the belief that there is very little that research has to tell her or that she has to tell research.

Returning for one last time to the big top, if an observer were to focus *not* on the rider (the bridge) straddling the two horses and not even on the two horses themselves, but instead focussed on the *gaits* of the two horses as they proceeded from walk to trot to canter and so on, the observer would be struck by the *similarity* of sequence and process rather than being overpowered by unique-ness and difference. It is, in fact, the similar gaits of the two that make accommodation possible, not the strength of the bridge. The "gaits" of child care research and practice *processes* are similarly striking in their similarity and compatability.

When one makes this mental and focal shift from the dissimilar-ity of product and procedures to the *parallel processes* inherent in research and in practice, a true accommodation between child and youth care practice and child and youth care research becomes pos-sible. Indeed, at the baccalaureate degree level, a program could not provide professional training in one without impacting on the other.

Elements that are similar for both practice and research are enu-merated below. Following that, other benefits of ongoing profes-sional development that emerge through a "unified" orientation to child and youth care research and practice will be considered.

THE SIX STEPS OF RESEARCH AND PRACTICE

Examples of similar elements of child and youth care research and practice processes include:

1. the ability to accurately *observe* and report observational data concerning human behaviour.
2. the ability to *interpret* observational data in light of *theoretical* constructs or perspectives (the ability to place specific obser-vational data into a theoretical context).

3. the ability to *plan* an appropriate intervention in that observed behavior sequence in order to effect a change in the specified behavior.
4. the ability to *implement* a plan and guide it through the host of unforeseen circumstances that can ensue.
5. the ability to *evaluate* if the planned intervention had the desired impact and, if not, to introduce corrective measures into the intervention.
6. the ability to *communicate* orally and in writing the above processes in a professional manner such that the above steps are replicable by other professionals.

The six steps of: observation, theoretical interpretation, planning, implementation, evaluation, and communication are as much a part of child and youth care practice as they are of child and youth care research processes. The degree to which one masters the constituent skills comprising each of the six steps noted above is, in large part, the degree to which one can claim to be a child and youth care *professional*.

Given the complementary nature of research and practice processes postulated here, it is important that undergraduate instruction integrate this unified concept from the earliest coursework. At the University of Victoria, Child and Youth Care courses commence in the second year of university work. During the second year students are introduced to fundamental observational practices and to several basic theoretical perspectives. They are then asked to integrate observation and theory in an entry level child or adolescent intervention. Issues of planning, implementation and evaluation emerge in the course of the exercise as do communication skills, primarily in a written form.

The research and practice perspective presented in this paper is one that has emerged over time within the School. Initially, the exercise of planned intervention was presented solely from a *practice* orientation. This orientation by-in-large continued through the third year so that when students entered their required fourth year research course, most entered believing that they did not possess a foundation in research procedures. This belief reinforced their perception that the research course was to be both an anomalous and painful experience bearing little relation to the "real world" of practice that they were eager to return to or to enter.

This dichotomous approach to practice and research training persisted for a number of years in the School until the research course instructors (author included) grew tired of the air of apprehension and dread permeating the early weeks of the course each year. The battle in the early weeks traditionally had less to do with the teaching of research than with efforts to sufficiently reduce anxiety so that instruction could commence. An approach the instructors have recently employed in an effort to reduce the students' dichotomous orientation is a more deliberate picking-up of the "strings" of research procedures that students have encountered in earlier years, but which they have known as practice procedures. These multifunctional strings are then used to weave a more practice-grounded understanding of research. What is impressed on the students in the grounding process is the concept that the interventions which they developed for second and third year practice, if properly designed, carried out and evaluated, can also be viewed as small research projects.

Given some preliminary successes in the fourth year re-interpretation exercises, the School is now looking towards such re-definition exercises in the earliest years of the program. Rather than students learning a set of procedures which they identify only (or primarily) with practice, those same procedures will be discussed in a more multi-functional context, embracing the "doing of" research as well as practice. The integrating element of the six steps common to the processes of practice and research will in the future help guide the School's incorporation of research into the overall curriculum.

CONTINUING PROFESSIONAL DEVELOPMENT

The six steps noted, when elaborated and embellished, constitute a necessary stream in an undergraduate child and youth care curriculum. In addition to their centrality to basic intervention and research processes, the mastery of such combined skills also provides the vehicle for an individual's continuing professional development beyond the bounds of a degree program.

Central to ongoing professional development and research practice is the acquisition of reliable and replicable feedback systems for professional child and youth care workers' activities and interventions. For many young child and youth care students there is a sense that what one must acquire is a "bag of tricks," the larger the better, from which can be pulled the appropriate response for a specific situation. The logic follows that workshops, training programs, and print materials should all exist primarily to help fill this bag. These tricks, like too much of the research orientation we present to students are, however, only products not processes. They represent the end product of some other individual's experience. They do not necessarily provide the tools for an individual to evaluate and refine his own practice. They are rather like the gift of a meal to a starving person, when what is needed is the knowledge of how to grow one's own food—the process whereby the product is generated.

With the gift of process—the process of observing, interpreting, planning, implementing, evaluating, and reporting—a professional can develop his or her own bag of tricks whenever needed and not be dependent on the oftentimes illusory wisdom of others. Through the process of acquiring research skills and practice skills one can learn what will be effective, under what conditions, and for which groups or individuals. And, ultimately, it is that ability, the ability to become a learner-practitioner utilizing systematic feedback and replicable procedures, which must serve as the foundation for the development of professional child and youth care.

REFERENCES

Alejandro-Wright, M. (1982). An inter-cultural perspective on research. *Child Care Quarterly*, *11*(1), 67-78.

Anderson, W. P., & Heppner, P. P. (1986). Counselor applications of research. findings to practice: Learning to stay current. *Journal of Counseling and Development*, *65*, 152-155.

Garduque, L., & Peters, D. L. (1982). Toward rapprochement in child care research: An optimistic view. *Child Care Quarterly*, *11*(1), 12-21.

Howard, G. S. (1985). Can research in the human sciences become more relevant to practice? *Journal of Counseling and Development*, *63*, 539-544.

Minor, B. J. (1981). Bridging the gap between research and practice (Special issue). *Personnel and Guidance Journal*, *59*(8).

Pence, A. R. (1983). Two worlds of day care: The practitioner and the researcher. *Monographs of the National Day Care Information Office*. Ottawa: Health and Welfare Canada.

Porter, C. J. (1982). Qualitative research in child care. *Child Care Quarterly*, *11*(1), 44-54.

Porter, C. J. (issue ed.). (1982). *Research issues in child care*. A special issue of *Child Care Quarterly*, *11*(1).

Powell, D. R. (1982). The role of research in the development of the child care profession. *Child Care Quarterly*, *11*(1). 4-11.

Shelly, M. H. (1982). The role of evaluation in child care research. *Child Care Quarterly*, *11*(1), 22-43.

Strauss, M. S., & Johnson, C. N. (1982). Academic perspectives: Applying research, teaching research and pursuing a career. *Child Care Quarterly*, *11*(1), 55-66.

Webster, C. D. (1982). How to fail as a child care researcher. *Child Care Quarterly*, *11*(1), 79-89.

19

Transforming Perspectives in Child and Youth Care Education

Michael Demers

ABSTRACT. The purpose of this chapter is to present a new understanding of child and youth care education. The competence perspective, adequate for the training of workers in a specific role, is less effective in a diversified and maturing profession. To develop new perspectives that can provide flexibility to perform effectively in a variety of contexts an educational model must be employed. One distinction between a training and an educational model is the opportunity for students to become aware of the assumptions that they maintain about themselves and their world. A transactional perspective is a complementary and necessary component of an educational model in child and youth care, enabling a professional to apply skills and knowledge in a variety of contexts. Child and youth care educators are presented with the task to adjust their curriculum in a manner that facilitates a process of perspective transformation.

The literature provides several models for the education and training of child and youth care workers (Anglin, 1983; Bayduss & Toscano, 1979; Blase & Fixsen, 1981; Goocher, 1978; Peters, 1981; VanderVen, 1979; VanderVen, Mattingly & Morris, 1982). These models incorporate research from areas such as adult development and humanistic psychology, but rarely refer directly to developments in the study of adult education.[1] Among adult education models, Mezirow's (1981) perspective transformation parallels cur-

Michael Demers is currently completing an MA in the School of Child and Youth Care, University of Victoria, P.O. Box 1700, Victoria, B.C. V8W 2Y2.

rent developments in child and youth care education. While child and youth care educators describe the need for contextual application, Mezirow describes the process students go through while developing this ability. This chapter will examine developments in child and youth care education and the potential role of Mezirow's work in future educational models.

Two main approaches to child and youth care education can be identified in the child and youth care education literature. The first, the competence perspective, includes those models that attend primarily to the development of core skills and knowledge while the second, the transactional perspective, refers to the contextual application of skills and knowledge. These two approaches will be discussed in relation to changes in the emerging field of child and youth care.

THE COMPETENCE PERSPECTIVE

Over the past 20 years the education of child and youth care students has focused primarily on the development of core skills (communication and relationship building, case management and assessment, observation, intervention strategies and professional presentation) and knowledge (theories of behavior change, human growth and development, research, principles of intervention, and ethics) (Principles and Guidelines, 1982). In the course of 2 to 4 years of college or university education, a student can attain a level of skill and knowledge often identified as "basic competence" (Bayduss & Toscano, 1979; Blase & Fixsen, 1981; Denholm, Ferguson & Pence, 1987; Goocher, 1978; Mattingly, Tittnich & VanderVen, 1986; Peters, 1981; VanderVen, 1979). However, competence in one setting does not necessarily translate into competence in other settings. The graduates' ability to remain effective in different contexts (settings, roles, populations, etc.) depends, in part, on their ability to break away from established ways of thinking and to engage a fresh perspective.

Changes in the nature of the practice of child and youth care have resulted in an increasingly more complex task for educators. While several education programs were developed in response to the expansion of residential and child day care services in the 1970s, an expanded definition of child and youth care in the 1980s now includes a variety of roles in different settings with different populations (Denholm, Pence & Ferguson, 1983; Denholm, Ferguson & Pence, 1987; VanderVen, 1986; Whittaker, 1979). Educators, preparing students for an assortment of employment possibilities, are also faced with the responsibility of educating personnel other than direct care workers in the roles of supervisor, administrator, trainer, educator, consultant, researcher, writer, advocate and policy maker (VanderVen, 1986, p. 7). The social and economic forces that have led to the professionalization of the field have shifted the focus of education from that of producing workers to preparing professionals.

In developing and refining programs that would fill the need for practitioners in the child and youth care delivery system, educators sought to better understand the "competencies" that employers in the field were expecting of graduates. For example, Anglin's (1983) needs assessment outlined the tasks of child care workers in a variety of settings and then compared the tasks in these roles to other human service roles. This led to a later work in which Anglin (1986) presented a nine step model for the design and implementation of a needs assessment in curriculum development.

While it is important to identify the tasks of effective child and youth care practice, there is a danger, to which many programs have fallen prey, that curriculum will be developed around a core body of knowledge and skills resulting in more of a training than an educational approach. Peters, in making a distinction between the two approaches, describes training as "job or task related" while education is considered "broadening, increasing the individual's capacity for responding in acceptable ways to a variety of situations" (1981, p. 5).[2] Despite this distinction made between training and education (Peters, 1981; VanderVen, 1986) educators strive to graduate "competent" students (that is, those who behave in a manner that reflects the analysis of child and youth care functions or tasks). The competence perspective, therefore, refers to the models of child and youth care education which focus primarily on the development of identified skills and knowledge. While this approach can be effective in developing competent workers, this type of education, narrow in focus, does not provide the broadening that flexible professionals require.

There are several weaknesses in the competence model. One of the greatest concerns has been that few child and youth care professionals remain in a front line position for an extended period of time. This is a particular concern with university graduates who appear to have higher expectations for advancement than do college graduates or experienced professionals who have chosen to advance through an agency. Educated front-line workers (who are not necessarily competent) are often quickly advanced in a child and youth care system where as many as 80% of front-line workers are hired with no child care pre-service training (Phelan, 1985). Advancement within the field often involves taking on a new role (e.g., supervisor), dealing with a different population (e.g., hospitalized children), returning to university for further education and perhaps even moving to another part of the country. This transitory aspect of well-educated professionals has only added instability to a field that, for an assortment of socio-economic reasons, has been inherently unstable.

Another concern with the competence model is that the general functions of the child and youth care worker have, historically, changed approximately every five to eight years in response to governmental policy changes and advances in the field. The institutional workers of the mid-seventies were first challenged to change their approaches when reemployed in community-based group homes, and then again in the early 1980s as preventive and family-oriented programs were developed. Gabor (1987) suggests that many of the competent institutional child care workers are "ill-prepared" for the complex tasks required in a community setting.

A third concern with the "competence perspective" is that an employer cannot be guaranteed that a "competent" front line worker will become "competent" in other child and youth care roles as described by VanderVen (1979). The "component" front-line worker who is moving into a supervisory position must acquire new skills and information that are pertinent to the role. The challenge of the educator, therefore, is to assist the student in preparing for a variety of roles, in different settings, and for an ascent up the child and youth care career ladder while avoiding the "treadmill of incompetence" (Peters, 1972).

Suppose that Marilyn, a recent graduate of a child and youth care program, has focused her studies on the needs of children in hospitals. The year that she graduates there are no positions available in local hospitals so she takes a position in a local group home for troubled teenagers. If Marilyn has been through an education program that has focused on developing the core skills and knowledge needed to work in a hospital, she may have difficulty dealing with adolescents in a relatively unstructured environment. With this transfer to a new setting, Marilyn can also anticipate changes in her lifestyle including new social contacts, a perceived shift in social status along with a change in her professional identity. If she has the opportunity to become aware of her beliefs and attitudes about this new context, Marilyn is much more likely to adjust and apply the skills and knowledge she has gained in her "specialized" training.

The concerns mentioned above describe some of the inadequacies of the competence education model which prepares the individual for a focused, task-specific career. Recognizing that four years of "competence" education may not be enough time to train any one individual in all of the potential career areas, educators must provide learning opportunities that involve a shift in perspective "so impactful that students can transfer their learning to corresponding situations in other relevant tasks" (Maier, 1986). In order to transcend the competence perspective, which is rooted in the training of front-line workers, new educational approaches must be considered. The transactional perspective, presented in the literature by several educators, offers the theoretical rationale for these changes in child and youth care education.

THE TRANSACTIONAL PERSPECTIVE

In part because child and youth care professionals deliver services in a variety of settings, the field is described as a leader in an "ecological approach to human services" (Mattingly, Tittnich & VanderVen, 1986). The ecological approach, working with children in their life space, calls for a reexamination of conventional education and the consideration of alternative approaches.

Oriented in an ecological view of child and youth care, Beker and Maier (1981) call for a move away from "traditional reductionistic" educational programs that are preoccupied with course content and the mastery of a "constellation of courses." What Beker and Maier propose is a holistic perspective that emphasizes patterns of thought and skill that would allow workers to interconnect their ongoing experience. Faithful to a systemic point of view, they warn that the manner in which the material will be organized and presented to students will be as important as the content. Broader than the content of the program, the process of child and youth care education should be organized so that, "the learner is required to deal effectively and integratively with the interconnectedness of what he or she is learning, and of life events."

This process of transforming one's perspective has been overlooked by competence models which have relied primarily on "first order change," which is step-by-step learning. Maier's (1986) discussion of learning processes and his introduction of "second order change," or contextual learning, provides an introduction to an educational approach that could facilitate a "transactional perspective." Rather than simply developing a "tool kit" of knowledge and skills, students must experience "interaction" in order to become aware of limiting biases and assumptions. While calling for a new philosophy of child and youth care education, Maier, and other writers, do not present an educational model that would facilitate this new perspective. The description of such a process, however, is outlined in the process of perspective transformation.

PERSPECTIVE TRANSFORMATION

Perspective transformation is a process through which a student can gain a new perspective in a new context, developing what Mezirow calls a level of "critical self awareness" (1981, p. 5).[3] Awareness of patterns of thinking and behavior is the first step towards developing new ways to act, thereby enabling one to become effective, not only in the specific position one has been trained for, but in a variety of roles encountered throughout a career. Developing the flexibility to use skills and knowledge in different contexts, and learning how to enhance this way of thinking in others, Beker and Maier call the "most critical learning of all" (1981, p. 205).

Mezirow (1981) discusses two types of psychological assumptions that can generate strong feelings and inhibit personal and professional growth. The first, "internalized cultural assumptions," includes those beliefs which are "expressed in terms of sex roles, social conventions and expectations and taboos." The second type includes those assumptions that are the result of "unresolved childhood dilemmas." Often a block in clinical effectiveness can be traced to "childish" beliefs which have not yet been flushed out, confronted and transformed. For example, workers dealing with a child whose life circumstance is very similar to their own can become "hooked" and react to the child and family in a manner that resembles their reactions to their own family. Brendtro, in his discussion of "roadblocks to effectiveness," maintains that "all those who work with disturbed children [must] make an honest attempt to assess the degree to which their own philosophical outlook is determined by their unique personality rather than the needs of disturbed children" (1969, p. 219).

The model of perspective transformation describes the process of facing old patterns and developing new perspectives of oneself and the world consciously as opposed to the unaware inheritance of beliefs and values in childhood (see Table 1). This is not always a joyous learning experience as many find the process to be "an unsettling, painful struggle in which glimpses of insight alternate with confusion, uncertainty, and ambiguity" (Brookfield, 1986, p. 22). A student, in interaction with other students who are also experiencing similar types of "assumptions," has the opportunity to move beyond these patterns. The insights gained from interaction and the subsequent critical awareness are "emancipatory in the sense that at least one recognizes the correct reasons for his or her problems" (Mezirow, 1981).

CONCLUSION

Child and youth care professionals, through contact with children, youth and families, relive aspects of their own childhood and adolescence. Therefore the degree to which they are aware of areas

Table 1

Dynamics of Perspective Transformation

1) a disorienting dilemma;

2) self examination

3) a critical assessment of personally internalized role assumptions and a sense of alienation from traditional social expectations;

4) relating one's discontent to similar experiences of others or to public issues - recognizing that one's problem is shared and not exclusively a private matter;

5) exploring options for new ways of acting;

6) building competence and self-confidence in new roles;

7) planning a course of action;

8) acquiring knowledge and skills for implementing one's plans;

9) provisional efforts to try new roles and to assess feedback and;

10) a reintegration into society on the basis of conditions dictated by the new perspective.

* adapted from Mezirow (1981).

of limiting assumptions will determine their ability to adapt to situations in which these issues reappear. To become aware of, and confront, these aspects of self, is the challenge facing students hoping to be effective child and youth care professionals. Mezirow's model is not just an interpersonal exercise: it is a process through which students can receive the support needed to transform perspectives preparing one for a career of different roles in a vibrant and evolving profession.

NOTES

1. In the child and youth care literature, Tittnich's (1986) article, "Training that takes: Adult learning and adult teaching are the key" is a notable exception.
2. While recognizing the value of learning in a training environment, Brook-

field, a noted adult educator, points out that "education is centrally concerned with the development of a critically aware frame of mind, not with the uncritical assimilation of previously defined skills or bodies of knowledge (1986, p.17).

3. The term "self-awareness," as used by child and youth care educators, generally refers to awareness of a thought, feeling, sense, intention, or action in the moment (Miller, Nunnally & Wackman, 1975). "Critical awareness" is the awareness of patterns of thinking and behavior which includes moments of "self-awareness" (Mezirow, 1981).

REFERENCES

Anglin, J. (1983). Setting the sights: An assessment of child care functions and training needs in British Columbia. In Denholm, C., Pence, A., & Ferguson, R. (Eds.). *The scope of professional child care in British Columbia*, Part 1, 2nd edition, [Monograph]. University of Victoria.

Anglin, J. (1986). Needs assessment: The initial step in curriculum design for child care practice. In VanderVen, K. & Tittnich, E. (Eds.). *Competent caregivers — Competent children: Training and education for child care practice*. New York: The Haworth Press.

Bayduss, G., & Toscano, J. (1979). The development of child care workers: Correlates between occupational and socio-economic growth. *Child Care Quarterly, 8*(2), 85-93.

Beker, J., & Maier, H. (1981). Emerging issues in child and youth care education: A platform for planning. *Child Care Quarterly, 10*(3), 200-209.

Blase, K., & Fixsen, D. (1981). Structure of child care education: Issues and implications for education and practitioner. *Child Care Quarterly, 10*(3), 210-225.

Brendtro, L. (1969). Avoiding some of the roadblocks to therapeutic management. In Trieschman, A. E., Whittaker, J. K., & Brendtro, L. K. *The other twenty three hours: Child care work with emotionally disturbed children in a therapeutic milieu*. Chicago: Aldine.

Brookfield, S. (1986). *Understanding and facilitating adult learning*. San Francisco: Jossey-Bass.

Denholm, C. J., Ferguson, R., & Pence, A. (Eds.). (1987). *Professional child and youth care: The Canadian perspective*. Vancouver: University of British Columbia.

Gabor, P. A. (1987). Community-based child care. In Denholm, C. J., Ferguson, R., & Pence, A. (Eds.). *Professional child and youth care: The Canadian perspective*. Vancouver: University of British Columbia.

Goocher, B. E. (1978). Ages and stages in professional child care training. *Child Care Quarterly, 7*(1), 7-20.

Maier, H. (1979). Child care workers development within a transactional perspective: A response to Bayduss and Toscano. *Child Care Quarterly, 8*(2), 94-99.

Maier, H. (1986). First and second order change: Powerful concepts for preparing child care practitioners. In VanderVen, K. & Tittnich, E. (Eds.). *Competent caregivers—Competent children: Training and education for child care practice*. New York: The Haworth Press.

Mattingly, M., Tittnich, E., & VanderVen, K. (1986). Positive signposts towards the future in training and education for child care practice. In VanderVen, K. & Tittnich, E. (Eds.). *Competent caregivers—Competent children: Training and education for child care practice*. New York: The Haworth Press.

Mezirow, J. (1981). A critical theory of adult learning and education. *Adult Education*, *32*(1), 3-24.

Miller, S., Nunnally, E. W., & Wackman, D. B. (1975). *Alive and aware: Improving communication in relationships*. Minneapolis: Interpersonal Communication Programs Inc.

Peter, L. J. (1972). *The Peter prescription*. New York: Bantam.

Peters, D. L. (1981). New methods for educating and credentializing professionals in child care. *Child Care Quarterly*, *10*(1), 3-8.

Phelan, M. (1985). Alberta's Child Care Counsellor Training and Certification Program. *Journal of Child Care*, *2*(3), 39-46.

Principles and guidelines for child care personnel preparation. (1982). Proceedings from Conference-Research Sequence in Child Care Education, University of Pittsburgh. *Child Care Quarterly*, *11*(3), 221-244.

Tittnich, E. (1986). Training that takes: Adult learning and adult teaching are the key. In VanderVen, K. & Tittnich, E. (Eds.). *Competent caregivers—Competent children: Training and education for child care practice*. New York: The Haworth Press.

VanderVen, K. (1976). A compendium of training programs in child care professions in the United States and Canada. *Child Care Quarterly*, *5*(4), 319-329.

VanderVen, K. (1979). Developmental characteristics of child care workers and design of training programs. *Child Care Quarterly*, *8*(2), 100-112.

VanderVen, K. (1986). "You've come a long way baby": The evolution and significance of caregiving. In Vander Ven, K. & Tittnich, E. (Eds.). *Competent caregivers—Competent children: Training and education for child care practice*. New York: The Haworth Press.

VanderVen, K., Mattingly, M. A., & Morris, M. G. (1982). Principles and guidelines for child care personnel preparation programs. *Child Care Quarterly*, *11*(3), 242-249.

Whittaker, J. (1979). *Caring for troubled youth*. San Francisco: Jossey-Bass.

20

Child and Youth Care Education
for the Culturally Different Student:
A Native People's Example

Carol Stuart
Mary Lynne Gokiert

ABSTRACT. The authors discuss the issue of how to educate child and youth care workers to work with culturally different children using the example of educating Native students. In order to educate Native students, educators must be prepared to adapt curriculum and child care methodology within the total education program. In addition, the needs of the culturally different child must be addressed within the mainstream programs.

The college education system in Canada has been developed by, and primarily serves, a group of people with a white European background. Similarly, the services provided to children by provincial child welfare authorities use a philosophy and methodology consistent with white European values and norms. In the past five to ten years there has been an increasing awareness that people from a different cultural background (Canadian Indian, Metis, Vietnamese, East Indian, etc.) hold differing values that may conflict with the educational system or the child welfare system. With the awareness that there is a difference, service providers must begin to address the issues of how to treat culturally different children who

Carol Stuart, Training Consultant, 9119-81 Avenue, Edmonton, Alberta T6C 0W9, and Mary Lynne Gokiert, Head, Youth Development Program, Grant MacEwan Community College, 7319-29th Avenue, Edomonton, Alberta T6K 2P1.

come into contact with child care services and how to educate adults who want to provide services to children from their own culture.

In Canada in 1980, 4.6% of all status Indian children between 0 and 19 years of age were in the care of child welfare authorities. Overall, .96% of all Canadian children between 0 and 19 years of age were estimated to be in the care of child welfare authorities (Johnston, 1983). Status Indian children were represented at over four times the rate of all children. These estimates do not include Metis and non-status Indian children for whom accurate statistics are not available. The status Indian population is 1/70 of the Canadian population. There are, however, very few Native child and youth care workers caring for these children. The Native people themselves are gradually moving to provide care for these children. In 1980 the Spallumcheen Band in British Columbia passed a by-law to authorize the band to care for their own children. In 1981 the Dakota-Ojibway Child and Family Service signed a tri-partite agreement in Manitoba giving them the authority to provide these services. The Dakota-Ojibway Service provided an intensive 3 month pre-employment training program for social workers with a curriculum geared toward Native people (Johnston, 1981). In the spring of 1984 the Saddle Lake Reserve in Alberta opened a group home and requested a child and youth care education program from Grant MacEwan Community College. The people of the Saddle Lake Reserve wanted a program which would provide an education and the skills equivalent to any other child care worker. The experience of the authors, and the examples used here, are drawn primarily from that program, which was offered at Blue Quills Native Education Centre in St. Paul, Alberta.

Educators in child care worker programs must be prepared to adapt curriculum, selection procedures, and traditional approaches to education in response to the needs of culturally different student populations. At the same time they should consider the needs of the culturally different child and address those within their mainstream programs.

Native people, particularly the Indian people but also the Metis, are stating that because of their different culture the care provided by non-Native child care workers is inconsistent or conflicts with the cultural background of the Native child (Andres, 1981). In discussing the issues involved in responding to the needs of culturally different students the authors make two basic assumptions: First, the educational program for a culturally different group of students *must* be equivalent to that offered to any student. If it is not, the implication is that the student is not as highly valued. Second, the students upon graduation must be qualified to work in any setting. The majority of Native children are in the care of mainstream child welfare agencies rather than in agencies operated by Native people, hence, the Native child and youth care worker may choose to work in a mainstream agency or may choose to work in an agency operated by a Native organization.

ISSUES ENCOUNTERED
IN PROVIDING CHILD CARE EDUCATION
TO CULTURALLY DIFFERENT GROUPS

The Child Care Worker Program offered at Blue Quills admitted two cohorts of students. The students completed the same program offered to on-campus students and graduated with a two-year diploma in Child Care. Slight adaptations to the program included longer course hours, a shorter summer break, incorporation of Native content in applicable courses, and the use of field placement blocks. The course content otherwise was identical to the on-campus program and in fact many of the same instructors were used. Two sets of issues encountered in the program will be addressed under the themes of cultural bias and changes to curriculum.

Cultural Biases

In educating students from a different culture the educator must begin by questioning some basic assumptions about the student's entry level skills, values, and attitudes. Students from a different culture have a greater likelihood of having learned English as a second language. The reading and writing skills that they bring to the program initially will be affected by this. Approximately 90 percent of the students completing the Child Care Worker Program at Blue Quills required upgrading in reading and writing skills. Textbooks are written in a sophisticated manner which the student may have difficulty comprehending. The educational level a student has achieved prior to entering the college program is also likely to be atypical. About half the students at Blue Quills had not achieved a grade 12 diploma. In comparison, the on-campus program had less than 35 percent of their students requiring upgrading. The culturally different student, in the authors' experience, is older with a broader range of life experiences, and is more likely to have a family.

The field of child care work places a strong emphasis on interpersonal communication skills. The assessment of such skills is "culturally-biased" and in assessing the suitability of a candidate the educator must be aware of the cultural norms. Some Native groups, for example, have strong norms around eye contact and whether it is appropriate and with whom. As an interpersonal communication skill, eye contact is evaluated in society at large as an indicator of attention, interest and validation of the speaker. A student who comes from an Indian band where eye contact is seen as disrespectful could be viewed as unsuitable for the program on the basis of initial interpersonal communication skills.

Typically the educational system places an emphasis on competition, achievement of high grades, attendance in the classroom, and completion of assignments on time as evidence of learning. The values held by the culturally different student may at times conflict with these requirements in the educational program. The educator must consider how to deal with this conflict. The students in the Blue Quills program, for example, often struggled with the need to care for their families as a first priority. Family was defined as anyone connected to the student. This meant that the death of a cousin, illness of a niece or nephew, as well as the needs of the student's own children could be seen as a priority more important than attending class or completing an assignment.

On the other hand, the culturally different student is likely to see the achievement of a recognized diploma as a means of getting ahead of their peers and achieving equality in the mainstream population. The educator needs to consider the equality of the program and demand the same standard of excellence from the student. The previously mentioned priority on family could make this a difficult balance.

Culturally different students, because of their minority status, may have developed different perceptions of authority figures and, in particular, the educator as an authority. For example, according to Hudson and McKenzie (1981), the Native people developed a colonial relationship whereby their beliefs, customs, and language were ignored or denied by the government, the educational system, and the child welfare system leading to their passive withdrawal from agents of that colonialization. In the classroom this may mean the student will not approach the instructor for assistance, to negotiate extensions, or to discuss classroom material. If students are not ready for a test they may choose not to write it rather than experience the associated feelings of failure.

For Indian students education is guaranteed as a right by the treaties agreed to between the government and the Indian people. This guarantee implies that the Canadian Department of Indian and Northern Affairs pays all costs for the students' post-secondary education. This may include living costs. As a result, the educator may be placed in the position of having to provide an attendance report. This raises two issues: the student may lose a portion of funding, or the student may be attending courses simply to support themselves financially and not as a carefully considered career choice. The instructor must be clear with students about the requirement for attendance reporting and that the student is responsible for being in class. The instructor will not "cover" for the student in the area of attendance. Additionally, the instructor must realize that the student may be less aware of the field of child care and may have chosen to enter the field based to some extent on finances, only later developing an interest in the child and youth care profession. The stereotypes and beliefs of the culturally different student about the dominant culture will influence the students' perceptions of the individual educator. The educator must be prepared to receive and deal with the feelings of the student about what he or she represents in terms of discrimination, oppression, and lack of sensitivity and knowledge about the student needs. Initially, at least, the educator can be a symbol for the students of all the pain that the dominant society has inflicted on their culture.

Changes to the Child Care Curriculum

In recognition of the differing value system, beliefs, and accompanying behaviors evidenced in a different culture some changes and additions must be made to the child care curriculum. Obviously each college or university will have a slightly different course program, sequence and emphasis. The authors assume, however, that the core areas of interpersonal communication, counseling, child development, family dynamics, activity programming, abnormal psychology and behavior management will be addressed by any child care education program. Adaptations can be made in any or all of these areas dependent upon the needs of the cultural group.

In sequencing the course work it may be important to begin with a life skills or personal awareness course prior to teaching basic communication and counseling skills. The Native student whose previous experience of the educational setting has been to feel put down and wrong in any attempts to communicate in class will be lacking in the confidence required to speak out and practice communication and counseling skills.

The educator needs to be aware of the cultural norms of the students surrounding particular interpersonal communication or counseling skills. In the traditional Native culture, for example, advice around personal problems is sought from the elders who hold the role of teaching and guiding. Thus the student has experienced a directive model of counseling. If the program teaches a non-directive model the student may have great difficulty changing old learning. The mature student profile means that the old learning has had more time to solidify and will be more difficult to change. The educator should address the issue of whether to develop a new curriculum consistent with cultural practices or recognize different cultural practices and teach the student skills which will enable him to work in mainstream child care agencies. The latter approach requires an integration of child care skills with Native philosophy as it is traditionally defined. In the counseling course used in the Grant MacEwan program, the student is expected to practice with a partner and to use real-life issues when practicing counseling skills and self-disclosure skills. In programs offered to a group of students from a common, close-knit community this has implications for confidentiality and the student's willingness to self-disclose.

When teaching the theory of child development the educator should consider that the theory was developed primarily based on white European children and youth. There is little recognition of cultural differences. Certain developmental issues, however, may be applicable. The identity crisis of the teenage years, for example, is of greater significance for Native children because they are coping with both their identity as a person and also their identity as a Native. The theory surrounding the development of values and morals provides the educator with a forum for discussing the different values held by members of the Native population. The students need to examine their own values and how those may conflict with the dominant culture or be similar to those held by members of the dominant culture.

In a course on families the educator must make adaptations to teach the child care worker about the differing family dynamics in their own culture. In the Native culture there are differences in the extent of inclusion of family members, child rearing practices, male and female roles, and attitudes toward children. These are all areas that should be addressed in a course on families. In Native families, for example, children are given much freedom to explore their surroundings, they learn by observation and practice and are not formally taught skills, and older siblings take on parenting roles at an early age.

In a course which teaches students skills to program activities for children there are some culture-specific considerations. The educator should include activities which are a part of the student's cultural background. The therapeutic rationale for programming cultural activities with the children also needs to be addressed. Native students could be taught beading, leatherwork, quillwork, and traditional dances and games by Native artisans and dancers. Native children in care need to learn about the beautiful and unique aspects of their culture so that they may feel a pride in their identity as a Native person.

The curriculum of an abnormal psychology course should reflect an emphasis on those problems common to the cultural group. Because child care workers deal with disturbed behavior patterns they must learn how to address those most relevant to the particular children with whom they will work. The Native population has a suicide rate six times that of the national population in Canada (Department of Indian & Northern Affairs, 1980). Alcohol and drug abuse is another area requiring emphasis for Native child and youth care workers. The students in the Blue Quills program requested additional information on dealing with child sexual abuse.

In the area of behavior management as in the area of counseling, specific skills are taught which have been developed based on the norms of the mainstream culture. The child and youth care educator must again consider whether to change the curriculum to reflect cultural practices or to identify for the student areas where there may be differences, and to teach mainstream skills so that the Native child and youth care worker is equivalently competent in a mainstream agency. The native cultures, for example, hold a strong ethic of non-interference which would imply that active intervention to change the child's behavior through the use of reinforcement or structured re-education programs may be culturally inconsistent.

Practicum presents a potential difficulty for the student, especially in a mainstream agency, because differences in cultural values and practices are then highlighted. The students notice differences in child rearing practices, discipline, expectations of children and youth, and the behavior of caregivers. The conflict is intensified for the student when there are Native clients in the setting for whom a Native approach would be more appropriate. Similarly, supervisors of students have a tendency to demonstrate a cultural bias in their expectations of students. It is useful to provide an orientation to supervisors prior to the practicum. A benefit observed for Native clients has been the opportunity to learn from the Native student about culturally appropriate practices and to develop a relationship with a Native role model.

SUMMARY

The idea of meeting the needs of culturally different children through the provision of care by adults from the same culture is not yet a common practice in North America. The traditional child care curriculum and methodology has been developed over the years based on the services provided by agencies within the cultural mainstream. There are few agencies that have been developed by other cultural groups and no research into child care practices that are culturally consistent with minority groups. At present it would seem that curriculum changes within child care programs can only examine the issues rather than teaching different skills from those already being taught. The authors believe that the most effective way to raise these issues and adapt curriculum is across the spectrum of all child care courses, enabling the student to achieve an integrated and holistic approach. As well, this approach provides the graduate with the choice of working in a setting developed specifically by their own cultural group or in a mainstream agency to assist children from their own culture.

REFERENCES

Andres, R. (1981). The apprehension of native children. *Ontario Indian*. Spring, 32-37.

Department of Indian and Northern Affairs. (1980). *Indian conditions: A survey*. Ottawa: Author.

Hudson P. & McKenzie, B. (1981). Child welfare and Native people: The extension of colonialism. *The Social Worker*, *49*(2), 63-66.

Johnston, P. (1981). Indian control of child welfare a historic step. *Perceptions*, *1*(2), 7-8.

Johnston, P. (1983). *Native children and the child welfare system*. Toronto: Lorimer and Company, Publishers.

Kershaw, J. (1986). *An evaluation of the Blue Quills child care worker program*. Unpublished.

21

Distance Education:
Catch the Wave

Roy V. Ferguson

ABSTRACT. Part-time adult learners have become the new majority in post-secondary educational institutions and are having a significant effect on colleges and universities. One of the major changes noted is the rapid growth of distance education activities within educational institutions. An examination of the factors contributing to this evolution is provided as well as a look at the implications for universities and colleges. It is suggested that educational resource networks are a key adaptive mechanism to be considered and that the child and youth care field is particularly suited to the development of such structures. The benefits of establishing an educational resource network are examined.

Contrary to what the title might suggest, this chapter is not about surfing. Rather, it is about adapting to a major trend which is sweeping across the continent and affecting all post-secondary educational institutions—the part-time adult learner. This "new majority" (Campbell, 1984) is no longer the wave of the future but is a phenomenon which exists now and cannot be ignored. It is important that educational institutions are able to ride the wave and, in this context, the present chapter will consider some adaptive mechanisms beginning with an examination of how distance education structures are necessary to meet the needs of the flood of part-time adult learners. Then, as a vehicle to facilitate efficient and inte-

Roy V. Ferguson, Associate Professor, School of Child and Youth Care, University of Victoria, P.O. Box 1700, Victoria, B.C. V8W 2Y2.

grated distance education within the child and youth care field, a proposed educational network will be outlined.

PART-TIME ADULT LEARNERS:
THE "THIRD WAVE"

The traditional clientele of universities, colleges and most post-secondary educational institutions have long been persons between the ages of 18 and 24 years who were engaged in full-time study. Recently, adult learners in part-time credit courses and in formal non-credit programs together outnumber the full-time student body (Campbell, 1984). This "new majority" is the result of a combination of technological, social, and economic changes and is a force which has considerable implications for the post-secondary educational system. Who, then, are these new learners and how will they impact on the educational system?

Toffler (1981) described "second wave" industrial citizens of the recent past as highly skilled persons of fairly similar lifestyles who are prepared to assume roles in factory-like environments. The institutions and systems which developed to serve the educational needs of these citizens are characterized by an emphasis on classroom instruction, similar curricula, and a common knowledge and skill base.

Toffler then went on to describe "third wave" civilization as being comprised of citizens who are likely to require educational structures which are increasingly individualized and decentralized:

> More learning will occur outside, rather than inside, the classroom . . . education will become more interpersonal and interwoven with work, and more spread out over a lifetime. (Toffler, 1981, p. 384)

Toffler's 1981 analysis of the future provides an increasingly accurate picture of the present state of affairs and educational curricular content and delivery mechanisms must adapt to the needs of "third wave" civilization. This means that educational institutions will no longer be able to provide programs which are offered only on a full-time basis in on-campus locations. Educators will have to adapt to the demands of "third wave" individual learners for more flexible mechanisms providing decentralized and individualized educational opportunities. Much of this adaptation will involve the use of new information technologies in a distance education format.

THE NATURE OF DISTANCE EDUCATION

Although terminology such as adult education, further education, extramural studies, continuing education, extension learning and distance education are used interchangeably, distance education appears to be emerging as the preferred term and will be used most frequently in this chapter. Keegan (1980) notes the main elements of distance education as:

1. the separation of teacher and learner which distinguishes it from face-to-face learning
2. the influence of an educational organization that distinguishes it from private study
3. the use of technical media, usually print, to unite teacher and learner and carry the educational content
4. the provision of two way communications so that the student may benefit from, or even initiate, dialogue
5. the possibility of occasional meetings for both didactic and socialization purposes (p. 33)

Simply stated, distance education involves the delivery of course material to adult learners at a distance through the use of multiple delivery technologies and strategies.

FACTORS CONTRIBUTING TO THE GROWTH OF DISTANCE EDUCATION

While the history of distance education dates back to the correspondence instruction developed in Great Britain in the 1850s, the period of greatest growth and innovation has been very recent. There are a variety of forces, outlined below, which are driving the rapid evolution of distance education.

1. *Technological advances*. Rapidly changing technology means that it is no longer possible to acquire a complete education at the beginning of a career. Lifelong learning and recurring education are universal needs which account for the increasing demand for continuing professional education.
2. *Role of women in the workforce*. Women now comprise approximately half of the workforce and are a significant element in creating an increasing need for part-time educational programs.
3. *Leisure time*. As more leisure time is available to individuals, they are using part of it to pursue a variety of educational interests.
4. *Non-sequential learning formats*. It is much more common today for periods of educational activity to be interspersed with periods of work or travel.
5. *Movement across educational systems*. Today's students quite typically move across a variety of educational institutions such as community colleges, universities and open learning structures. They are seeking a mix of educational experiences suited to their own particular and changing needs.
6. *Increased life expectancy*. As members of the population live longer they will have more time to be active in their various educational interests.
7. *Life changes*. The occurrence of divorce, illness or death within a family creates a situation where, often, the surviving spouse will require some form of educational upgrading.
8. *Mid-career change*. An increasing proportion of the already well-educated population are involved in distance education to enable voluntary or required mid-career change.
9. *Occupational licensing requirements*. Various occupational groups are requiring that their members be involved in a certain amount of continuing education each year in order to maintain practice credentials.
10. *Economic restraint*. The restricted economic outlook existing throughout the continent has resulted in a tighter job market in which fewer persons are willing to leave their places of employment to seek out further education. Curiously, these same conditions create a situation where employers, because of

greater competition for existing positions, can demand higher educational credentials of candidates.

It is interesting to note that half of all adults, males and females, are engaged in some form of formal learning and that half of these are between the ages of 25 and 39 years. Nearly one-third have a college degree or graduate education and over half are professional or technical people. Within the university sector, 39% of adult education programs are involved in continuing professional education with specific percentages of programs as follows: medicine (95%), nursing (90%), accounting (57%), engineering (48%), and education (38%) (College Board, 1980). Unfortunately there were no continuing education figures for the child and youth care profession.

There are a variety of reasons for participating in continuing professional education. Professionals are concerned about keeping up with the new knowledge and skills necessary for competent and responsible job performance. They want to understand new orientation shifts within the field and to stay aware of changes in the basic principles underlying the profession. Some professionals want to maintain a fresh outlook on their work while others want to concentrate their skills in a particular area. Certain professionals participate in continuing professional education to retain the will and capacity to learn while others are involved because it is required by their professional association in order to maintain their certification. Whatever the reasons, the demand on post-secondary educational institutions for continued professional education offerings (particularly for credit) is rapidly growing.

IMPLICATIONS FOR UNIVERSITIES AND COLLEGES

Throughout North America universities and colleges will be faced with a fixed, or perhaps even dwindling number of conventional, on-campus students and a rapid increase of part-time learners. In order to successfully adapt to these changes educational institutions will need to carefully determine who the adult learners are as well as their instructional needs. They will need to devise instructional materials which meet the requirements of the target audience in terms of content and methodology and create delivery mechanisms which are flexible in regards to scheduling, location and duration. Campbell (1984) notes that "This is reason to speculate that the university which neglects the continuing education of its graduates will have cause to regret it" (p. 23).

Although the continuing education of adults represents a mass movement which is as large as post-secondary education has ever experienced (National Advisory Council on Extension and Continuing Education, 1975), the phenomenon has been met by many universities with an attitude of indifference. Perhaps this is due in part to the fact that the provision of distance education questions a number of traditional university assumptions:

1. the requirement of on-campus attendance by the learner
2. the requirement that courses be offered by an institutional staff member
3. the assumption that education must fit within a set time frame
4. the assumption that conventional classroom study is the only valid way of acquiring knowledge and skills appropriate to credit towards a degree
5. the assumption that distance education offerings will dilute the academic integrity of the institution
6. the assumption that effective teacher/learner interaction can only be achieved in a traditional classroom setting

Fortunately, as institutions become increasingly involved in distance education activities they usually realize that these traditional assumptions do not hold and that the goals of university continuing education are not apart from the nature of the goals of the university as a whole. In fact, over time the conceptualization which most often develops is one of parallel on-campus and off-campus programs having the same academic standards, objectives and course content as well as utilizing the same instructors. Under these circumstances it is typical for students to move from the off-campus program into the on-campus one in order to accelerate their progress towards a degree. The reverse also occurs when, for economic or family/personal reasons, an on-campus student is unable to continue as a full time student and moves into the off-campus program. As can be seen, the establishment of parallel programs offered on-campus as well as off-campus provides a considerable increase in the educational alternatives available to the new "third wave" learner.

This is not to say that distance education programs are without their own unique set of problems. Issues such as professional socialization, clinical supervision, availability of library resources, access to consultation/advising and inter-institutional transfer credit arrangements, to name a few, arise in the provision of distance education. However, for the most part, they are not insurmountable and simply represent new problems for the educational institution to address.

EDUCATIONAL NETWORKS

To date, the development of most distance education resources has occurred within single institutions on a relatively isolated and somewhat competitive basis. This is not a very efficient approach to meeting the complex and diverse educational needs of the "third wave" society, particularly in times of fiscal restraint. Economies of scale are necessary in order to provide the spectrum of educational resources required by the large and disparate group of part-time adult learners. It will not be possible for individual institutions to meet all distance education needs within their geographic area so that interagency mechanisms will need to develop to increase student access to existing resources, regardless of where they were developed. Some softening of regional mandates of educational institutions will need to occur and a new spirit of cooperation develop. Educational networks will need to be set up to assemble the material and human distance education resources which have been developed in universities, colleges, technical institutions and service agencies. Such networks would play a key role in identifying existing resources, marketing programs, assessing needs for new programs and coordinating their development. They would also be instrumental in addressing some of the problems (Gregor, 1979) in coordinating educational programs across different institutions.

In brief, the "third wave" of part-time adult learners has arrived and educational institutions must develop distance education programs to meet their diverse continuing education needs. Resource networks are a key mechanism for educational institutions to consider in developing the distance education facilities they need. The remainder of this chapter will examine the potential for developing such a resource network within the context of professional education for the child and youth care field.

A CHILD AND YOUTH CARE
EDUCATIONAL RESOURCE NETWORK

Perhaps the single greatest incentive for considering the development of a resource network is the general tone of economic restraint which is evident throughout Canada and the United States. The reduction of funding support for post-secondary education means that new educational programs, as well as new courses within existing programs, are much slower to develop.

Ironically, at a time when education and training resources are static or diminishing, the press for admission to professional preparation programs is increasing. Partly, this is accounted for by the time-honoured observation that when unemployment increases, so does the number of students wishing to attend post-secondary educational institutions. The press on college and university programs is also due to an increasingly competitive professional job market. While child and youth care workers were previously able to find employment largely on the basis of clinical experience, human service agencies are increasingly requiring more academic credentials of the staff they hire.

Not only are child and youth care workers needing more academic credentials to find new jobs, but workers who are employed are requiring more education in order to advance their careers, or sometimes, even to continue in the jobs they have. This is quite typical in times of high unemployment where an ''employers' market'' is created. Increasing numbers of child and youth care workers are seeking educational upgrading but find themselves unable to leave their jobs to attend campus-based programs. The only available alternative, under these circumstances, is to find continuing education coursework designed for part-time students. Since not all child and youth care workers in this situation are located in large urban centres with college and university programs, the need for off-campus credit coursework becomes urgent.

Another trend noted is a movement towards a broader definition of the field of child care (Denholm, Ferguson & Pence, 1987). The scope of practice is moving beyond the traditional residential care and daycare settings to also include children, youth and families receiving care in community settings, hospitals, schools and recreation centers. As the scope of practice increases, it becomes more evident that the similarities in educational preparation of practitioners in these various settings is considerably greater than the differences. This observation then results in movement on the part of educators towards a greater generic emphasis in coursework developed for professional preparation programs. For example, at the Conference-Research Sequence in Child Care Education held in Pittsburgh in 1981 and 1982, it was recommended that the professional education curriculum content in all educational programs should include coverage of the following three generic domains: (a) human growth and development, (b) child care methods and skills and (c) personal and professional development.

It is highly unlikely, however, that all colleges and universities are going to have the necessary resources available to develop all the distance education coursework they require. Fortunately this press occurs at a time when there is a growing awareness of the generic nature of professional education curriculum content within a broadening child care field. Consequently, the time is ideal for educational institutions to consider pooling their resources in developing generic, interchangeable coursework packages which are of mutual benefit.

An educational resource network, then, is a structure in which a number of child care educational institutions develop distance education coursework in a coordinated and standardized manner so that these resources can be exchanged among the participants.

BENEFITS OF AN EDUCATIONAL RESOURCE NETWORK

The most obvious benefit of a resource network is that it will offset restrictions being placed on educational programs by fixed or diminishing resources. Rather than having to develop all of the distance education coursework required, each setting would concentrate only on certain of the generic or elective courses. In addition to having less coursework to develop, each educational institution would be able to focus on module development in their areas of particular strength so that all of the resources within the network are of higher quality. For example, one setting may be particularly strong in the area of human development and would be responsible for the development of this module while another institution may develop the family systems or interpersonal communications coursework because of unique resources and expertise in these areas.

Another advantage of a resource network is that coursework exchange will facilitate the development of increased distance education activity across a number of educational programs enabling more students access to professional training in their own geographic region. In fact, the network may make the difference between certain educational settings having a distance education program or not. The prospect of developing an entire off-campus program may be overwhelming to a college or university program while the development of only certain modules may be considerably more realistic.

An interesting side benefit of a resource network is that the courses produced by this type of cooperative effort would constitute a major step towards achieving some degree of standardization in the professional preparation of child care personnel. Greater standardization would facilitate the transfer of students across both educational programs and service delivery settings. A resource network would represent the beginning of a universal academic credit bank for child care students which would allow them to move about the continent without jeopardizing continuity in their professional development. Further, the resulting standardization and continuity created by a resource network would also be instrumental in helping to define the child and youth care profession more clearly.

A last benefit, one which has been recognized by educational programs with experience in developing distance education coursework, is that the resources prepared for off-campus delivery can, in large part, also be used for on-campus course offerings. The process of developing distance education courses usually results in improved curriculum design of the on-campus counterparts as well as providing extra resources, such as manuals, videotapes, progress assessment scales, etc.

Newly developed educational programs are in a particularly good position to benefit from involvement in a resource network because they can develop their on-campus and off-campus coursework on an integrated basis right from the start. It is much easier to establish good curricular continuity between on-campus and off-campus course offerings if they are developed on a coterminous basis.

SUMMARY

Now that part-time adult learners constitute the largest segment of university and college student populations, the "third wave" is no longer a future prediction, but is a reality of the present and particularly pertinent to the child and youth care field. In order for educational institutions to survive and thrive they must adapt to this new phenomenon. A primary aspect of this adaptation is the development of flexible distance education structures which complement and augment existing on-campus programs. Parallel on-campus and off-campus credit coursework needs to be developed within university and college programs involved in the preparation of professional child and youth care workers. These are not good economic times to be building new educational programs and careful consideration should be given to the establishment of an educational resource network to facilitate cooperative course package development among post-secondary educational institutions. The child and youth care field, because it is relatively young compared to allied disciplines, has the flexibility necessary to move quickly on this issue in order to establish a leadership role in setting up an educational resource network. In the words of a current media icon, Max Headroom, . . . "catch the wave."

REFERENCES

Campbell, D. D. (1984). *The new majority: Adult learners in the university*. Edmonton: University of Alberta Press.

College Entrance Examination Board. (1980). *Americans in transition: Life changes as reasons for adult learning*. New York: The Board.

Denholm, C., Ferguson, R., & Pence, A. (1987). *Professional child and youth care: The Canadian perspective*. Vancouver: University of British Columbia Press.

Gregor, A. (1979). The re-alignment of post-secondary education systems in Canada. *Canadian Journal of Higher Education*, *9*(2), 35-79.

Keegan, D. J. (1980). On defining distance education. *Distance Education*, *1*(1), 13-36.

National Advisory Council on Extension and Continuing Education. (1975). *Equity of access: Continuing education and the part-time student*, 9th. Annual Report. Washington, D.C.

Toffler, A. (1981). *The third wave*. New York: Bantam Books.

22

The Transition from Student to Practitioner in Child and Youth Care

Sharon Moscrip
Adrien Brown

ABSTRACT. The transition from child and youth care student to child and youth care professional can be an anxiety producing experience. The purpose of this chapter is to identify the challenges regularly encountered by beginning practitioners in order to provide a frame of reference for entry into this type of work. Anticipating and preparing for these events may facilitate an easier transition into the world of work. This chapter addresses the following areas: finding work, readiness to practice, defining the child care role, supervision, agency structures and suggestions for the beginning practitioner.

BACKGROUND

The transition from child and youth care student to child and youth care professional can be an anxiety producing experience. The purpose of this chapter is to identify the challenges regularly encountered by beginning practitioners in order to provide a frame of reference for entry into this type of work. Anticipating and pre-

Sharon Moscrip, Executive Director, Esquimalt Neighborhood House, 102-527 Constance Street, Victoria, B.C. V9A 6N5 and Adrien Brown, District Elementary Counsellor, Sooke School District, John Stubbs Special Services, 301 Zealous Crescent, Victoria, B.C. V9C 1H6.

The authors wish to acknowledge David Greer, Carey Denholm and Chris Balmer for their editorial assistance.

paring for these events may facilitate an easier transition into the world of work.

Evidence suggests that levels of involvement and types of concerns experienced by child and youth care workers change noticeably during the first three years of employment (Sutton, 1977). Sarata (1979) examined three phases of work experience of new cottage parents. Initially, they were preoccupied with mastering standard operating procedures. During the second phase they tended to compare their work attitudes and philosophies to those of co-workers and supervisors, and in the third phase, the major focus was their appropriateness for and commitment to the child care role.

Sheahan et al. (1987) identified three developmental stages that residential child care workers within one institution seemed to move through. Each of the stages is described by approximately twenty worker behaviors characteristic of the stage. Beginning workers are given a copy of these behaviors upon commencement of employment. The intended goal is to reduce worker frustration, anger and disappointment around predictable events and to provide an opportunity for supervisory intervention in a supportive manner based on the worker's particular stage of development.

Research examining actual phases in moving from student to professional is limited. Sarata (1979) states that "most observers of child care practitioners have failed to distinguish between working in the role, and the process of beginning employment or adjusting to the role" (p. 298). A successful adjustment to initial employment is seen as critical if the worker is to continue practicing in the field.

BECOMING EMPLOYED

Finding Work

The challenge of finding full-time employment in child and youth care often begins towards the end of a student's final practicum. In addition to broadening awareness, skills, and knowledge, the practicum provides an opportunity for students to make professional contacts. That is, a positive impression generated in the mind of a field supervisor may open "employment doors" to the student's future.

As graduation approaches, the student begins to assess the job market, realizing that the graduate in the late 1980s is entering an employers' market. Many employment areas have suffered cut backs in government funding of social services and it is not unusual for employers in major urban areas to receive several hundred applications for a single vacancy. Applications are often received from persons whose qualifications far exceed the job requirements both in training and in field experience. Subsequently, students who are at last relieved of the pressures of academic competition with classmates may now find themselves in an even tougher competition for jobs.

This situation permits employers to make additional requests of candidates. For example, an agency director may ask a prospective employee to give a commitment to remain employed with the agency for two years. The employer, however, may only be able to offer minimal job security, due to dependency upon renewal of government funding each fiscal year and the availability of contracts. The successful applicant may more readily agree to a solid commitment in an uncertain environment given the competition from the throngs of applicants.

Typically, students attempt to seek employment in their area of specialization or interest. Depending on level of training, workers are qualified for a broad range of jobs; however, given the scarcity of employment opportunities, the tendency may be to apply for child care related positions in areas in which they have less adequate training. Employment in an area for which one has little experience can be an unsettling prospect. For example, students specialized in preschool or daycare may feel ill-prepared to work with troubled adolescents.

Relying solely upon traditional job search strategies appears to be inadequate given today's market conditions. Results from Attison and Glassberg's study (1983) indicate that the largest percentage of jobs were obtained through personal contacts (38.6%) rather than through newspaper advertisements (19%). One may conclude that child and youth care students who make professional connections and establish a network of contacts in the field will have an advantage in finding employment. Making contacts with other professionals, gaining experience, and establishing a reputation are all benefits gained through practica and volunteer work. Seeing the value in these experiences and taking advantage of the opportunities they may provide gives an added edge to the beginning job search.

In preparation for the interview, questions may arise about the job requirements and one's suitability for the position. The interview process requires a careful balancing act. The applicant realizes there are inherent risks in using the interview to explore whether or not the job will be suitable while wanting to appear enthusiastic and committed to a job they know very little about. This can lead to frustration if there has been little opportunity for information exchange, as often occurs in newspaper advertisements where an anonymous box number is given by an employer who wants to avoid being overwhelmed with inquiries. Although there may be initial frustrations and disappointments associated with the employment search, there is also an accompanying sense of excitement in beginning to practice in the field in which so much preparatory time and energy has been invested.

Readiness to Practice

Along with the initial excitement, novice child care workers need to grapple with the complexities of the new job, and will likely have questions about their career readiness. A general lack of confidence or a feeling of being in over one's head may accompany this experience. For example, "I've spent two years studying to be a child and youth care worker and I'm still not sure I'll be able to do the right thing, at the right time, with the right child." The graduate now realizes that the prior focus on learning has changed to one of accountability for the specific client interventions. The responsibility of intervening in another human's life can be overwhelming and beginning workers may see their approach as one of trial and error. Whereas this lack of clear focus can be confusing, with experience comes a clearer perspective and understanding of the process of intervention (Sheahan et al., 1987). Developing clear theoretical application in practice only evolves with time and with field experience.

A common tendency for beginning workers is to assume responsibility for client successes and failures. As a result workers may find themselves on emotional "rollercoasters," peaking when they perceive client success and "zipping down into the chasm" with lack of client progress. Ownership of client progress may subsequently result in the tendency for workers to contribute to client dependency. Not only do clients tend to become dependent on their workers for experiencing success, but beginning workers depend on clients for meeting their needs to be loved and admired (Vander-Ven, 1979). This need to be accepted can interfere with the worker's ability to set clear limits, particularly if in the setting of limits, the worker risks rejection by the child. The following case illustrates this type of dilemma faced by a beginning worker.

> Friday afternoon, when left alone with a class of six adolescents in an alternative school, the youth care worker was approached by a youth complaining of a stomach ache. He had already had two timeouts; and one more would result in a suspension. Intent on avoiding unnecessary conflict, the worker carefully weighed the options. Should the youth stay in the class and risk an inevitable suspension or would it be better to let the youth go home early and avoid further confrontation? After "careful" consideration the youth was permitted to leave. Five minutes later smoke filled the classroom; the student had set the school on fire as he left. The child care worker had the following thoughts. "I should have known something like this would happen! If only I'd paid attention to his nonverbal behavior."

Two issues emerge from this example. The first is the worker's choice of intervention, which was based somewhat on avoiding conflict or rejection; it was easier to send him home sick. The other issue is the worker's questioning of her own level of competence. New workers often believe they should know what to do in every situation. Learning to take a positive view of mistakes, by accepting and learning from them is a necessary part of adapting to work in child and youth care.

The beginning practitioner needs to be prepared for the processes involved in learning new skills quickly rather than expecting to be thoroughly versed in all areas (Baer & Federico, 1979). Assessing skills needed to function effectively in any position, and then identifying how and where to get these skills, is a key aspect to success in child and youth care work. Reading up-to-date publications, attending and participating in workshops, conferences and post graduate courses are additional opportunities for fine tuning or developing the necessary skills.

Defining the Child Care Role

Professional child and youth care has expanded rapidly over the last three decades moving from an almost exclusively institutional base to a broad range of services and programs (Denholm, Ferguson & Pence, 1987). As a result of the expansion of services to children and families, the focus and definition of child care work has changed dramatically. However, the continued professionalization of child and youth care workers has often been held back as agencies define their standards of practice by whom they hire. Although there may be intensive academic training now available, many agencies still tend to hire inexperienced and untrained personnel. This practice clearly affects the status of the profession.

Child and youth care workers who are new to the field may move into a new program where they are the only child and youth worker employed. They may be without a statement of philosophy, theoretical premise, or frame of reference for the role and yet are expected to define their role within the program, to the community, and to other professionals. Lack of role clarity can make it difficult for novice workers to present clear statements about who they are and what they do. A child and youth care worker may move into a setting where other professionals are unsure of the role and mandate of the profession and thus are unsure of the contribution that a child care worker can bring to a team or agency.

Perhaps one of the most prevalent situations in which lack of role clarity is evident is the school setting. Workers often walk a fine line in trying to clearly define their role without affecting the teacher's role by performing teaching tasks, yet still being viewed as a supportive person within this environment (Denholm & Watkins, 1987). Clearly, part of the challenge for the new worker is to educate and inform fellow workers of their role, skills and professional value. The new worker thus needs to become confident and assertive about role clarity and which functions they are, or are not, willing to perform.

While this lack of role clarity can be difficult for some, it is nevertheless one of the most appealing aspects of this profession. Unlike other professions, the child care role has flexibility and provides child and youth care workers with the freedom to adapt their service to meet the "real" needs of the children and families with whom they work.

Supervision

The beginning worker may be reluctant to take complete advantage of the expertise of the supervisor. Instead, supervisory sessions tend to be used to *prove* one's competence and supervision time may see the worker attempting to convince the supervisor of her proficiency and commitment rather than gaining support and information related to the job. The benefits to be gained from supervisor feedback on areas of weakness or inexperience may be lost as confidence building takes precedence. This focus on competence at the expense of self examination may relate to the fact that mistakes now take on a new meaning as they may now affect one's reputation as a professional rather than simply indicating areas of focus for student learning. With this shift in emphasis, the novice practitioner can become fearful not just of making errors, but of these errors coming to the attention of the supervisor.

One aspect of professionalism is having a rationale for clinical intervention. Beginners naturally question their level of professionalism yet need to remember that whether they feel qualified or not, the job has been entrusted to them. At times there may be self-doubt, a feeling of being ill equipped to offer assistance or support to their clients. In retrospect, the beginning practitioner may not realize that this self-doubt surfaces at times for all those in the helping professions.

Sarata (1979) describes the initial months of first employment as a lonely time where "the workers find it difficult to request assistance for themselves and often relegate concerns and frustrations to another time" (p. 27). The beginning workers' inability to articulate their concerns often limits their capacity to obtain the type of peer support needed in the early stages. As Sarata (1979) comments, "maintaining a supportive atmosphere for discussion will not always be easy because a new worker's preoccupation with basic procedures will be less than intriguing to more experienced workers" (p. 33).

Another area of supervision that can create difficulties for the beginning worker is the worker's confusion with regard to the many roles performed by the supervisor. Workers may be requesting assistance as to the effectiveness of an intervention or simply identifying weak areas in order to request feedback and support from their supervisor, while the supervisor may be in the process of evaluating the worker's competence. Therefore, both workers and supervisors need to reach joint clarity about the purpose and structure of supervision and each others' expectations.

Agency Structures

Another area facing the novice child and youth care worker is the development of a thorough understanding of the agency functions, policies, procedures, rules, politics, and power structures, and an understanding of how these functions are related to their own role. As Fassett (1978) noted, "discovery of these realities without adequate preparations has had devastating effects on many of our new eager and creative talents" (p. 54). However, the new practitioner is rarely aware of or prepared for these realities when commencing employment.

The worker's limited perception of the agency may be traced to what Egan (1986) calls "the shadow side of organizations." These are the covert rules and complex sets of mutual understandings which are not written in any policy handbook yet govern how employees behave and how procedures are followed. An example of such a covert rule would be that no employee shall talk directly to the Director about a case without first consulting the program supervisor. The new worker usually stumbles over such covert rules through trial and error. Nevertheless, the worker's effectiveness will be influenced by the ability to quickly assess the informal agency structure. That which may initially have been perceived as a program restricted by the routine of tradition may in fact be a program held in place by a series of interrelated expectations cemented by years of practice. This view is supported by Fassett (1978) who commented, "untold energies are spent in attempting to reconcile what practitioners view as a conflict between their professional ethical structure and the demands of agencies" (p. 54).

VanderVen (1979) describes beginning child care workers as having "a feeling that administrative action and policies actually erect a barrier to the spontaneity and freedom they feel the children need and they can provide" (p. 104). That is, the position taken by the agency may seem antithetical to the workers' perception of human service needs. Subsequently, "new workers develop a sense of 'self-hate' from seeing themselves as purveyors of negative factors" (Fassett, 1978, p. 54). Learning to deal with disillusionment, when the realities involved in services to children and families offered by various agencies becomes evident, can be difficult. Due to political, economic and social factors, clients' needs will not always be foremost in service planning. The worker who feels responsible for poor service offered by agency constraints may feel helpless and victimized, identifying with the client and thus becoming less effective as a worker.

To increase effectiveness, the child and youth care worker, rather than feeling like a participant in a system that is self-serving, may chose to work towards becoming a political change agent. For example, rather than complaining about the elimination of a program, the option to contact the news media and publicly advocate for the continuation of the service, to participate in a cost/benefit analysis of this program, and to release these results to the public, are constructive alternatives. Thus, involvement in political change strategies may assist in maintaining a level of idealism and active commitment to services for children and families regardless of the program contents.

The idealism of beginning practitioners is an attribute that can provide energy and drive in advocacy for children and families and in working with demanding and difficult clients who, because of their experiences, are resistant to developing relationships with professionals. Keen, fresh perceptions can serve to revitalize an existing program. However, a critical aspect is the skill with which new workers share these perceptions and suggestions for change. Too much enthusiasm may be perceived as criticism of the program's inadequacies, thus putting staff on the defensive. The challenge for the beginner, then, is not just to identify program areas that need changing but to advocate for these changes in a way that staff feel supported rather than criticized. Over time, novice child and youth care workers will come to understand the adage, "real change takes time." Moreover, they will likely discover how best to work with colleagues to influence policy and program, in order to bring about realistic and effective changes which in turn bring better service to children, youth and families.

CONCLUSIONS AND IMPLICATIONS

Issues and challenges facing beginning child and youth care practitioners have been presented. Awareness of these issues and challenges may assist in facilitating a smooth transition from the years spent in study and preparation to employment within the work force. The following is a list of suggestions which may assist students about to undergo this transition:

1. *Join a Child Care Association*. Often child and youth care workers work in isolation and need the support, professional identity, and information provided through contact with their professional community.
2. While you are a student, begin a *professional network* that will help you with your job search and support system after graduation.
3. Don't expect to have all of the skills necessary for the ever-changing role of the child and youth care worker. Chart a course for your *continued personal and professional development*. Evaluate whether you have the skills needed and, if you do not, ascertain where and how you can obtain them.
4. Have your name put on *mailing lists* for training seminars, workshops, conferences and retreats.
5. Become proactive in *soliciting support and feedback from your supervisor* and from your colleagues concerning improvement in practice skills. Often colleagues will resist giv-

ing unsolicited feedback, yet when approached will offer valuable suggestions and insights.

6. Develop *interests and friendships outside of work* that provide support and help replenish your energies. This will assist your need to create a balanced lifestyle, and provide a "clean break" from the job.

7. Find *people to talk with who understand and support your work*. When things are going well and when problems arise, have someone you can share with who will listen, share ideas and will offer supportive understanding.

REFERENCES

Attinson, Z., & Glassberg, E. (1983). After graduation, what? Employment and education experiences of graduates of BSW programs. *Journal of Education for Social Work, 19* (1), 5-13.

Baer, B., & Federico R. (Eds.), *Educating the baccalaureate social worker: Report of the undergraduate social work curriculum development project*. Cambridge Mass.: Ballinger.

Denholm, C. J., Ferguson, R. V., & Pence, A. R. (1987). *Professional child and youth care: The Canadian perspective*. University of British Columbia Press: Vancouver.

Denholm, C. J., & Watkins, D. (1987). Canadian school based child care. Ch. 4. In Denholm, C. J., Ferguson, R. V., & Pence, A. R., (Eds.), *Professional child and youth care: The Canadian perspective*, (pp. 64-88). University of British Columbia Press: Vancouver.

Egan, G. (1986). Discussion at Clinical Skills Symposium at the University of Victoria, Faculty of Education.

Fassett, J. D. (1978). Overall practice concerns and issues. In Baer, B. & Federico, R. (Eds.), *Educating the baccalaureate social worker: Report of the undergraduate social work curriculum development project*, (pp. 51-59). Ballinger Publishing Company. Cambridge, Mass.

Sarata, B. P. V. (1979). Beginning employment as a child care worker: An examination of work experiences. *Child Care Quarterly*, 8 (4), 295-302.

Sheahan, E., Garbor, T., Graff, D., Hoffman, B., Mitchell, L., Stingley and Taylor, B. (1987). Developmental stages of child care workers. *Journal of Child and Youth Care Work, 3*, 55-59.

Sutton, B. (1977). Consideration of career time in child care work experiences. *Child Care Quarterly, 6*, 121-126.

VanderVen, K. D. (1979). Beginning employment as a child care worker: An examination of work experiences. *Child Care Quarterly, 8* (4), 100-111.

SECTION 6:
THE CHANGING WORK
ENVIRONMENT AND NEW ROLES
FOR CHILD AND YOUTH WORKERS

Introduction

Perhaps more than with any other profession, the major constant in child and youth care has been *change*. Whereas such fields as education, nursing, and psychology have experienced changing needs of clients and the periodic emergence of faddish approaches, child care has endured these as well as an even more dramatic explosion in the nature of the roles and settings in which its practice takes place. Each of the chapters which follows addresses current understandings of the work environment of child and youth workers and suggests future directions.

Victor Savicki sets the stage with an overview of trends affecting the work world in general in North America, and presents some of their implications for the field of child care. He identifies the need for the evolution of the child care worker's role into one of team integrator, orchestrating the diversity of services and professionals involved with children and youth. Savicki notes that the very milieu treatment skills developed in the context of group care prepare child care workers for such an integrative role.

For workers more used to occupying a small seat in the back of

the orchestra pit, the assumption of the role of conductor will undoubtedly seem rather presumptuous and far-fetched. We can discover, perhaps, in the subsequent chapter by F. Herbert Barnes and
Laurence Bourdon both the reasons for our current low status and a
model worthy of emulation which may offer a way forward.

Barnes and Bourdon describe how, through rigorous education
and training and recognized professional definition, the French
child and youth workers (éducateurs spécialisés) are prepared, and
expected, to assume a responsible role in the care of children and
youth. In the éducateur model we find the implementation of a vision so long haunting us in North America, but so seldom realized.
As the authors recount, even the best trained and most highly
skilled workers cannot perform basic child care functions effectively when their treatment role is devoid of sufficient content and
individual professional discretion. We can hope that through sharing their experiences of profound culture shock with us, these visiting éducateurs can help spur their North American colleagues into
developing and implementing a suitable conceptual (and working)
model for the profession.

Christopher Bagley and Loretta Young, with their concept of the
scientist practitioner, present an important dimension of just such a
model. Following on Pence's critique of the "two worlds" myth
(see Section 5), Bagley and Young describe a research study designed and carried out by child care workers in order to assist them
in better understanding and treating the children and families in
their care. This particular illustration is but one of very many viable
approaches that are possible, and our field can benefit from encouraging and supporting all such efforts to integrate these two central
dimensions of our work.

The two closing pieces in the section by Karen VanderVen and
Carey Denholm explore a broad range of career issues and options
for child and youth workers. VanderVen takes seriously the necessity for expanded career options in order to make direct clinical
child care work a viable life-long employment opportunity. Just as
Phelan (see Section 3) focused his consideration of supervision
around the stages of worker development, so VanderVen depicts
evolving clinical roles over the progressive stages of practice. If the
profession is to continue to be grounded in day-to-day work with

children and youth, it is vital for our future well-being to provide such clinical paths to many of our most gifted and competent practitioners.

Denholm, in his wide-ranging look at the training and development of workers for emerging career functions, extends Vander-Ven's analysis into a number of options for workers with particular interests and talents for less traditional child care roles. Neither VanderVen's nor Denholm's models should be seen as purely futuristic. At the major conferences now taking place on a regular basis, nationally and internationally, practitioners at all of the stages and representing all of the career options discussed are in evidence. Denholm's call for our profession "to continue to be characterized by equality, collegial support, and challenge and nurturance" is both wise and timely. As the field continues to mature, we shall experience ambivalence and conflict on numerous issues; such tension and challenging can serve as a source of energy *if* we hold fast to our commitment to the development of a new, sensitive, and grounded profession which genuinely understands the needs of children, youth and families, and unfailingly accords these first priority.

23

Modern Times:
Trends in the Context of Work
Suggesting Future Roles
for Child and Youth Workers

Victor Savicki

ABSTRACT. Possible future roles for child and youth workers are suggested based on an examination of trends within the world of work generally, and based on an analysis of child and youth care's goals, tasks, and work environments. Results of the analysis describes child and youth work as a complex, segmented, and dynamic job with high perceived uncertainty, and high needs for information, communication, and coordination. The prescribed decentralized, egalitarian organizational structure for child and youth services indicates communicator and integrator roles for child and youth workers as they use their milieu-based communication expertise to coordinate child and youth services. Specific suggestions are offered to prepare for these future roles.

In the classic movie "Modern Times," Charlie Chaplin finds himself both enthusiastic and disenchanted with his working world. What seemed in the beginning to hold promise and fulfillment turned confusing and even hostile. Much has changed since then. Our modern times in the world of work has been influenced by several powerful trends. To interpret how the maturing child and youth work profession fits within the flow of work trends, this

---

Victor Savicki, Director, Clinical Masters in Child and Youth Care, Western Oregon State College, Monmaith, OR 97361.

chapter will first examine a few of the most powerful trends and explain their effect on child and youth work service delivery today. Then, as an attempt to look through a window into the future, this chapter will analyze the child and youth care work context in order to suggest the most useful organizational structures that will maximize future quality of care and worker satisfaction. This chapter plots a trajectory of development and suggests methods to keep on target. Our modern times also promise fulfillment and excitement. Ideas on how to maintain the momentum may help the field from taking a different turn.

TRENDS OF WORK IN MODERN TIMES

In the world of large corporations and businesses, much discussion and soul-searching springs from the question of how to design an organization that facilitates the most production and the highest quality at the same time. Although different organizational designs may be appropriate for different conditions, a general trend in design has gained popularity. This trend now emphasizes a concern for the human side of the work place (Peters & Waterman, 1982). Such emphasis was not always the case.

The model of work settings as machine-like, stemming from the industrial revolution, has begun to be replaced by a more balanced model acknowledging the needs of workers as well as the needs of manufacturing a product or delivering a service. The "scientific management" approach (Taylor, 1911) sought to reduce human error by simplifying tasks and confining decision making to bosses and managers higher up the organizational structure. Modern approaches (Hackman & Oldham, 1980) seek to involve the line worker in complex, meaningful tasks with the assumption that those workers closest to the task have a unique knowledge and commitment to bring to bear on problems that may affect productivity and quality. The recent popularity of "Japanese management" reflects the surge toward this approach (Ouchi, 1981).

WORK TRENDS PARALLELED
BY CHILD CARE CHANGES

In a historical sense, the practice of child and youth work has paralleled the trends in the larger working world. Initially children and youth with problems were removed to specialized care facilities (like factories) to be served by a set of hierarchically distinct workers. At the top were physicians and psychiatrists, followed by psychologists, social workers and nurses; and on the bottom the child care staff. Child care, in these circumstances, was defined as a simple, custodial task in which decisions concerning treatment and rehabilitation were not made or carried out. "Real" treatment occurred only in the presence of the "experts."

Modern approaches acknowledge the unique perspective of child and youth care workers as the practitioners closest to the moment-to-moment opportunities to observe and treat the individuals in their charge (Brendtro & Ness, 1983). Additionally, as child and youth care practice becomes more holistic and systems-oriented, child and youth workers have moved into a variety of important environments of children and youth; into the families, schools, juvenile justice system; and into the streets.

As trends in the larger work context and in child and youth work move together, child and youth workers need to understand the flow that they are a part of in order to take advantage of that momentum rather than paddling upstream. As individuals, child and youth workers can shape the policies and events of their agencies. As a profession, child and youth work needs to adapt the aspects of general trends that will advance higher quality care for children, youth and families.

ORGANIZATIONAL STRUCTURE MODEL
APPLIED TO CHILD AND YOUTH CARE

This chapter will suggest conclusions for organization and structure of future child and youth work based on a decision-making model used in business and industry. The model, proposed by Duncan (1979), takes into account the unique aspects of an organization's goals, tasks, and environment. In order to draw conclusions about optimal organizational structures suggested by Duncan's decision-making model, two preliminary conditions must be met. First, the tasks and environments of child and youth work must be identified. Second, these tasks and environments must be analyzed according to Duncan's model. Finally, conclusions can be stated concerning approaches suggested by the model.

CHARACTERISTICS OF CHILD AND YOUTH WORK SERVICE DELIVERY

Child and youth work covers a multifaceted array of factors that emerge from the individual child or youth, from the family or primary living situation, and from important contexts with which the child or youth — family or living group interact; e.g., school, courts, community. At the individual level, the child or youth represents an holistic collage of physical, psychological, developmental, behavioral, cognitive, and emotional functioning. Each of these levels affects, and is in turn affected by all others. In other words, the individual child or youth represents a holistic, dynamically shifting balance of forces.

The family and primary living situation present another array of variables. Within the family many simple facts can impose complicated outcomes; e.g., who is in the family and who is out, what order they came or left, roles, norms, and multi-generational contacts. The child or youth's family can also be seen as an holistic collage of individuals and patterns of interaction which is at times helpful to the treatment process and at times hindering. Likewise the primary living situation (if it is other than the family) contains many of the same variables. Foster parents, child and youth care workers, peers in treatment or care all coalesce to present an impact more powerful than the sum of the separate individuals. In other words, the family or living situation represents a dynamically shifting balance of forces of which the child and youth worker often becomes a part.

Finally, beyond the child or youth and family or living situation fall the contexts that affect all the others. Various child and youth service organizations; e.g., schools, juvenile court, and mental health agencies, each exert an influence. And beyond all of those falls the community expectations for the performance of those service organizations. Cooperation or conflict with these organizations can help or hinder the progress of the child or youth. Ultimately, the community can restrict the ability of the child and youth care practitioner to deliver service at all; funds may be cut, practice may be regulated. In other words, the contexts beyond child or youth and family or living situation represent a potentially shifting balance of forces that encompass both the child and youth care practitioner and his or her work activities and clientele.

In summary, the practice of child and youth work embodies tasks that must show responsiveness to dynamically shifting forces within individuals and families or living contexts. Each of these forces can be explained and influenced by practitioners expert in that level of treatment. In addition, child and youth care practice takes place within a larger environmental context that also shifts dynamically as organizations which also impact on the children or youth in care exert their influence. As Ferguson and Anglin (1985) say: "Child care is concerned with *the totality of child development and functioning.*"

MODES OF WORK ORGANIZATION
SUGGESTED BY DUNCAN'S MODEL

According to Duncan's (1979) model of decision making concerning organizational structure, child and youth care practice exists in a "complex," "segmented," and "dynamic" environment (see Table 1).

That is, the goals and tasks of service and the environment in which they are accomplished are multifaceted, able to be divided into meaningful sub-units, and are changeable. Although individuals working in such conditions maintain their own role identity, they also experience a reciprocal interdependence; that is, the outcomes of their work become the material of other's work which generates materials for the original worker, and so on. As Table 1 indicates the organizational needs of such work contexts include high need for information and coordination, high need for skilled

TABLE 1. Analysis of child and youth care work-context using Duncan's (1979) decision tree

Duncan's questions	Child and youth work analysis	Organizational needs
What is the nature of the organization's goals, tasks, and environment: simple or complex?	<u>Complex:</u> • Multiple levels of treatment (medical, psychological, educational, nutritional, etc.) • Multiple clients • Multiple practice settings (residential or day treatment, school, family, community) • Multiple contextual influences (community, funding sources, legal and governmental regulations)	High need for information High communication skills
Can we segment the task and environment: segmented or unsegmented?	<u>Segmented:</u> • On the basis of expertise required (milieu organizer, teacher, psychological therapist community organizer) • On the basis of practice setting (residential or day treatment, school, family, community) • On the basis of clients seen (child/youth, family, community representatives)	High need for coordination
Do task and environmental factors change over time: static or dynamic?	<u>Dynamic:</u> • Child/youth changes--(developmental; outcomes of treatment) • Family/living situation changes (developmental-life cycle; outcomes of treatment) • Context changes (research, technology, funding priorities, legislative priorities)	High perceived uncertainty

individual and group communication, and a need to reduce the uncertainty that is a by-product of complexity and change.

Duncan's model suggests that organizations functioning under such conditions can best achieve their goals by structuring themselves in a decentralized manner, with flat hierarchy of authority, and with heavy emphasis on communication among the various specializations that may be identified within the organization. Specialized expertise needs to be acknowledged as unique and equal in status. Separate individuals or groups need to communicate and coordinate effectively with other specialized personnel. One of the biggest liabilities of a decentralized organization is its inability to provide integration and coordination among segmented components.

For the child and youth care profession, Duncan's model suggests a team approach involving specialists working together in a semi-autonomous structure in the service of the child or youth. The goals of quality care can be met by continuous coordination among practitioner specialists who address different aspects of the child or youth and family or living group-context. These coordination and orchestration skills are the very abilities that child and youth workers have developed in the milieu treatment approach. The major difference lies in the scope of the newly defined milieu which includes family or living situation and community context as well as the child or youth in a group living situation.

IMPLICATIONS FOR THE CHILD
AND YOUTH WORK FIELD

Duncan's writing assumes that a single organization contains the various segmented components. In the child and youth work field, the components may or may not come under the same organizational umbrella. A single agency may have child and youth workers, teachers, family workers, and community advocates. It may deal with children, schools, families, and other community agencies. It may see its clientele in a residential group living situation, a day treatment situation, a weekly interview format, and a consultation format both in and out of the agency. Such an agency clearly falls within the organizational purview of Duncan's decision analysis.

But what about the solo practitioner? What about the child and youth worker in a small independent group practice? What about the small agency that does not have the resources to hire the diversity of personnel that has been mentioned in this paper? Duncan's analysis still applies; yet has to be broadened in scope. Rather than seeing one agency as decentralized, we can view the resources for the child or youth being decentralized. Resources exist, but not all under one roof. In this situation, a heavy emphasis is placed on communication and coordination. Duncan suggests several methods of enhancing "lateral relations"; i.e., communication between segmented components. These methods include direct contact with others involved, task forces to coordinate around a specific case or issue, liaison role in which one individual maintains contact representing many other individuals, and an integrator role in which one person is assigned to maintain contact with all others involved for the purpose of keeping everyone informed.

Duncan's model does not support the generalist practitioner who incorporates all of the specialties within one person. Realistically, a generalist framework is needed by all of the individual practitioners involved; yet the level of expertise and differential access to community resources requires that coordination between disparate individuals be maintained regardless of generalist training. No one individual could contain all of the necessary capabilities at the requisite level of mastery. However, the analysis does support the continued development of multiple skills by child and youth practitioners so that they become more fluent with the various levels of influence on the child or youth's situation (VanderVen, 1981).

CONCLUSIONS

Several conclusions of the above analysis present themselves concerning the trajectory of the field. First, child and youth work cannot isolate itself from other human service providers. Turf and territoriality only raise barriers to communication and coordination. Second, child and youth work must hold fast to its area of expertise. Child and youth practitioners will be seen as equal members of a differentiated team only if they have something unique and valuable to offer. Third, child and youth workers can play the "integrator" role in developing and maintaining lateral relations among the segmented components of the treatment effort. As the trends in the world of work become better recognized, agencies and individuals will be searching for ways to structure child and youth work into decentralized, egalitarian, semi-autonomous work teams. Child and youth workers can call upon their milieu experience to assume the integrator role in order to coordinate the team in the service of the child. Training and education institutions need to orient future child and youth workers to this role and its many skill requirements. An awareness of, and willingness to play, this role may lead to an expanded definition of child and youth work.

REFERENCES

Brendtro, L. K., & Ness, A. E. (1983). *Re-educating troubled youth: Environments for teaching and treatment*. New York: Aldine.

Duncan, R. (1979). What is the right organizational structure? *Organizational Dynamics*. Winter.

Ferguson, R. V., & Anglin, J. P. (1985). The child care profession: A vision for the future. *Child Care Quarterly*, *14*(2), 85-102.

Hackman, J. R. & Oldman, G. R. (1980). *Work redesign*. Reading, MA: Addison-Wesley.

Ouchi, W. G. (1981). *Theory Z*. Reading, MA: Addison-Wesley.

Peters, T. J., & Waterman, R. H. Jr. (1982). *In search of excellence*. New York: Harper & Row.

Taylor, F. V. (1911). *Scientific management*. New York: Harper.

VanderVen, K. D. (1981). Patterns of career development in group care. In Ainsworth, F., & Fulcher, L. C. (Eds.). *Group care for children*. (pp. 201-224). London: Tavistock Publications.

24

Cross-Cultural Perspectives in Residential Youthwork: The French Educateur and the American Child Care Worker

F. Herbert Barnes
Laurence Bourdon

ABSTRACT. A look at the similarities and differences between French educateurs and their counterparts in the U.S.A., reveals that American child care workers' roles and responsibilities are much more narrowly defined. The differences in training, role and practice definitions and professional orientations are some of the issues discussed in this chapter.

French educateurs, participants in the International Learning Exchange in Professional Youthwork (ILEX), have been working in the United States side-by-side with American child care workers and, from this shared experience, have observations about the role they have met here. Contrasting what they do here as American child care workers with what their profession expects them to do in France, they find their responsibilities here to be more narrowly

F. Herbert Barnes, Director, and Laurence Bourdon, participant, The International Learning Exchange in Professional Youthwork (ILEX), 17 South Street, Portland, ME 04101. The authors acknowledge the participation of the following ILEX participants in sharing the results of their perspective and their analysis of observations and experience: Jean-Luc Descourtis, Sophie Jannin and Vincent Nicolais.

defined and with considerably more emphasis on social control of children and basic caretaking of their residential unit.

Their experience in France, while including these basic elements, supports a much more complex set of responsibilities and a larger scope for the role. Both elements, they believe, have significant implications for the ability of residential treatment programs to define the milieu as a major therapeutic agent.

This chapter discusses these issues and suggests ways that child care workers in North America might enlarge the scope and depth of their role without conflicting with the therapeutic turf of any of the more dominant professional disciplines. Role expansion might be achieved through making more psycho-educational use of the activities of cottage living and the group's program, and through more clearly defining the responsibilities of the child care worker. In so doing, the views of the ILEX program participants will be augmented by a range of earlier comments made on the need for a larger and more professional definition of this role, as well as on previous considerations of the educateur's role and practice as a conceptual model for building the profession. The professional development of the educateur in France and the commitments there in training and certification that make such a level of practice possible will be presented to establish a clear understanding of the background of the visiting educateurs.

BACKGROUND OF VISITING EDUCATEURS

We will begin by outlining the basis of the participation of the four educateurs who have contributed to this paper.

The International Learning Exchange in Professional Youthwork (ILEX) was begun in 1983 through the joint sponsorship of the Center for Youth Development and Research of the University of Minnesota and Youthorizons, a non-profit youth services agency in Maine. The ILEX Program is directed specifically to the development of youthwork practice through collegial affiliation of trained professionals from other countries and American youthworkers working side-by-side as colleagues and fellow team members in the direct practice setting of American youth service agencies. The program is based in the belief that international sharing of knowledge and expertise in the field of child care and youthwork will promote:

- professional development of youthworkers—those staff members who work directly with youth in the living situation of residential programs and have responsibility for the treatment impact of that milieu, or staff members of community-based programs who carry cross-disciplinary responsibilities in a milieu treatment approach;
- enrichment of the field of child care and youthwork through cross-cultural experiences which can link practitioners and agencies in an on-going international relationship and forum.
- continuing advancement in quality of youth service programs through the direct worker-to-worker exchange of ideas, concepts for practice, and program models by professionals who are actively engaged in carrying out these programs and approaches.

The French contributors to this paper all are Educateurs Spécialisé, a French professional discipline that is now of some forty years standing. It had its beginnings in Europe, immediately following World War II, as a way of addressing youth needs which were so urgent as to be unable to be met by then existing approaches based in benign substitute care. Though the war-ravaged children needed care, they also needed emotional support which they could not accept, and they required behavioral interventions which custodial workers were totally unprepared to provide. Teams of young workers were sent by the French government to the United States to do intensive short-term study in education and social work and returned to devise treatment programs for children and training programs for workers. In 1945, conferences about disturbed children were held in Paris and in 1946, the first educateurs graduated from two different French schools. February 1967 saw the inception of the National Diploma for Educateurs Spécialisé based on a defined three-year training which incorporated previously sectorized training for work with delinquency, disturbance, deficiency and physical handicap. Today's training, requiring three years of full-time involvement, is one-half coursework and one-half applied learning (practicum). Significantly, coursework is not restricted to psychology, anatomy, sociology, law, policy, health, normal human development and pedagogy (the way to teach children and youth) but includes equivalent attention to the acquisition of new skills or the development of personal skills into curriculum resources such as sports, handicrafts, camping, cooking, sewing, art, physical education, games, techniques of animation, and techniques of expression.

The three years study leads to a final examination which is both oral and written and includes a review of the journal kept by the student over the entire three years, and a thesis prepared on a selected topic during the last year of training. Upon successful completion of the training and examination, a national certification is granted identifying the person as a professional educateur.

Though the group of participants involved in the preparation of this paper are all French, and all educateurs, it is interesting to note that France is not the only country with such a highly developed profession of youthwork and concomitant training to support it. In Denmark (where the worker is called an "orthopedagogue") and in Norway (where the worker is called a "barnevernpedagog"), pedagogy is defined as:

> the teaching about how psychological, social and material relationships and differing value orientations promote or hinder an individual's or group's total development and growth. That which characterizes social pedagogy is that it takes its starting point from aforementioned relationships and, with conscious methodic work over time in the client's environment, attempts to influence the individual or group to better social functioning and increased well-being. Social pedagogy includes curative and preventive work. (Norges Kommunal-Og-Sosialhogskole, 1985, p. 3)

The education of Danish and Norwegian workers is also a three-year professional study at the college level, including both course study and field work, and leads to the diploma in child welfare which is the basic credential for practice in the profession.

OVERALL OBSERVATIONS
OF THE VISITING EDUCATEURS

The visiting educateurs, participants in the 1985/86 ILEX Program year, were placed in agencies in New Hampshire, Maine and New York State. The perspective they share comes from the combining of their own training and experience with their experience here, as well as from a synthesis of the experience of other participants, a product of the program's Mid-Year Seminar. They felt that the child care worker in the U.S. "does not look like the French counterpart for a variety of reasons, among which are the lack of a required training and the lack of specific expectations towards a defined profession." They felt that the American child care worker is more often defined by what each individual agency wants child care workers to do rather than by any centrally held definitions which are then applicable broadly, or even licenseable, as in France. They likened this situation of being unable to account for what a child care worker really is and does to a famous remark of General DeGaulle, questioning his task when he assumed the presidency of the French Republic: "How do you propose to govern a country that has 436 different kinds of cheese?"

The French participants suggested that this question was the same question confronting the building of a profession here: How do you propose to define and build a profession with so many different names for the same thing—child care worker, residential advisor, group life supervisor, youth life educator, milieu therapist, house parent, cottage worker, child care counselor? In an earlier attempt to address this issue, Barnes and Kelman (1974) suggested the importance of formulating concepts for an educative model that utilizes the elements of daily living as curriculum for growth and behavioral change. Out of this proposal originated a conceptual design for the role and practice of a professional who could manage this curriculum and interrelate the helping processes of both the group and its component individuals. Albee (1968) proposed twenty years ago that this had not happened because we were in a "Manpower cul-de-sac" that has been generated by over-reliance on the "illness model of mental disorder" as the conceptual model for the design of services and professional roles. At the same time, the then president of the International Union for Child Welfare, Dan Mulock-Houwer, observed that:

> It is curious that the United States, which has had such an influence on Europe regarding case work and group work, is overdoing specialization but it is not giving the right instruction to the people who live twenty-four hours a day with the children in residential care. . . . The United States has been one of the least developed countries in the world in regard to providing a professional training program for residential child care workers. (Linton, 1971, p. 167)

Linton (1973) subsequently commented on this further by noting that in many treatment facilities, "the therapeutic intervention process is formally separated from the daily life activities of the child though it is far more realistic and in line with empirical evidence to make the two a completed integrated operation."

The director of a training school for educateurs in France commented on this same phenomenon on a visit to the United States. Jean Ughetto explained that in France these two functions are unified because of a conviction that

> the person who works with the child in the daily living situation is closest to the child and will be the person with whom the child most wants to share his feelings and his innermost fears and concerns, while the person who accepts those feelings, far from being neutral and remote, is best equipped to use that knowledge to help the child negotiate the demands of daily living and the exigencies of group interaction. (Ughetto, personal communication, 1971)

The educateur is strategically placed to do that.

We can chart the two orientations by illustrating first the role location which the non-professional care worker occupies.

As seen in Figure 1, this worker, who does not appear with the other specialist disciplines, is largely expected to supervise the children and maintain both social control and a climate conducive to treatment. It is interesting to note that one French educateur, given such an assignment during her ILEX year in an American agency,

Treatment & Care - Illness Orientation

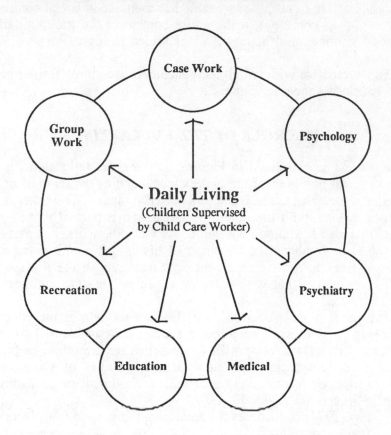

Fragmented Model in which the Child Care Worker or Youth Worker manages the daily living situation and provides social control while sending the children to individualized special services which are percieved to be the treatment.

FIGURE 1

was completely unable to carry out the task. There was simply not enough content in her role to enable her to maintain social control, which should come out of the entire content of the group's daily living, learning, and activity, all of which needs to involve the worker.

The alternative with which the educateurs are more familiar can be charted as shown in Figure 2.

THE ROLE OF THE EDUCATEUR

In the scheme outlined in Figure 2, the worker (educateur) is a fundamental part both of the child's world and of the team of professional specialists, and is the link between them. The worker is a co-professional with the other specialists and is part of that high-level therapeutic strategy ensemble. As well, the worker is part of the child or youth milieu by virtue of his unique position and responsibilities for providing on-the-spot treatment in the life-space and coordinating that with care, management, nurture and social control.

The International Association of Educateurs defines the educateur role as follows: "The job of a specialized educateur is to encourage character development in disturbed people while helping them to mature socially through various activities of situations, spontaneous or contrived, in a natural environment or an institution" (Ginger, 1971, pp. 19, 20).

Lemay (1974) contributes the following thinking to this elaboration of role:

> The specialized educateur lives continuously beside the disturbed child, sharing his difficulties and utilizing daily situations to lead him towards a gradual reorganization of his personality. He is identified in certain respects with the psychologist who looks for an understanding of human behavior, which can be a response to the needs of the maladjusted child; he also is like the social worker who searches in the wealth of his knowledge of social problems for that which can be adapted to the child's group and to the interrelationships developing within the core of the group. If the educateur is in a

Milieu Treatment - Integrated & Holistic Orientation

Integrated Model in which the joint action of children and educateurs provide care, social control, and treatment opportunities. Specialists are still used but as technical resourses outside the milieu.

FIGURE 2

certain sense a teacher who, instructing children in the art of living, has to interest himself in questions of discipline, regulations, the acquisition of habits, he is also a specialist in leisure time activities since it is useless to understand a child if one is unable to offer him activities to which his interest attaches. Finally he is a parent substitute with all those transference problems connected with his last role which he must recognize, control and utilize to the degree that is possible. (pp. 6 & 7)

The ILEX participants, from their own experience, identify the educateur as:

Having a central role in the client's treatment. Depending on the situation, the educateur is a role model, a parental substitute, and a society representative. But first and foremost, the educateur is a technician of the relationship and the environment and one who takes advantage of both to intervene in a therapeutic way.

In managing the milieu, they see the worker having three responsibilities:

1. organizer — setting up situations;
2. animator — helping the clients to get involved in activities;
3. utilizer — using the clients' reactions in a therapeutic way.

These three dimensions are seen as being present even in the simplest acts of the daily life which should not be understood merely as cottage routines or, worse, as chores. Daily life provides a real wealth of opportunities to help the clients in their task of growing up, in feeling more confident with themselves, and in functioning more productively with higher levels of satisfaction and efficiency. A client who begins to take care of his appearance and who now experiences pleasure in this makes as great a victory for the professional as the milestone of progress he provides for himself. Serge Ginger, who chaired the Technical Committee of the International Association of Educateurs (AIEJI) and directed residential treatment programs in France, describes the educateur role and its operation in terms of its aims and means:

Where the aims are concerned, it is a question of acting on a person in light of a social environment to help the individual to become himself while still being one of the group but not necessarily conforming.

Where the means are concerned, it is a question of overall action through constant contact based on a more or less shared day-to-day existence; a constant contact practitioner. (Ginger, 1971)

Today's educateurs endorse the concept of the "constant contact practitioner" and in their experiences and observations here, note many settings where this kind of practice is taking place. They bemoan, however, that these dynamic definitions with truly professional performance expectations are an idiosyncratic function of individual agency definition rather than being universal. They recommend a definition that sees the milieu worker, by whatever name, as a specialist among specialists whose specialty is being a generalist. This generalist characteristically uses all of the opportunities of the environment to promote individual growth and welfare and builds a close relationship with children through being a full part of the children's lives. This relationship uses all of the worker's skills and requires openness, authenticity, honesty, lucidity, and human caring.

THE EDUCATEUR AND ACTIVITIES

The visiting educateurs also suggest that an approach to building the above professional definition might be found in implementing a more dynamic definition of activities. Their experience suggests that an important practice difference exists between themselves and many of their American colleagues in how activities and routines of daily life are perceived. Building further on the points made earlier by Linton and Ughetto, they see involvement in these daily events as high-order professional tasks so that the activity is much more than a good way to burn up some energy or have the cottage be clean. Activities of daily life are really a tool for the development of children and the implementation of goal objectives that have been defined as necessary to the work with the group and the individuals.

The educateurs' involvement with these activities and aspects of daily life is much less for control purposes and more for educational purposes. However, it is out of the entire matrix that social control, as well as group and individual development, take place.

It is much less likely, given this concept of practice, to find in France a separation between living and treating, or a perception that some activities are merely recreational while others are therapeutic. Lemay (1974) makes the point that:

> the educational program and the life milieu play a therapeutic role themselves when utilized in a coordinated and well thought-out manner. . . . The content of the program is no longer the essential matter, although it plays an important part in the establishment of the educative relationship. The adult in charge looks to create a way of living in order to evoke a new way of acting. (pp. 27-28)

Elsewhere in this volume, Arieli, Beker, and Kashti reference this point as they note the value of "expressive curriculum" as a means of producing alternative opportunities for achievement. In the work previously cited by Barnes and Kelman, curriculum is seen as the combination of specific activities, routines, regular jobs necessary to group survival, and special projects that evolve in the context of group life. As workers share in the living situation and in its curriculum directly with children it becomes "not child-centered but people-centered and no longer an aggregate of children who are off-duty from their clinical hours . . . a laboratory for kids' learning which includes both learning and learning to learn" (Barnes & Kelman, 1974).

OTHER SETTINGS

Though this sharing and utilizing of daily life is a primary responsibility of the educateur in residential treatment, it is not the only setting in which this approach is applicable. Educateurs may also be found in daycare and treatment settings where their skills in participating directly in the milieu are well expressed. The ability to manage a milieu, to assist people in finding useful activity and to enable their interacting helpfully and supportively has now propelled educateurs into community and in-home services to children and families in order to prevent removal of children from home. Educateurs have moved as well into preventive work where they use their skills as organizer, animator and utilizer to meet children and youth in their own social environment. They provide support and leadership designed to help youth to resist becoming enmeshed in drugs, alcoholism, prostitution and crime. As one visiting educateur, Jean-Luc, described this role: "I am an educateur on the back stairways in the worst neighborhood of Paris." Philosophically, this is a logical extension of practice for workers who perceive their competence as relationship and environmental specialists who have the ability to use both these elements in therapeutic interventions. The same skills needed to work in residential settings are applicable in other service delivery settings and, indeed, it is this portability of the discipline which gives it credibility as a profession.

CONCLUSIONS

The American child care scene, as viewed by visiting professional child care workers (educateurs) from France, is perceived as globally unconceptualized and lacking coordination of many very interesting definitions of the task developed by different agencies. The educateurs observe that an American child care worker's lot in life as a professional is determined in the main by the agency of employment. Child care workers have the role that the agency determines. This is quite different when contrasted with their home country where a professional determination for this work had its beginnings as early as 1945 and now exists as a nationally certified discipline for which there are clear definitions of role and practice, and forty training schools to prepare people for entrance into the profession. Because of different professional priorities and, therefore, a different evolution of services and manpower, the conceptual model of American child care work is not nearly as developed as the conceptual model of the educateur. Similarly, the elements of practice for which the American worker is responsible are not as clear as those for his counterparts in France.

Though the building of clear conceptual models for both role and practice is a task that a number of agencies have elected to work on, coordination among these efforts is lacking and, in many situations, there still appear to be questions about defining child care work as professional. Alt (1969) specifically addressed this problem years ago in a paper advocating the development of a technology in child care:

> Those who harbor doubts about the usefulness of a defined body of practice for a function such as child care contend that child rearing is an art and contributes most to child growth when it is performed by adults intuitively capable of constructive parental attitudes and behavior. It is our view, however, that the value we place on expanding and improving technology in this field does not minimize the concept of child care as an art. All arts incorporate technical skills that need to be learned by those who practice them. As a matter of fact, the utilization of such skills can serve to enhance spontaneity and intuitive response.

Such a technology, clearly defined and broadly accepted, would seem from the international observations of our visitors from France to be a critical ingredient for a more sophisticated development of child care work. And perhaps in North America we have now a sufficiently similar emergency situation comparable to that which confronted post-war children and youth in Europe and which gave rise to the educateur. Perhaps it is time to build a similar profession in North America. The social emergency presented by increasing numbers of physically and sexually abused children, adolescent pregnancies, unemployed youth and violent crimes committed by children at progressively younger ages, coupled with the desire to serve children in less restrictive settings which are more normalizing in their context and more developmental in their purpose, may well indicate that the time is right to recognize the need for building a profession of transdisciplinary workers who, like their colleagues in Europe, can be "technicians of the relationship and the environment."

REFERENCES

Albee, G. (1968). Conceptual models and manpower requirements in psychology. *American Psychologist, 23,* 317-320.

Alt, H. (1969). Toward a technology of child care for children in residence. *Mental Hygiene, 53*(4).

Barnes, F.H., & Kelman, S.M. (1974). From slogans to concepts: A basis for change in child care work. *Child Care Quarterly, 3,* 7-30.

Ginger, S. (1971). "The problem-educateur," social unrest. *International Child Welfare Review, 9* (no vol.), 17-23.

Lemay, M. (1974). *The Functions of the Specialized Educateur for Maladjusted Youth* (V. Jarvis, Trans.). Brewster, NY: Green Chimneys Children's Services and the Edwin Gould Foundation for Children.

Linton, T.E. (1971). The educateur model: A theoretical monograph. *The Journal of Special Education, 5*(2), 155-190.

Linton, T.E. (1973). Services for "problem" children: Contrasts and solutions. *International Journal of Mental Health, 2*(1), 3-14.

Norges Kommunal-op Sosialhogskole (Norwegian State College of Public Administration and Social Work). (1985). Curriculum of Study for Diploma in Child Welfare. Oslo: Author

25

Taxonomy and Treatment:
The Role of the Scientist Practitioner
in Child and Youth Care

Christopher Bagley
Loretta Young

ABSTRACT. Child and youth care stands at the threshold of a development in which the movement to full professional status involves, among other things, the initiation of and participation in, descriptive, taxonomic, evaluative and follow-up research of programs for children and youth. It is argued, in particular, that if progress is to be made, then there must be a fit between carefully-designed programs and clearly-defined client groups. This principle is illustrated by a taxonomic analysis of data on 518 residents at two residential centers for emotionally-disturbed children and youth. A special study has been made of 58 adopted children within this population: these 58 children can be allocated to at least eight different groups, each identifying a different pattern of adoption breakdown and psychological need in the child. The implications for child care programming are discussed.

A true professional is constantly reflecting on the technicalities of his or her craft, thinking about why and how certain techniques work, how practice can be improved, evaluating techniques of intervention in controlled or natural experiments, and reporting on

Christopher Bagley, Professor, Faculty of Social Welfare, University of Calgary, 2500 University Drive N.W., Calgary, Alberta T2N 1N4 and Loretta Young, Social Worker, Alberta Children's Hospital, 1820 Richmond Road S.W., Calgary, Alberta T2T 5C7.

new developments and techniques, in professional journals. The degree to which a profession does this is a sure indicator of its maturity, effectiveness and status. A semi-profession is one in which members accept passively, or at least without rational criticism, activities for working with client groups. In a semi-profession, members innovate, if at all, intuitively rather than rationally; in such a profession, members do not reflect on or write about professional development and they rarely try and understand the nature of the clients they are serving, through, for example, statistical analysis and description. Members of such a semi-profession rarely undertake systematic evaluations of practice, or undertake follow-up work with clients. Such a semi-profession has low status, little say when it comes to decisions about the admission, referral and disposition of clients, and is poorly paid.

There is evidence that child and youth care workers in Canada are strongly motivated to leave behind this semi-professional status. A significant development in this respect was the First National Child Care Workers' Conference held at the University of Victoria in 1981. Hundreds of child care workers from across Canada attended this Conference, and among the developments which emerged was the founding of the *Journal of Child Care*, a professional outlet for Canadian child care workers. The influence of this Journal (now edited from the newly-founded professional child care centre, the Hull Institute in Calgary) extends not only across Canada, but also to the United States. The *Journal of Child Care* has had a particular role in encouraging front-line child care workers to write about professional problems and program developments.

THE CHILD CARE WORKER
AS SCIENTIST PRACTITIONER

The type of role for child care workers which we are advocating is that of scientist-practitioner, a role which has emerged in psychiatry and psychology, but which is still struggling to emerge in the child care profession. Ideally, the professional should be not merely a practitioner; rather, he or she should constantly describe, analyze and evaluate the basis for practice. The ultimate aim, of course, is to improve the service given to clients.

Jung and his child care colleagues (Jung, Bernfeld, Coneybeare & Fernandes, 1984) have described how this scientific-practitioner model can work, using the example of group psychotherapy for adolescents in residential child care. As these authors note:

> While adolescent group psychotherapy is a popular and accepted form of treatment, there is little research on the process of adolescent group therapy—that is, how and why it works. (pp. 16-17)

These authors designed or adapted a number of measures which showed the various processes in group therapy at work over a six-month period. Over this period, it was found that there were consistent increases in frequency of positively-oriented task and group behaviors, while no changes were found in the frequency of individual, negative behaviors.

> Another finding indicated that both the observer and group leader ratings of group development reliably increased, thus validating the increase in observed group behaviour. Ratings of both the adolescents' verbal and non-verbal functioning also showed an improvement over time. Pre-post ratings of group leader behaviour . . . indicated a decrease in their control-directiveness and an increase in the group-oriented questions they asked. (Jung et al., 1984, p. 21)

These systematic investigations by a team of child and youth care workers showed not only what the processes of group therapy were, but also how the process was succeeding in some aspects and not in others (lack of change in some negative behaviors). This study pointed to, but did not investigate, some other pertinent research questions—for example, how did changes of individual behavior in the group relate to other behavioral changes in the child care facility, and to long-term changes in behavior and adjustment, following discharge from the facility?

Systematic follow-up of the clients of child care and child welfare agencies is still the most crucial, and the most neglected aspect of child care work. Systematic efforts in this respect have been both interesting and discouraging (Bagley & McDonald, 1984; Hunter,

Webster, Konstantareas, & Sloman, 1982; Pettifor, Perry, Plowman, & Pitcher, 1983). These studies, combined with case history data (Allison, 1984; Popp, 1983; Bagley, 1985) do suggest, however, that much child care activity is often irrelevant and in some cases dysfunctional, neglectful or actually harmful. As Jung et al. (1984) emphasize, if we are to serve "the best interests of the child" we must, as child care professionals, constantly re-evaluate and seek to improve the basis for practice and professional service.

ASSESSMENT AND TAXONOMY OF RESEARCH TASKS FOR CHILD CARE

Before we can treat adequately, before we can evaluate, predict and follow up, some more basic tasks have to be performed systematically. These initial tasks include a full and systematic assessment of our child care clients; and secondly, a systematic classification or taxonomy of clients must be undertaken. As Luborsky, Chandler, Averbach, Chandler and Jacobs (1971) have observed in their analysis of outcomes of psychotherapy, if counseling is to be effective, the type of treatment has to be systematically matched with the type of client. Likewise, to be effective as child care workers, we must know how to classify the majority of our clients into clearly-defined sub-groups, in order to innovate and evaluate appropriate treatment. Indeed, this is an essential beginning task in any scientific enterprise: we need to know how the phenomena under study can break down into smaller groups. Psychiatry, of course, has long since recognized this fact, and much enterprise has been devoted to diagnostic and statistical classification in this profession. While some of our child welfare clients can be classified according to psychiatric criteria, many cannot, and we need to measure developmental, social background and interpersonal variables connected with symptom clusters (Bagley, Jacobsen, & Rehin, 1976).

An excellent account of the critical role of assessment in child care has been presented by Altrows (1983). These assessments include, not only the results of formal testing and observation when the child is first seen, but also the recording of hypotheses of how treatment might proceed and the making of process and outcome measures in such treatments. Altrows advises child care workers to:

. . . advocate the use of research methods, keeping systematic records of test results and recording selected measures when treatment programs are employed. These are unobtrusive ways of helping to direct future activity. It is no longer meaningful to ask whether child care and treatment programs ought to be evaluated. In fact, they are continually evaluated: by politicians, the press and the public. They also ought to be carefully examined by persons more directly involved in the field! (Altrows, 1983, p. 74)

It is the argument of this chapter, that the efficiency of treatment can be improved if, in addition to unique methods tailored to fit the picture which an individual presents, we are able to specify some common types of "syndromes" of childhood and adolescent disorder which are experienced in child care settings, and if in addition, we are able to devise and evaluate specific therapies for these subtypes.

A Taxonomic Study

The study which we will briefly report here was undertaken at two residential centers for acutely-disturbed or deviant children and adolescents in Calgary, Alberta. The case notes of 518 individuals admitted over a five-year period were carefully screened, and a wide range of information was abstracted. Inter-rater reliability was established for the judgements of the four people involved in abstracting these data (Young, 1985). Data collected included socio-demographic, family, scholastic and behavioral variables.

First of all, correlational and principle components analyses were undertaken of the behavioral pictures presented by the children (Nie, Hull, Jenkins, Steinbrenner, & Brent, 1975). Four main clusters of components emerged. These are as follows:

Component I: *Delinquency* including:

- Serious offenses (theft over $200.00; break and enter, etc.);
- Sexual delinquency (including prostitution);
- Use of drugs;
- Running from home;
- Fire-setting (before running or soon after);

- Hyperactivity (before running);
- Aggression to both mother and father;
- Demographically: usually adolescent on admission; males and females equally represented.

Component II: *Organic Problems* including:

- Neurological signs on medical examination;
- Prior medication for C.N.S. problem;
- Hyperactivity;
- Aggression to peer/siblings;
- Running from home;
- School problems (refusal to attend/suspended);
- Fire-setting;
- Encopresis or enuresis;
- Speech problems;
- Demographically: usually pre-adolescent on admission; Eighty percent males.

Component III: *Depression* including:

- Clear signs of depression;
- Suicidal behavior or gestures;
- Sexual acting-out (promiscuity, prostitution);
- Use of drugs;
- Demographically: usually adolescent on admission; Eighty percent females.

Component IV: *Running From Home* including:

- Running from home (strongest loading item);
- Aggression to father;
- Fire-setting;
- Sexual acting-out;
- Demographically: no clear age trends; Sixty-five percent males.

While some of these behavioral profiles are intuitively obvious (and are reflected in such formal procedures as cottage allocation), the particular combination of symptoms could not have been easily predicted. Some symptoms failed to load significantly on these four components—for example, children in all four groups showed diminished self-esteem, and this variable had no particular relevance for classification. But previous fire-setting (a characteristic of only nine percent of children overall) does emerge as a significant variable on two of the components.

Analysis of background factors indicated that significant antecedents of Component I (Delinquent Behavior) were: marital separation in the three-year period prior to admission; mental health or behavior problems in mother (but not father) in three years before admission; gross instability and marital conflict in an intact home prior to child's admission; prior physical abuse; harsh, authoritarian discipline of child; and presence of a step-parent. The disturbed behavior in this group is wholly explicable in terms of family disruption, combined with various kinds of abuse in the family setting.

Antecedents of Component II (Organic Problems) included both physical and sexual abuse of the child. It appeared that the child's early maladaption (reflecting an organic syndrome likely related to neonatal trauma) had led the child to be scapegoated and abused.

Antecedents of Component III (Depression and Suicidal Behavior) included the presence of a step-father, sexual abuse of child (often by her step-father), mental health problems of mother, absence of mother, and unrealistic academic expectations by a parent.

Antecedents of Component IV (Running From Home) include mental health problems or alcohol abuse in a parent, family disruption, physical or sexual abuse, and harsh and authoritarian discipline.

It should be stressed that the principal components method classifies *variables* relating to individuals, rather than the individuals themselves. Thus, an individual child could be represented on both Component I (Delinquency) and Component IV (Running).

The classification of individuals involves a further process, examining individual scores on each main component of behavior, and carrying out a cluster analysis with individuals, rather than variables as the units of analysis.

The present study (which is reported here as an example of how taxonomic research can help child care practitioners, rather than as an example of completed research per se) had a particular aim of identifying the problems of adopted children in child care settings (Young, 1985). It was found that 61 (11.7%) children in the two residential centers had been adopted, compared with an expected four percent (based on the number of adopted children of similar age in the general population). Relatively complete data were available for 58 of the 61 adopted children and a cluster analysis of individual cases was undertaken (see Table 1). The cluster analysis allows quite small groups to be identified which are uniquely different from all other groups. While it is not the purpose of this chapter to design or discuss treatment strategies, it is obvious that classifying children according to clusters of current problems, together with antecedent circumstances, implies both strategies for prevention and avenues for treatment.

These eight sub-clusters collapse logically into four major clusters (see Table 2); Type A (11 cases) represents children adopted early in life; Type B (13 cases) groups children adopted past infancy, with a history of previous trauma, and who are currently depressed and suicidal; Type C (9 cases) represents children who suffered abuse within their adoptive homes; and Type D represents children who were adopted by a step-father (but who were never separated from their mother), and who are now delinquent and aggressive in the community. It should be noted that nine children (15%) could not be classified in any taxonomic analysis; there will always be some unique cases which defy classification, and which present a particular challenge to child care workers.

Treatment Implications

Treatment in child care needs to meet the specific needs of the client, and has to be as individualized as possible. Taxonomic analysis can be of considerable help in this task. For example, if we can identify children in Group A (neurological problems) we already know that medical treatment and assessment are vital, and systemic observations of how behavior may change in relation to medication are important. Behavior modification techniques can often be useful too for such children. Family problems often reflect rather than cause behavioral problems in the child, though often there has been a negative cycle of mutual reinforcements. The purpose of family therapy is to break this cycle, giving the parents a set of coping skills which can enable the child to return to the family, with consistent medical, emergency and relief-time support. Adoptive par-

TABLE 1

Cluster Analysis of 58 Adopted Children in

Residential Care for Maladjusted Children

Cluster I - 11 cases

Age: younger;
Age of onset of behavioural problems (younger);
Symptom cluster: hyperactivity, neurological problems; lower IQ, aggressive to peers/siblings;
Health problems early in life, and still persisting;
Child difficult in infancy (restless, crying, slow in milestones);
Adoptive mother's poor mental health (depression);
Child's age at adoption (younger);
Sex: male.

Cluster II - 9 cases

Gross marital tension in home in three years before child's admission;
Step-father;
Mental health/behavioural problems in father;
Inconsistent discipline, veering from lax to harsh, without rational cause;
Age of onset of behavioural problems (older);
Child has been unable to relate or bond to step-father;
Symptom cluster: Delinquency; running; drug use.

Cluster III - 9 cases

Child has experience of marked physical abuse and neglect prior to adoption;
Child had problems in bonding to adoptive parents;
Age adopted: older;
Mental health/behavioural problems in father (in 4 out of 5 cases in biological father);
Mental health/behavioural problems in mother (in 3 out of 5 cases in biological mother);
Parents have unrealistically high academic expectations for child;
Child has experienced sexual abuse prior to adoption;
Symptom cluster: Anxiety/depression; suicidal behaviour; sexual acting-out;
Child sexually abused in the community after adoption.

Cluster IV - 5 cases

Sex: male;
Number of other adopted children in family: more;
Age of onset of behavioural problems: younger;
Behavioural problems in sibling(s);
Discipline consistently harsh and authoritarian;
Social status of family: lower;
Symptom cluster: Delinquent; runs; drug use.

TABLE 1 (continued)

Cluster V - 4 cases

　　Social status of family: higher;
　　Age of onset of behaviour problems: older;
　　Adoption of a foster child;
　　Number of other adopted children in family: more;
　　Symptom cluster: Anxiety/depression; suicidal behaviour

Cluster VI - 4 cases

　　Suspicion of sexual abuse in family;
　　Discipline harsh and authoritarian;
　　Age at adoption: older
　　Number of biological children of adopting parent(s): more;
　　Symptom cluster: Delinquent; runs; drug use.

Cluster VII - 4 cases

　　Gross marital tension in home in three years before admission;
　　Sex: female;
　　Age at onset of behaviour problems: older;
　　Symptom cluster: Aggression to mother; aggression to father;
　　Symptom cluster: Anxiety/depression; suicidal behaviour; sexual
　　acting-out;
　　Suspicion of sexual abuse in existing family.

Cluster VIII - 3 cases

　　Mother single parent when child five or younger;
　　Death of father;
　　Step-father at present time;
　　Symptom cluster: Delinquent; runs; drug use;
　　Age: older;
　　Behavioural problems in a sibling;
　　Age behavioural problems began: older.

Note:　Characteristics assigned to clusters if more than half of the cases
　　　　possessed the characteristic. For symptom or behavioural group-
　　　　ings, at least two of the symptoms had to be present in a marked
　　　　degree for the behavioural cluster to be assigned to the group.
　　　　Rank of listing within each group reflects prevalence of item in
　　　　association with the cluster.

ents often experience a great amount of guilt over problems which
may not be their fault: they are usually anxious to welcome the child
after residential treatment, and attempt rebonding.

　　Parents of children in Group B (children with prior disruption
adopted past infancy) also have considerable emotional investment
in making the adoption work, and should be involved as closely as

TABLE 2

Groupings of Clusters of 58 Adopted Children

Cluster I	Cluster III plus Cluster V	Cluster IV plus Cluster VII	Cluster II plus Cluster VI plus Cluster VIII
becomes	becomes	becomes	becomes
GROUP A (11 cases)	GROUP B (13 cases)	GROUP C (9 cases)	GROUP D (16 cases)
"Neurological problems in children adopted in infancy; hyperactivity"	"Children adopted past infancy; previous trauma; depressed and suicidal"	"Abuse in adoptive home"	"Adoption by step-parent; delinquency in child"

Unclassified: 9 cases undifferentiated by any behavioural profile.

possible in continuing specific therapies initiated by the child care team. For Group D, dysfunctional relationships with a step-parent present special challenges for the child and youth care worker, which we will not elaborate here. Similarly, Group C, who have experienced abuse after being adopted, require therapy which addresses these experiences. Return to the adoptive family is not automatic in such cases.

CONCLUSIONS

As Krueger (1982) has argued, if child care workers are to be truly professional, they must be involved with research at some level. Of course, as Krueger argues, this research role is always a secondary one to the child care worker's primary roles—those of treatment of children, and the administration and organization of child care facilities and programs. However, research has to be an essential aid to this process, since only by systematic measurement, assessment and evaluation can we increase the efficiency of these core professional roles.

Beker (1979) has observed that the need for child workers to become involved in research at some level has clear implications for training and education. We suggest the following: at the diploma level of education, child care workers should understand the importance of research, and be able, with supervision, to collect research data. At the bachelor's degree level, they should be able to read, understand, and criticize research articles, collect data on their own initiative, and conduct straightforward data analyses. At the master's level, child care workers should have a clear understanding of research and analysis (both qualitative and quantitative), and should be able to initiate and supervise research programs in their fields of speciality.

Such educational programs in Canada are still the exception rather than the rule. Krueger's observation, made in 1982, is still highly relevant today:

> It's time that child care workers, program managers and instructors throw aside their doubts and concerns about research. They can and must be overcome. The field is crying out for the knowledge base enrichment that only child care workers can provide. (p. 64)

REFERENCES

Allison, J. (1984). The Who Cares young people. *Journal of Child Care, 2*(2), 59-66.

Altrows, I. (1983). The discovery of the child: The critical role of assessment in child care. *Journal of Child Care, 1*(3), 65-76.

Bagley, C. (1985). Child abuse by the child welfare system. *Journal of Child Care, 2*, 63-69.

Bagley, C. & McDonald, M. (1984). Adult mental health sequels of child sexual abuse, physical abuse and neglect in maternally separated children, *Canadian Journal of Community Mental Health, 3*, 15-26.

Bagley, C., Jacobsen, S., & Rehin, A. (1976). Suicide: A taxonomic study. *Psychological Medicine, 6*, 424-438.

Beker, J. (1979). Child care education and the trainers. *Child Care Quarterly, 8*, 159-160.

Beker, J. & Baizerman, M. (1982). Professionalism in child and youth care and the content of work. *Journal of Child Care, 1*(1), 11-20.

Hunter, D., Webster, C., Konstantareas, M., & Sloman, L. (1982). Children in day treatment: A child care follow-up study. *Journal of Child Care, 1*(1), 45-58.

Jung, C., Bernfeld, G., Coneybeare, S., & Fernandes, L. (1984). Toward a scientific-practitioner model of child care. *Journal of Child Care, 2*(1), 13-26.

Krueger, M. (1982). Child care involvement in research. *Journal of Child Care*, *1*(1), 59-615.

Luborsky, L., Chandler, M., Averbach, A., & Cohen, J. (1971). Factors influencing the outcome of psychotherapy: A review of quantitative research. *Psychological Bulletin*, *75*, 145-184.

Nie, N., Hull, C., Jenkins, J., Steinbrenner, K., & Brent, D. (1975). *Statistical package for the social sciences*. New York: McGraw Hill.

Pettifor, J., Perry, D., Plowman, B., & Pitcher, S. (1983). Risk factors predicting childhood and adolescent suicides. *Journal of Child Care*, *1*(3), 17-50.

Popp, J. (1983). Leaving care: A personal account. *Journal of Child Care*, *1*(5), 73-79.

Ricks, F. & Charlesworth, J. (1982). Role and function of child care workers. *Journal of Child Care*, *1*, 35-44.

Young, L. (1983). *Adjustment in adoption*. The University of Calgary: Unpublished M.S.W. thesis.

26

From Two Years to Two Generations: Expanded Career Options in Direct Child and Youth Care Practice

Karen VanderVen

ABSTRACT. A full profession includes roles in both direct and indirect career functions for its members. As the field of child and youth care has developed, career paths for practitioners primarily focusing on indirect functions have been proposed. This chapter proposes a career trajectory in clinical work that allows for increasingly responsible, complex and autonomous practice as the practitioner becomes more mature and experienced both personally and professionally. Actualization of both career path options should contribute towards the retention of practitioners, and to the long term advancement of child and youth care as a profession.

NEED FOR DIRECT PRACTICE CAREER OPTIONS IN CHILD CARE

"You're going to be a child and youth care worker? Well—that's great—I hear it's interesting and certainly worthwhile work. But what is it like and what kind of future is there in it? I heard that most people don't stay in child care more than 2 years, and of those that do, most end up as administrators. There's no way to be able to work with kids the rest of your life."

Two years. Everyone in child care is familiar with the notion that

Karen VanderVen, Professor, Program in Child Development and Child Care, School of Social Work, University of Pittsburgh, 1717 F Cathedral of Learning, Pittsburgh, PA 15260.

direct line child care workers have about a two-year period of job longevity. New practitioners learn via the "grapevine" that they can be expected to stay in direct child care not more than two years almost as quickly as they learn the names of the children on their units.

Frequent job turnover or *short job longevity* in child care presents a serious problem to both individual practitioners and to the field as a whole. However, it is by no means insoluble, since there are now *career path options in child care that can enable long term career development*. If child care workers are aware of these career possibilities, and of the qualifications they must have, or develop, in order to achieve them, both individual satisfaction in the field, and the number of sophisticated practitioners who can contribute to its ongoing advancement, have the potential to increase.

BACKGROUND

Issues in Worker Retention
and Career Path Options

Job Turnover. Frequent job turnover has negative implications for children and youth, child care practitioners, and the field itself. Loss of those staff whose major function is to provide predictability and stability in primary care and in relationships obviously diminished the overall quality of service to children and youth. Furthermore, in a field already beleaguered by economic constraints, costs are escalated by the need to continually recruit, hire, and orient new child care practitioners.

Indirect Practice Career Paths. It has often been said in order to remain in child care at all, and to attain any increased responsibility and remuneration, that it is necessary for practitioners to move away from direct to indirect practice in such activities as supervision, administration, and teaching of other adults. The fact that it is important for persons in these roles in child care to actually come from the front-line ranks has been underscored by others, including this writer, who has previously described career path options in "indirect" work (Vander Ven, 1980; 1981).

Direct Practice Career Paths. However, to fail to have opportunity for practitioners to achieve long-term careers in *direct* practice is to compromise the development of a field into a full profession. Rather, it will remain in the form of a "semi-profession." The "semi-professions" are human service fields such as nursing, teaching, and social work. They are practiced in bureaucratic, hierarchical settings in which direct service is tightly supervised. In order to achieve increased compensation, status, and responsibility, the practitioner must move sequentially away from direct client contact into supervisory and managerial roles (Etzioni, 1969). This, it is important to underscore, is different from the case of "full professions" such as law and medicine which allow practitioners to deliver direct clinical service throughout a life time. They are retained in the profession because the clinical practice option allows for increasingly responsible and autonomous practice. The importance of extended "direct" practice careers as well as for managerial tracks has been recognized in the business sector as well as the human services (Deutsch, 1986).

That a career path which serves as an "elaboration and extension" of the entry level of direct child care work is needed to accompany those proposed for indirect work has been underscored by Thomas (1982, p. 147). To have one would certainly seem to be one way of attacking the multiple problems for children, workers, and the profession as a whole that are generated by short job longevity in direct work in child care. Although this writer has previously suggested such career paths (VanderVen, 1985 a; 1985 b), they have not been formally published.

PURPOSE

This chapter will therefore describe a model for expanded, long term career options in *direct* clinical child and youth care work. Hopefully it should prove useful to those who are embarking on work in the field to recognize the many opportunities that are actually possible for gratifying and increasingly challenging careers. The model is based on the concept that different skills and attributes, such as ways of thinking about problems encountered in the course of work, are related to the ability to perform at different career levels, and that the ongoing process of development as an adult encourages the acquisition of these abilities. The concept of adult development, implying personal growth throughout life, supports the notion that advancing levels of practice that involve greater responsibility and more complex functions, require the abilities that increasingly unfold in a maturing person.

THE MODEL FOR EXPANDED CAREER OPTIONS IN DIRECT CHILD AND YOUTH CARE PRACTICE

The model for expanded career options in direct child and youth care practice will be presented in three sequential, increasingly responsible and demanding stages: *Initial, Informed,* and *Complex* (VanderVen, 1988). For each, a comprehensive description will be provided that includes the scope and context of practice at that stage, including clients served, sites and location of practice, and interventions utilized: the attributes and skills required of practitioners, the kind of supervision involved, and the job functions that can be filled.

Stage 1—Initial Practice: The Beginning Direct Line Practitioner

General Description

Stage 1, Initial Practice, is the entry, or beginning level, of child care work. Almost all practitioners at this stage are involved in *direct care*, usually in a group setting. Their decision to enter child care is frequently based on a planned choice and wish to pursue a career working with children and youth, and is determined by practitioners' own childhood experiences that are the origins of strong personal motivations to do so (VanderVen, 1980). However, there are some who take a position in child care simply to provide financial support while they prepare for another field.

The initial experience may play a major role in determining whether these practitioners remain and subsequently move on to more advanced activities, or whether they indeed leave within two years or so. Practitioners at the *Initial Stage* differ widely in educational preparation. Some taking this first major (full time) position may have no more than a high school diploma; others may have some informal training. At this stage in their lives, they are concerned with *establishing* a career (Hall, 1986) whether or not they expect it in the long run to be in child care.

Scope and Functions of Practice

Clients. At this stage, the worker is most likely to work with groups of children or youth within their daily living situation. Should the setting be one in which there are exceptional children with special needs for behavior management, the newer practitioners will usually be assigned to work with those who are comparatively "easy." Entry level workers in general do not work with children's families, or with professionals outside of the immediate work setting. In some settings they may have little active participation in the clinical team effort of treatment planning; an unfortunate occurrence since these child care workers can bring fresh observation and enthusiasm to the team, as well as use it as a learning situation for their own professional development.

Settings. Organized group settings specifically operating to provide care to children are the primary site of practice of those in Stage 1.

Interventions. Direct line practitioners at the Initial stage are generalists forming relationships with individual children and youths within the group context, and providing direct group care and activities in the daily milieu. They are not likely, at this stage, to work in identifying and securing community resources and to set developmental care plans. At Stage 1, child care workers' practices are pitched at the *behavioral* level. That is, they are oriented to hygienically managing children's behavior as it is occurring in the immediate situation. It should be stressed that this is an invaluable service: to provide children with a nurturant, orderly, safe and stimulating living situation is indeed the basic core of the child care function.

At Stage 1, practitioners customarily are appropriately closely supervised. What they lack in experience or formal knowledge is often filled in by "common sense" or their own memories as to how things were done when they were children. They may be directly responsible to a senior child care worker (a preferable situation), to a director of a clinical discipline in the setting (e.g., nursing or social work), or to a unit director, reflecting the fact that child care, on its way to becoming a semi-profession, is still primarily practiced in hierarchical settings, at least by those in the Initial Stage. These practitioners are team members (assuming that their programs utilize the team approach). In this capacity they can provide, as already mentioned, valuable observations and possibly suggestions in team planning, but in general do not give leadership to this effort or make major conceptual contributions.

Cognitive and Affective Attributes

Depending to some extent on the life experience and educational preparation of entry practitioners, they bring varying degrees of "professionalism" to their work. By definition, "professionalism" in child care is practice that is informed by knowledge of children's developmental dynamics and needs, and of specific skills for relating to them. At best, non-professional practice is hygienic (does not harm) and supportive; at worst, it can reflect attitudes and actions that actually are harmful.

In general, Stage 1 practitioners are most likely to feel that "common sense," "love of kids," and, for older workers, "having raised children of my own" is sufficient background for handling the tasks of daily practice. Often these "good feelings" underlie valuable contributions, but these practitioners usually will not know *why* they handled a situation a certain way, will not be able to explain it to somebody else, and may not, therefore, be able to repeat the action in a subsequent occurrence of a similar situation.

Most Stage 1 practitioners are still "close" to their own childhood and its related issues. As a result, they are closely identified with *children* and their needs. This may result in "rescue fantasy" behavior in which novices "take on the pain" of a specific child or children—often those who are most vulnerable, needy, or demanding of attention. Initial stage practitioners usually eschew the possibility of movement into indirect practice (VanderVen, 1980).

The Stage 1 practitioners with some educational background may be familiar with some of the theoretical and applied positions in the field, e.g., psychoanalysis, behavior modification. However, they are likely to view these in an "either-or" framework, the approach being either "good" or "bad" in all situations, rather than in an eclectic way in which advantages and disadvantages within the *same* perspective might be recognized; and in which various aspects might be differentially utilized in different situations. In line with their identification with children themselves, and their developmental tendency to think in "either-or" terms, novice practitioners often tend to see parents as "bad" and to avoid the notion of actually working with them (VanderVen, 1980).

Those Stage 1 practitioners who find their initial work engaging and meaningful, may begin to make the transition towards Stage 2; those who, for whatever reasons, don't become similarly involved will be among the "two years" casualties.

Stage 2: Informed Practice

General Description

Having survived the "two years in-and-out" phenomenon, Stage 2 practitioners now feel a commitment to the field and a sense of personal identity as child care practitioners. In Hall's (1986) formulation, they will be in an active process of *establishment* of their careers. At this stage they still are involved primarily in group care in organized settings. But through a combination of educational preparation and work experience, they now offer a background that *informs* their practice; in child care worker parlance, they might be considered more "seasoned." Some of these practitioners as they enter this stage are graduates of established academic programs with considerable work and field experience; others may have received in-service training and participated in continuing education, such as the growing number of conferences offered in the field.

Scope of Practice

Clients. Primary clients for Stage 2 practice are still the children in care in group settings. By this time, these workers may be looked upon to work with the more difficult or challenging children within the setting, and also to deal with the individual within the group in a crisis situation. Furthermore, at this stage practitioners may begin to have contact with *parents* as well, in order to ensure continuity. Such contact would usually occur at points of exchange of the child between worker and parent, around the logistics of visits, or within the structure of a parent education or parent participation program. With regards to the latter, Stage 2 practitioners may serve to demonstrate or describe positive ways of managing children's behavior to parents (VanderVen, 1988). Thus, in general, the scope of practice with clients at Stage 2 is broadening.

Settings. Similarly, the scope of settings for practice for workers at Stage 2 widens. These more experienced workers may not only work within the organized group care setting, but also in other settings, e.g., in the child's home. Furthermore, more practitioners are more likely to be employed within other institutions of society that have responsibility for children, e.g., schools, recreational centers, the community, and mental health programs, for their ability to contribute the particular skills of child care.

Interventions. In *informed* practice of child care, the child care activities are carried out in a richer, targeted, more complex fashion. For example, their use of self as a model and communicator might include the employment of more sophisticated techniques, e.g., life space interviewing and crisis intervention methods. The use of activities of daily living is undergirded by an effort to deal with developmental issues and competencies that might be associated with these areas, e.g., eating, dressing, and sleeping. Activity programming may be utilized in a more focused manner, e.g., when a specific activity is selected to meet identified therapeutic goals. Work with the group may go beyond basic hygienic management to encompass specific use of group process or more tightly organized group activities to deal with a crisis or a specific issue, e.g., sexual concerns, or general participative planning for the living unit.

While Stage 2 workers who have major responsibility in the daily lives of children still manage surface behavior, they are able to deal with it in a more dynamic fashion. Basic, hygienic management is transcended by a concern with the reasons for, and meaning of, the behavior within the situation in which it is occurring.

Control of Practice

Stage 2 practitioners, in general, still work in hierarchical organizations in which there are levels of supervision. Thus, they are still responsible to a senior person for both guidance and accountability. However, at this stage the focus of supervision may be less on development of basic skills and more on joint consideration and solving of more complex problems, with, at least in the optimal situation, a concomitant concern for the professional development of the practitioner. Stage 2 practitioners are expected to be capable of making some independent decisions in those areas most specifically related to delivery of the child care perspective. In those settings that have child care worker career ladders, they may be responsible for orienting and even serving as the immediate supervisor for newer, Stage 1 workers.

As team members, Stage 2 practitioners now are able to take a more active role in goal setting and establishment of developmental care plans, with identification of the interventions that can serve to achieve them, as well as in providing input in policy, program development, and handling of individuals.

Cognitive and Affective Attributes

The term *informed* practice means that practitioner responses are now *professional*. These workers now know, and can state, why they select a certain intervention from a wider repertoire of possibilities, and monitor the resultant outcomes. They no longer believe, as they may have at Stage 1, that to plan and act consciously as a child care worker somehow restricts relationships or decreases spontaneity. Common sense indeed gives way to informed action.

Since Stage 2 practitioners are, in general, older and more mature, they have moved further away from their ties to their own childhood and are thus able to take a broader perspective on persons and activities that they earlier may have felt were antithetical to child care. Interestingly, either through parental contact "forced" by the structure of their jobs, or by actually becoming parents themselves, some practitioners develop both greater empathy for, and interest in working constructively with, parents.

At this stage, the earlier "either/or" thinking gives way to an ability to take a broader perspective. Practitioners are more able to take the variables in a particular situation into consideration, a characteristic of "contextual" thinking (Beker & Maier, 1982).

As well, knowledge of relevant theoretical concepts and systems has become more expanded, and practitioners are able to evaluate their potential for differential application to various issues or situations they encounter. For example, to deal with a specific problem, the worker might identify, utilize, and apply specific approaches gleaned from a variety of methodologies.

Stage 2 practitioners today form the crux of the child care field; they are those who are increasingly demonstrating the significance of the informed *child care perspective* in the array of services intended to promote the welfare of children and youth. There are options for further expansion of practice beyond this stage; those who have found success, a sense of commitment, and even hidden capacities for growth, have the option of moving on to Stage 3.

Stage 3: Complex Practice

General Description

The term *"complex"* practice reflects just that: there is a greater amount of *complexity* in the populations served, the settings in which services are delivered, and in the interventions provided, both in terms of variety and impact.

Stage 3 in direct child care practice is the one in which there is the least numerical representation among practitioners in the field, and is also the one whose potentialities are least recognized. One reason for this is that *child care work at an advanced clinical level* has not really been defined, although there are now a number of persons in the field whose career activities reflect progress to this stage. Traditionally, some of the functions that will be explicated for Stage 3 child care have been performed by clinicians in related mental health disciplines. The premise here is that *the special skills of child care* have applications at a high level of conceptualization and sophistication, and to be able to implement these is a unique contribution to the total array of disciplines oriented towards serving children. By this time, or at sometime as they progress, practitioners at this stage will probably have achieved an advanced educational credential. More and more often this is actually in child care or in a program that allows for specialization with children and child care work. These individuals have often begun to develop a reputation within the field; they may serve as conference speakers and workshop leaders, as consultants; and as authors of articles and reports describing some aspect of their work.

Scope of Practice

Clients. Child care practitioners at Stage 3 have a greatly expanded array of clients: children, youth, parents, families, and even people of age groups not traditionally served by child care, e.g., older adults and elderly. They can work with individuals and groups. Practitioners at earlier stages, particularly Stage 1, may, due to lack of experience, feel that they can only work with a single age group, or type of child. By the time Stage 3 is reached, practitioners recognize that the core components of the child care perspective are applicable across diagnostic categories and age groups. At this stage, the organization of their work may be more oriented towards specialty areas rather than to age and broad diagnostic groups. For example, practitioners may work with abused or sexually molested children; with children in transitional family situations, such as divorce or reconstituted families, contributing their skills in the child care perspective at an advanced level. In general, Stage 3 practitioners are the ones who may be steered towards direct involvement with the most complicated, difficult, or demanding cases. In work with parents and families, many aspects of the child care perspective have direct relevance. For example, environmental design skills may be used to help a parent arrange her own living area to more effectively accommodate both her own and her child's needs.

Settings. Stage 3 practitioners likewise may deliver their services in a variety of settings. Some may serve as senior workers in organized group care settings, and are viewed as leaders and models for sound practice. They may combine direct work with a supervisory or program management responsibility. Others may serve as clinical therapists with individuals, families or small groups in community-based mental health programs. Still others may actually be in private practice as *advanced clinical child care specialists*. Within this group, some may have their own offices; others may work with an organized group of clinical practitioners from other disciplines. It should be pointed out that the terms "private practice" and "therapy" are not synonymous; private practice of child care might include specifically therapeutic activities in the traditional sense but in general focus on other advanced applications of child care knowledge.

Interventions. At Stage 3, the interventions represent highly specialized applications of the generic skills in the child care perspective. They are highly goal-oriented and may be targeted towards both promoting specific competencies or remediating identified conditions. They may be delivered to two sub-groups simultaneously, for example, in holding a conjoint play interview (Griff, 1983) with parents and child together. Some interventions by a Stage 3 practitioner are dynamically oriented; that is, they go beneath surface behavior to identify and deal with deeper meanings and previous experiences that may have contributed to a current situation.

Control of Practice

Stage 3 practitioners have by this time achieved the competence prerequisite to highly independent practice. If they work within an organized setting, they will, of course, be responsible to a person of higher rank in that setting. However, they will practice with a great deal of individual responsibility, with much or all of their work performed outside the direct purview of their supervisor. They will be able to set their own tasks, perform them with a minimum of external guidance, and evaluate their effectiveness.

As team members in such settings, Stage 3 child care practitioners might find themselves either as major contributors to the treatment goal setting and treatment planning process, or, in some settings, as the team leader. It has been proposed (Krueger, 1983) that the advanced child care practitioner, as the person most tied into the daily life experience of the child in care, is the ideal person to serve as coordinator and integrator of the child's life space, and thus can be an ideal leader of the clinical planning and treatment team. These practitioners can help make the contributions of other clinical specialties to the child's total program be experienced by the child as a meaningful cohesion of relevant activities, rather than as a ride along an assembly line in which each discipline simply "lays" a different experience on him.

In a community or outpatient agency, the integrative and coordinating function for children might be served by the child care practitioner as case manager. This invokes the component of the child care perspective in which the practitioner utilizes various community resources to empower the child and his family to achieve competence and well-being.

Cognitive and Affective Attributes

The term *complex* practice means that the child care workers' responses are not only professional, e.g., informed, but also that they are *highly and richly* informed. Practitioners are able to take past experiences, the dynamics of the current situation, established treatment goals, future needs, and possible appropriate interventions all into consideration in dealing with a particular situation. In short, they are capable of "systems" thinking, taking a variety of complex, interacting variables at different levels into account when planning or making a clinical decision.

Like practitioners at the *informed* stage, they demonstrate clinical eclecticism, but in their more advanced development they may also look outside human services to other fields and disciplines, such as religion, literature, politics and science, to further enrich their thinking about child care.

Because of their personal maturity, they are able to abandon the more rigid adherence to codified "professional" behavior standards characteristic of some at earlier stages. They may know, for example, how to reveal something about their personal selves to a child in a way that conveys warmth and caring without stirring up undue fantasies in the child. This might be in contrast to the less mature worker—probably one at the *informed* stage, who would, probably appropriately, feel a need to adhere to the more traditional caveat against personal disclosure, the rescue fantasies that earlier stage practitioners direct at individual children would be now transformed into not only a healthy investment in those children, youth and families with whom they work directly, but also an interest in modifying those wider institutions, systems and values of society that inevitably affect societal welfare.

Many of these practitioners in the *complex* stage have moved considerably away from their own childhoods; some may be middle-aged. They, and their field, should realize that in attaining the ability to provide a high level of clinical child care, to do it without reliance on close supervision, and to be able to tell others what they have done, is a major advance. The best news is that there is still further opportunity for both their individual development and their ability to further advance in the child care field.

SUMMARY

This chapter has described a three-stage model for career development in direct clinical child and youth care work. Presence of such a cadre of child care practitioners at all levels of clinical practice is a fundamental component of the task of building the profession. Providing career path options as described, the working conditions and career ladders that enable practitioners to progress into them, will enable the field of child care as a whole to continue its journey along the continuum from job to full profession. The best result of this progress will be the betterment of the quality of care delivered to children, youth and families.

REFERENCES

Ainsworth, F. (1985). Direct care practitioners as promoters of child development. *Journal of Child and Youth Care Work, 1*(2), 62-70.

Anglin, J. (1983). Setting the sights: an assessment of child care job functions and training needs in British Columbia. In *The Scope of Professional Child Care*. Victoria, B.C.: The University of Victoria.

Bayduss, G., & Toscano, J. (1979). The development of child care workers: correlates between occupational and social-emotional growth. *Child Care Quarterly, 8*, 85-93.

Beker, J., & Maier, H. (1981). Emerging issues in child and youth care education: A platform for planning. *Child Care Quarterly, 10*, 200-209.

Deutsch, C. (1986, November 16). Holding on to technical talent. *New York Times* business section, p. 4.

Etzioni, A. (1969). *The semi-professions and their organization*. New York: Free Press.

Griff, M. (1983). Family play therapy. In Schaefer, C., ed., *The Handbook of Play Therapy*. New York: John Wiley.

Hall, D. (1986). Breaking career routines. In Hall, D. & Associates. *Career development in organization*. San Francisco: Jossey-Bass.

Katz, L. (1977). *Talks with teachers*. Washington, D.C.: National Association for the Education of Young Children.

Krueger, M. (1983). *Careless to caring for troubled youth*. Milwaukee: Tall Publishers.

Thomas, D. (1982). Stages of professional development in child care work: a proposed model. *Child Care Quarterly, 11*, 147-149.

VanderVen, K. (1979). Developmental characteristics of child care workers and design of training programs. *Child Care Quarterly, 8*, 94-99.

VanderVen, K. (1980). A paradigm describing stages of personal and professional development of child care practitioners with characteristics associated with each stage. In *Proceedings of the Ninth International Congress of the International Association of Workers With Maladjusted Children*. Montreal.

VanderVen, K. (1981). Patterns of career development in group care. In Ainsworth, F., & Fulcher, L., (eds.) *Group care for children: concept and issues*. London: Tavistock.

VanderVen, K. (1985a). From two years to two generations: life long career paths in child care. Keynote speech delivered to Kansas Association of Child Care Workers Third Annual Conference. Topeka, Kansas: Washburn University.

VanderVen, K. (1985b). Educating child care practitioners for life long careers in the field: strategies for achieving the "Two C's" Model. Presented at Trainers and Educators' Day at "The Empowerment of Youth: First International Child Care Conference." British Columbia, Canada: Vancouver.

VanderVen, K. (1988). Pathways to professional effectiveness, for early childhood educators. In Spodek, D., Saracho, O., & Peters, D. (eds.) *Professionalism and the early childhood practitioner*. New York: Columbia University Teachers College Press.

VanderVen, K. (1988). Working with families: expanded roles for child care professionals. In Olson, D., (ed.) *Family Perspectives in Child and Youth Care Work*. New York: The Haworth Press.

27

2000 and Beyond:
Future Career Directions
for Child and Youth Care Professionals

Carey J. Denholm

ABSTRACT. Established child and youth care training programs attempt to ensure that students become skilled and knowledgeable in core competencies appropriate for the breadth of work settings with children and youth. Providing direction about employment areas also now requires information for students contemplating study at the graduate level. Six future career pathways are described, including preparatory skills, work characteristics and realities about each career area.

This chapter describes emerging future career functions for child and youth care professionals. Further, it suggests that the point of entry into a child and youth care education and training program is an appropriate time to expose students to opportunities and attendant competencies needed for work within employment areas requiring these functions.

Historically, many child and youth care training programs were characterized by "curricula pragmatism," maintaining a predominant focus on goal attainment and skill development, and oriented to specific approaches within single environments with identified groups of children (e.g., residential care for developmentally handicapped). In the past twenty years, the development of two and three

Carey J. Denholm, Associate Professor, School of Child and Youth Care, University of Victoria, P.O. Box 1700, Victoria, B.C. V8W 2Y2.

year college and four year university undergraduate generalist programs preparing graduates for a range of positions across a breadth
of environments has occurred (Denholm, Ferguson, & Pence,
1987). The option of advanced study at the graduate level has also
now become a reality. Not only has this brought an infusion of new
approaches, a stronger research base, and a wider perspective to the
scope of the field, but more graduates now enter traditional "front-
line" work with the intention to eventually specialize and rise
within a career hierarchy.

In tandem with Savicki and VanderVen (see chapters 23 and 26),
the suggestion is made that child and youth care practice of the
future will reveal expansion in the way in which the profession
historically has been conceptualized. Change in how we presently
think about the field may produce anxiety for some, yet paradoxically, it is postulated that such growth will bring stability and an
inherently stronger professional self-definition.

In terms of future areas of employment, it will be noted that some
trends discussed in this chapter are now occurring. However, these
six proposed career options (consultant, educator, clinician, researcher, administrator, political lobbyist), have yet to be seriously
considered as appropriate career pathways. They are all areas in
which a variety of educational experiences and advanced clinical
training are required.

REFLECTIONS ON THE CHILD
AND YOUTH CARE PROFESSION

Beginning child and youth care professionals currently face a
range of societal and professional issues: the growing adult and ger-
ontological population, reduction in government resources allocated to human services, emphasis on evaluation and accountability,
development of quality standards of care, accreditation, licensure,
impact of the media, sexual abuse, quality therapeutic foster care,
and delinquency with violence. More and more, workers are called
on to be effective and credible communicators with parents, agencies, and government officials. With the development of national
and international associations that are fast becoming the vanguard
of causes for children and youth, developing both professional

knowledge and sensitivity to local and global needs and issues is becoming a more central concern of the profession.

The urgency for the child care professional to adopt and cope with change has been stated (Ferguson & Anglin, 1985). Responsiveness to local, national and international trends is not only part of the necessary development of the profession, it is critical to understanding the scope of the entire child and youth care field. Subsequently, anticipation of emerging career pathways in relation to that scope is the next logical extension of this evolutionary process.

One model found useful in conceptualizing related child and youth care career pathways has been depicted as an umbrella (Figure 1).

To incorporate any change within this model, one is limited to vertical (hierarchal) expansion within existing areas designated as child and youth care and potential horizontal additions of fields of service currently considered outside the range of child care practice. Each approach requires linearity of thinking. That is, an addition could be made on this graphic in one direction or the other. For example, on this model, international and intercultural child and youth care might be added as a major new segment to the umbrella, or, between front-line worker and supervisor an intermediate step such as "shift head" could be included.

One of the limitations of this model in relation to emerging careers is the appearance of a series of fixed boxes, or slots. In reality, many roles, settings and levels of employment exist on a continuum and involve overlapping functions. Many undergraduate and graduate students of the future will, in addition to the core grounding in child and youth care theory and application, seek to develop competencies which traverse current work settings in order for them to function simultaneously within a range of systems. As a result, this type of work will require contact with a broad range of professionals who have varied academic, political and cultural backgrounds.

This direction *will not replace the need for the day to day care of child and youth* in a variety of settings. However, as students recognize the expanded career opportunities occurring in allied professions such as nursing, education, psychology and social work, discussion of the following six career options involving a number of competencies during their training becomes not only desirable, but

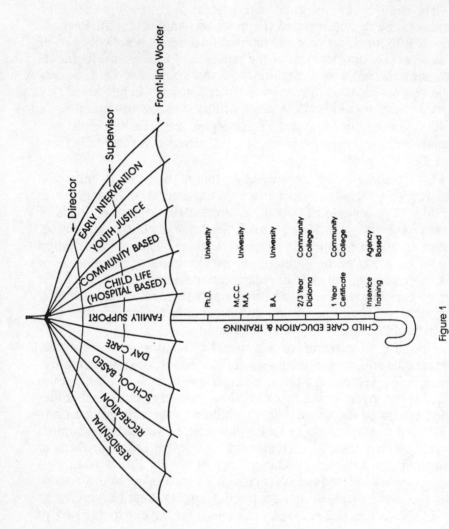

Figure 1

The umbrella model of child and youth care

essential. This need is also in response to the range of serious questions being asked of child and youth care educators by beginning level students in relation to career direction, potential for advancement, and future educational opportunities. These six areas are represented as part of the supporting structure for the canopy in the previously presented model, likely developing as distinct pathways, primarily at the graduate level of education (see Figure 2).

Although it is difficult to depict in this graphic, these areas *traverse* the standard work settings identified in Figure 1. This supporting structure can, in effect, be rotated through all of the settings. For example, it is possible to be employed as a child care educator responsible for coursework focusing on three or four settings with varied age groups, all having a range of needs, and teach-

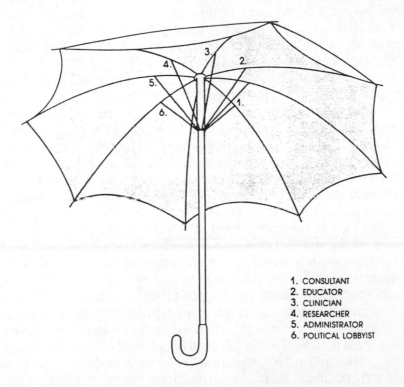

1. CONSULTANT
2. EDUCATOR
3. CLINICIAN
4. RESEARCHER
5. ADMINISTRATOR
6. POLITICAL LOBBYIST

Figure 2
Emerging functions for child and youth care professionals

ing a number of creative arts modalities within a counselling frame-work. Each of these six areas involves a complexity of functions and professionals optimally would have had experience in a number of settings with various individuals and groups, comprehensive and credible education and training, and some opportunity to work at various employment levels (e.g., supervisor, director) prior to spe-cializing in any of the six areas. Each career option will be consid-ered below.

1. THE ROLE OF CONSULTANT

Consultation is considered a second-order intervention strategy involving a temporary, short-term relationship between a profes-sional helper, a client, and an issue or system. Second-order means that the client (or target) does not directly engage the services of the consultant, rather the services are arranged by the consultee (Male, 1982; Parsons & Meyers, 1984).

The provision of consultation services by child and youth care professionals may provide either short- or long-term employment. The nature of the contract may involve, for example, providing direction concerning the design and implementation of new policy or standards, individual and management issues with clients, inter-nal staff conflict, or the training of staff. Often, consultants are faced with the problem that the organization has lost its direction or is unclear about its philosophy. Obtaining a complete organiza-tional history, knowing methods of problem solving, and under-standing the current management structure are critical.

One setting in which consultation has been extensively developed and researched is within the education system. In a review of 21 separate studies on the effectiveness and role of consultation by school counselors, Bundy and Poppen (1986) conclude, "18 (86%) studies provide outcome data that show significantly positive effects of consultation by counselors" (p.220). In this review, consultation was utilized in 67% of studies to change behavior of students, teach-ers or parents and in 50%, significant changes in attitudes or percep-tions were obtained. In addition, significant outcomes included im-provements in student grades, student attention, parental confidence, student motivation and parent-child communication.

Of particular note to the child and youth care profession is the close attention paid to evaluation and research by school counselors. Similar emphasis and constant demonstration of clinical effectiveness needs to be maintained with the development of consultation within child and youth care settings. For child and youth professionals, consultation as an intended key function, requires advanced level relationship and communication-building skills, comprehensive understanding of group processes, knowledge of change processes within systems, imaginative and divergent thinking ability, strategies and pragmatic approaches for skill development within organizations, problem-solving and "brainstorming" skills, and realistic approaches to staff resourcing. Writing ability and computer literacy may be particularly critical when short turnaround periods are required. These skills may also be useful in providing direction on new advertising brochures and strategies for publicity.

2. THE ROLE OF EDUCATOR

With the advent of new community college and university-based programs, this career route continues to be legitimized. Child and youth care educators have traditionally come from a broad spectrum of professional training such as education, nursing, counseling education, psychology and child and youth care. Whereas level of clinical skill, credibility in the field, and research interests have traditionally been of primary concern, the focus on actual teaching ability and teaching performance have been considered less critical factors. However, educators within these programs are now having to meet not only the curricula needs of the particular program, but also a range of multi-dimensional aspects required for basic competence within the particular institution. These include conducting research, design of grant proposals, successful and significant publications in academic and professional journals, and community involvement and consultations to boards and committees.

The dimensions of teaching have also continued to expand and greater emphasis on obtaining educators with an adult learning background who exhibit innovative instructional techniques and who have demonstrated the ability to cope with a range of advanced technological aspects, is now a reality. Often included in job descriptions are the development of off-campus learning packages, involvement in curriculum design, and theoretical perspectives on curriculum in relation to standards and needs within the field. In addition, development of suitable assessment and delivery strategies in perennially difficult areas such as practicum and clinical skills development, in-service training of supervisors, and development of policies and text resources are often expected. Constant public relations on behalf of the program is also a reality.

Clearly, teaching within a college or university environment is not simply a matter of talking about one's clinical experiences. Students intending to make this a career direction need, at a formative stage, to have an opportunity under guidance to organize and conduct workshops, to understand the assessment, objectives, organization, and management of adult learners within a range of educational situations and environments. In addition, principles of questioning, familiarity with adult learning theory and principles, knowledge of classroom management strategies, awareness of one's own competencies and strengths, clarity and practice with instructional approaches and techniques, understanding principles of assessment, giving feedback, grading strategies, and well developed writing skills, are all key aspects.

The potential instructor should be clearly motivated and have demonstrated aptitude and a sense of presence within classroom situations; that is, the good clinician does not necessarily make a good teacher of clinical skills, and vice versa. Examination of the personal motives for teaching, removing the need for the "performance factor" and demonstrating a passion for questions relating to learning and education environments, are essential.

3. THE ROLE OF CLINICIAN

This field is littered with workers who add to their resume, "private practice." Realistically, private practitioners often need to supplement income with part-time work, both inside and outside their field of expertise, in order to maintain their practice for the years before it becomes self-supporting. With clinical experience and supervision at the Masters level, child and youth care professionals *can* justifiably think of themselves as clinicians, who can compete on an equal basis with graduates from psychology, psychiatric nursing, social work and education. Work as a child and youth care clinician may be in a private clinic, an assessment and treatment center, or on a contracted fee-for-service basis with community agencies.

Students contemplating this direction should carefully select a strong and credible graduate program, and enter with clarity of intended career direction. If the program falls short in relation to particular clinical interests, the student should ask for program support and direction in order to obtain the necessary experience.

As a clinician, a minimum of one year supervised clinical internship is recommended. During this time, graduates should seek every opportunity to conduct workshops and demonstrate new approaches, speak in public meetings, and make submissions to professional journals. These activities become the corner stones of a solid clinical foundation.

4. THE ROLE OF RESEARCHER

The book in which this chapter appears represents the accumulated wisdom, reflections, and abilities of many practitioners and each contributor offers some expansion to child and youth care research. Publishing research findings is not simply seen as an additional task, but is an essential part of the entire research and evaluation process. Similarly, good clinical work involves sound and thorough assessment, appropriate and theoretically-based intervention, client evaluation and sufficiently detailed written and planned reports. Yet, as Pence points out elsewhere in this volume, the world of the clinician and that of the researcher are not separate, but integral. That is, the same kind of systematic thinking needs to go on in the mind of the clinician as in the mind of the researcher.

Research per se, both to the front-line and supervisory-level worker, has been viewed as something to be left for university professors. However, given the current and future need for quality researchers, data collectors and interpreters, analysts and writers, this area represents an area of emerging opportunity. Whether it be the preparation of documented support for new policy, analysis of literature in support of a particular therapeutic trend, study on the profession (such as employment and turnover trends), the need for full- and part-time researchers is being recognized. Approaching research from a clinical perspective, the need to provide evaluations of client interventions on an ongoing basis and to teach clinical research methods to agency staff and co-workers, makes the need for education in applied research a critical aspect.

Child and youth care students interested in conducting research and pursuing a career in this area need to have demonstrated competencies in the following areas: computer applications, advanced critical writing, research design and statistics, applications of research approaches within clinical populations and settings, and life-span development and its research implications.

5. THE ROLE OF ADMINISTRATOR

Clearly, as far as professional associations are concerned, the late 1980s could be considered the era of accreditation and registration. The advent of mandatory registration of mental health counsellors in the U.S. and oral and written examinations required of child and youth care professionals in Alberta and Ontario, legitimizes the need for strong child and youth care associations. Thus the need to provide management, leadership, and organization of a legislated body of professionals charged with the task of self-monitoring, continues to develop. Attendant to this trend for the development of an infra-structure within organizations and professional associations, are associated tasks for administrative personnel; presenting to conferences, workshop and seminar organization, communication with politicians and community and volunteer groups, fund raising, raising community profile, national and international networking, and working with research groups.

Whereas this career direction is seen as specific to such things as professional membership, organization and the development of standards and ethics, the position of administrator may also occur in treatment centers, non-profit societies and community groups, hospitals, government offices or agencies, remand centers, infant development and family resource centres. Clearly, training in administration, finance, group management and written and oral communication skills, clinical work in the specific area of employment, and comfort in relating to business issues, are essential. Where the particular job relates to such tasks as accreditation, knowledge of the historical development and sensitivity to the needs of the specific organization, are also important. An ability to deal with volunteer boards, maintain consistency with membership, and implementing set policy are also requisite skills.

6. THE ROLE OF POLITICAL LOBBYIST

This final category may seem a little unusual. Historically, child and youth professionals have considered themselves to be "above" politics, and communication with the media. Therefore, these areas have not been seen as appropriate vehicles through which to address issues of children and youth. Alternatively, it could be that the profession has been somewhat blinded by the need to maintain an interpersonal relationship focus to the exclusion of political realities. Meanwhile, services to children are reduced due to economic and political decisions and nothing (or little) is said by the profession. Separate from this area of employment, the issue of political advocacy in general needs to be seriously addressed. For example, how many child and youth professionals have been assisted, groomed and supported by local associations in seeking political office?

An unelected lobbyist, however, needs training in law and in journalism; if these are not present they need to be acquired. This work also involves advocacy at its highest level and demands a national and international perspective, without loosing sight of day-to-day, seemingly trivial, issues. It involves a love for politics, a sensitivity and discrimination of the "elephant" (as distinct from the "peanut") issues and causes, all demanding long-term commitment and enthusiasm. This position requires patience, intuitive timing, a sense of both the elegant and absurd, and the vision to redefine small gains as great leaps.

Gaining confidence and ability for this task requires both a determination and clarification of personal values, taking the opportunity to "work through" many of these values in volunteer community and political groups, and an internal resiliency to work for long hours with little opportunity for advancement and with minimal financial rewards. The payoff, however, in terms of community and national profile, is potentially great.

SUMMARY

The child and youth care profession of the future offers a range of exciting new developments. Each level of work should be respected, with none seen as greater than the other. Although recognition of each distinctive career direction, contribution or particular area of work *is* important, this profession needs to continue to be characterized by equality, collegial support, and mutual challenge and nurturance. The traditional roles and functions carried out by professional child and youth workers in a variety of settings remains central to the integrity of the profession.

By reflecting on the breadth of the field with its emerging and changing career parameters, the profession continues to become more clearly defined, and thus stronger. Established professions have developed levels of career advancement and specialization in which well-educated practitioners assume key positions of leadership and profile. This chapter proposes that child and youth care is facing a time where developing a unique body of knowledge (researcher), teaching (educator) and demonstrating to students (clinician), advocating change (political lobbyist), providing alternative perspectives to fellow professionals (consultant) and assuming key responsibilities for the many professional associations (administrator), emerge as separate career directions.

The child and youth care profession stands at the precipice of the present, facing the distant cliff of the future. Will the response be retreat, ambivalence, a leap of blind faith or the building of a carefully designed bridge? The provision of credible, realistic and innovative career options, needs to become a component of the accepted framework into which the year 2000 and beyond is entered with confidence.

REFERENCES

Bundy, M. L., & Poppen, W. A. (1986). School counselors' effectiveness as consultants: A research review. *Elementary School Guidance and Counseling*, *20*(3), 215-222.

Denholm, C. J., Ferguson, R. V., & Pence, A. R. (Eds.). (1987). *Professional child and youth care: The Canadian perspective*. Vancouver: University of British Columbia Press.

Ferguson, R. V., & Anglin, J. P. (1985). The child care profession: A vision for the future. *Child Care Quarterly*, *14*, 85-102.

Male, R. A. (1982). Consultation as an intervention strategy for school counselors. *The School Counselor*, *30*(1), 25-31.

Parsons, R. D., & Meyers, J. (1984). *Developing consultation skills*. San Francisco: Jossey Bass.

Index
for Parts I and II